D0705680

The Television Handbook

The Television Handbook is a critical introduction to the practice and theory of television. The book examines the state of television today, explains how television is made and how production is organised, and discusses how critical thinking about programmes and genres can illuminate their meanings. This book also explores how developments in technology and the changing structure of the television industry will lead the medium in new directions.

The Television Handbook gives practical advice on many aspects of programme making, from an initial programme idea through to shooting and the post-production process. The book includes profiles giving insight into how personnel in the television industry – from recent graduates to television executives – think about their work.

The Television Handbook bridges the gap between theory and practice. There are chapters on the vigorous debates about what is meant by quality television, how news and factual programmes are responding to interactive technologies, and how formats such as Reality/Talent TV have risen in prominence, as well as how drama, sport and music television can be discussed and interpreted.

The Television Handbook includes:

- Profiles of TV news and drama producers, editors and TV studio personnel.
- Case histories of important TV genres and series.
- Practical programme-making advice.
- Explanations of key theoretical perspectives in television studies.

Jeremy Orlebar is an experienced radio and television producer, freelance writer and lecturer. He has over twenty-five years experience with BBC radio and television producing and directing programmes. His publications include: *Digital Television Production* and *The Practical Media Dictionary*.

Media Practice

Edited by James Curran, Goldsmiths College, University of London

The *Media Practice* handbooks are comprehensive resource books for students of media and journalism, and for anyone planning a career as a media professional. Each handbook combines a clear introduction to understanding how the media work with practical information about the structure, processes and skills involved in working in today's media industries, providing not only a guide on 'how to do it' but also a critical reflection on contemporary media practice.

The Advertising Handbook
3rd edition
Helen Powell, Jonathan Hardy, Sarah Hawkin and Iain MacRury

The Alternative Media Handbook
Kate Coyer, Tony Dowmunt and Alan Fountain

The Cyberspace Handbook
Jason Whittaker

The Documentary Handbook
Peter Lee-Wright

The Fashion Handbook
Tim Jackson and David Shaw

The Magazines Handbook
2nd edition
Jenny McKay

The Music Industry Handbook
Paul Rutter

The New Media Handbook
Andrew Dewdney and Peter Ride

The Newspapers Handbook
4th edition
Richard Kebble

The Photography Handbook
2nd edition
Terence Wright

The Public Relations Handbook
4th edition
Alison Theaker

The Radio Handbook
3rd edition
Carole Fleming

The Television Handbook
4th edition
Jeremy Orlebar

The Television Handbook

Fourth edition

Jeremy Orlebar

Routledge
Taylor & Francis Group

LONDON AND NEW YORK

Fourth edition published 2011
by Routledge
2 Park Square, Milton Park, Abingdon, Oxon OX14 4RN

Simultaneously published in the USA and Canada
by Routledge
711 Third Avenue, New York, NY 10017

Routledge is an imprint of the Taylor & Francis Group, an informa business

British Library Cataloguing in Publication Data
A catalogue record for this book is available from the British Library

Library of Congress Cataloging in Publication Data
Orlebar, Jeremy.
  The television handbook / Jeremy Orlebar. — 4th ed.
  p. cm. — (Media practice)
  Rev. ed. of: The television handbook / Patricia Holland.
  Includes bibliographical references and index.
  1. Television—Production and direction—Handbooks, manuals, etc.
  2. Television broadcasting—Handbooks, manuals, etc. I. Title.
  PN1992.5.H63 2011
  791.4502'3—dc22   2011005510

ISBN: 978–0–415–60413–0 (hbk)
ISBN: 978–0–415–60414–7 (pbk)
ISBN: 978–0–203–80647–0 (ebk)

Typeset in Helvetica and Avant Garde
by Florence Production Ltd, Stoodleigh, Devon

Printed and bound in Great Britain by the MPG Books Group

This book is dedicated to Amanda and Tessa
for all their love and care

Contents

7 Schedule and audience   78

PART 3
FACTUAL TELEVISION   **93**

8 Documentaries   95

9 Reality TV   111

10 Making factual programmes   119

PART 4
NEWS AND SPORT   **135**

11 Television news   137

12 Television sport   158

Figures

Acknowledgements

The author would like to thank Jonathan Bignell for permission to reproduce his significant theoretical contributions from the third edition of *The Television Handbook*.

All photographs by Jeremy Orlebar.

Introduction

MEDIA LITERACY

The fourth edition of *The Television Handbook* takes account of recent and current developments in broadcast television and in the ways it can be studied, building on the theoretical work by Jonathan Bignell in the third edition, and continues with the exploration of television production and programme areas. Parts 1 and 2 of the book set the agenda and present important information about the development of contemporary television, and provide an initial overview of the state of television in Britain today, and some of the key areas of work in academic Television Studies. The subsequent parts of the book focus in greater detail on the practices of television makers and the institutions they work for, and on programme areas and points of debate that are central to teaching about television today.

Television Studies is in a continual process of development, and the ongoing production of new television programmes, made by new and changing institutions under changing conditions and with new technologies, continually generates new questions and ways of answering them. British television has aimed to represent a relatively unified culture, even though the nation has been divided into local TV areas like the Midlands, Scotland or Northern Ireland. The great majority of program-mes shown on British TV are made in the UK, and there are important differences between the way TV is organised in Britain compared to other nations such as the USA or Italy. In a similar way, the shape of the critical approaches to television taught in British colleges and universities is relatively distinctive compared to other nations. Despite the international flow of ideas (not unlike the international trade in television programming), there is a strong and healthy interest in television among

British students, critics, teachers and enthusiasts. This book is for that broad constituency of people who want to participate by working in or learning about television. Although there are many books that address aspects of this field (some are listed in the Further Reading sections), the fourth edition of *The Television Handbook* balances up-to-date research and information, ideas and arguments and television programme production in a way which is both distinctive and easy to access.

Because of the deep embedding of television viewing in everyday life, Television Studies also has a strong connection with studies of the sociology of culture (see Brunsdon 1998). The sociological strand of television study addressed television in the context of a political critique of the forces of social control, since television's institutional and industrial production could be seen as the carrier of ideological values. By analysing television as one of the means by which social life is given meaning, and aspects of contemporary society are represented and debated, Television Studies with this sociological focus can contribute to social and political education. It has been especially important in considering society as a dynamic and changing thing, in which more powerful and less powerful definitions of issues, groups of people and expectations of the future compete to establish themselves as the accepted common-sense understanding of the world. Analysis of television with this sociological and political agenda could therefore reveal the negotiation between the sanctioned 'official' values of a ruling elite or governmental institution and the world-views of ordinary people. Television programmes' meanings could then be regarded as a site of struggle between different 'official' and 'popular' discourses.

In this analytical tradition, study of television is one of many ways to discover how social meanings are created, perpetuated or modified, and how television representation connects up with the broader media landscape of a particular historical moment, especially the present.

The other significant strand of teaching about television is the imparting of professional skills and knowledge that enables students to understand how programmes are made technically, industrially and institutionally, providing them with the potential to find employment within the media business. However, while this kind of training may sometimes seem merely to be creating a workforce to serve the current state of the media industry, the great majority of television professionals aim for a committed engagement with the technical resources of the medium, a concern for its relationships with society at large, and an interest in the creative possibilities that are possible in television production. This assumption that working in television is creative, socially engaged and personally enriching is matched by the syllabus of many courses that primarily focus on the acquisition of professional knowledge and skills. Work in television is understood as the deployment of a body of professional knowledge, working practices and technical expertise. The key aspects of these professional competencies are outlined in Part 6 Practical Programme

Making and Part 3 of this book where they relate to factual television and Part 5 where they relate to television drama production. The possession of these competencies is also a means for the expression of ideas and an opportunity to contribute to the evolution of the television industry and also the broader society to which that industry belongs.

Television training entails the understanding of social responsibility and the recognition of opportunities for creative intervention. So television training is close to the agendas of the theoretical studies of television described above, in that it deals with questions of quality, aesthetics and politics. In this book, we take the position that the two strands of television education are mutually compatible and interrelated.

REFERENCES AND FURTHER READING

Brunsdon, C. 'What is the Television of Television Studies', in C. Geraghty and D. Lusted (eds), *The Television Studies Book*, London: Arnold, 1998, pp. 95–113.

Part 1

Television in transition

CHAPTER 1

Television today

TELEVISION TODAY

Television Studies focuses on broadcast television in the English language and is concerned with the sociological and cultural context and content of the main UK broadcasting companies (Bignell 2004). It is perhaps then a worry that over the first ten years of the twenty-first century television audiences for the UK's five main 'terrestrial' channels – BBC1, BBC2, ITV1, Channel 4 and Channel 5 – declined. Glanfield interprets the data starkly: 'The five main terrestrial channels have recorded a combined average viewer share decrease of 32.5 per cent . . . and since 2006 every one of the channels has reported a year-on-year decrease in their market position' (Glanfield 2011). Some of that audience is clawed back by the growing popularity of the big five's digital channels such as ITV4 and E4 – the BBC has seven multi-channel options as well as BBC1 and BBC2, so this apparent decline in audiences on the main channels is not the whole story.

In 2010 there was a turning point in the television landscape. The long heralded convergence of online video, broadcast television, the internet and mobile media services finally arrived in the living room and not just on the laptop. Large audiences for the well-received costume drama *Downton Abbey* helped return ITV to profitability and an adventurous Christmas schedule in 2010, including a classy *Doctor Who* special, delivered high audiences for the BBC. Audiences are watching television on more channels and in different ways. Glanfield notes:

> Now the main terrestrial networks would argue that their influence in the new digital age is even more far reaching than their TV portfolios, as they all now

offer extensive on-demand services on the Internet, through various cable networks and even on video games consoles. This is true; BBC iPlayer, ITV Player, 4OD and Demand Five add more bang to the networks' buck. For example, BBC iPlayer had 1.3 billion requests in 2010.

(Glanfield 2011)

The story in the second decade of the twenty-first century is that all around the world there is a resurgence of interest in traditional broadcast television but it is being accessed differently. Television is able to live confidently alongside online services, video on demand and social networking sites. Television programmes are often the topic of discussion on Twitter and Facebook. Viewing of 'live' television shows such as sports and talent contests (ITV's *The X Factor*) is the currency of communication across the age groups.

The history of television shows that developing technology has been the driver of change in viewing habits and content. As television changed to colour in the 1970s and then widescreen in the 1990s and now High Definition and limited 3D so viewers have bought into the technology and the programmes, but new media knocked this progress off course. Curran in *New Media, Old News* (2010) advises a cautious approach, as technological advances in television rarely live up to their promise, and he cites the overblown benefits of cable TV, community TV and interactive digital TV: 'Even *Big Brother* discontinued the option of red button voting in 2004 to retain voting by telephone' (Curran 2010). Where he agrees new technology did change television was in offering many new channels, up to 1000, by 2011.

Each new technical media development has been greeted as the death of old media, whether it was the demise of newspapers because of the advent of radio, or the end of cinema because of the ubiquity of television. In nearly all cases old media has adapted and flourished and enhanced its role in the media landscape.

Media convergence does offer challenges to broadcast network television. Plunkett argues:

> The most significant recent innovations have actually happened away from television sets and the broadcast networks that serve them . . . the huge success of iPlayer and similar catch-up TV services – as well as Hulu, YouTube and others – have changed the expectations of PC savvy viewers.
>
> (Plunkett 2010)

Modern viewers prefer to be in control of what they are watching and crucially when it is watched. Choice of content came with multi-channel digital cable and satellite broadcasting in the 1990s, but the viewer was still the victim of the scheduler. That changed with the advent of catch-up TV, with the BBC's iPlayer, and digital video recorders such Sky + and YouView.

The viewer is now the scheduler. These services are augmented by on-demand television/internet systems where the viewer is even more in command of not just the schedules but where and how TV can be watched. The viewer is now a participant in the media world.

The internet is part of the future for the delivery of television, and this means that quality programmes and TV content are at a premium. Some quality television programmes made today will still be broadcast in the next decade and so networks are investing in quality drama, sitcoms that will appeal across frontiers, like *Friends* did, and quality shows for young people such as *Glee* (E4).

Broadcast television will continue to be the main form of information and entertainment for most people around the world. However, the way audiences use and receive this content will change to a more interactive mode. The modern viewer delights in multi-tasking. The television programme is the catalyst to text a friend or Tweet with comments on the programme, and the TV is the constant companion while the viewer keeps an eye on Facebook on the laptop, and the football scores on the Blackberry. Far from being displaced, broadcast television is doing what it does best which is to provide varied and well-produced high-quality entertainment, and illuminate the world around us. It is both a reflection of society and a window into society.

In the field of news the main TV broadcasters are possibly vulnerable as the internet is the fastest growing platform for news and information, although the BBC and Channel 4 (ITN) particularly have comprehensive high-quality broadcast and online news presence. Quality news acquisition is both costly and open to cheaper online only alternatives where citizen journalism has created a new market with alternative news sites, blogs, Twitter feeds and Wikileaks. Redden and Witschge argue that abundance does not lead to a plurality of approaches on the internet:

> The content of mainstream news outlets is largely the same, with different outlets – often with a very different ethos and editorial stance – using identified quotes, images and very similar text . . . these sites paint, for the most part, a one dimensional picture of online news homogeneity.
>
> (Redden and Witschge 2010)

Peter Lee-Wright is concerned that the real worry is the destruction of investigative skills as traditional investigative journalism has all but disappeared from television (Lee-Wright 2010: 77). Holland is also concerned with the decline in mainstream current affairs programming although she argues that new programming styles have helped to keep the genre alive:

> Although the project of current affairs has been challenged by many factors – including stunts, hype and infotainment – it has been at its most creative when it has been able to make use of and derive value from these things while at

the same time maintaining a space for consistent, persistent and disrespectful reporting.

(Holland 2006: 219)

Undoubtedly news, current affairs and infotainment will continue to excite and interest audiences on television and online. The blogosphere has been credited with taking on major news corporations and the interactive and participatory nature of the internet means that everyone can be a journalist. Gillan makes a compelling case that it is the muscle of combined media that is also television's strength: 'Broadcast television still has power, but its impact is more dramatic when it works in conjunction with new media' (Gillan 2011: 244).

Ofcom's *Annual Communications Market Report 2010* found that television remains a central part of daily life for all age groups. Each day we spend on average three hours and forty-five minutes watching television and this is up by 3 per cent over five years. It is not, however, just scheduled linear mainstream television that we are watching. The number of people watching satellite services and catch-up TV also increased by more than a third over the twelve months from 2009 to 2010 (Ofcom 2010). The decline of broadcast television – if there ever was one – appears to be halted. Gillan confidently asserts: 'People will continue "to watch television", although what it means to follow a television program and through what devices content is accessed and how viewers are measured will continue to evolve' (Gillan 2011: 244).

CONVERGENCE

Convergence is the coming together of multimedia digital technologies allowing for great flexibility in delivery and storage of data. A television set linked to broadband – satellite, telephone line or cable – becomes an interactive communication module. It is able to download music and video, receive on-demand films, and offer two-way interactive communication with social networking sites, as well as receive broadcast television programmes.

The value of convergence is that it liberates the consumer from the power of monolithic media corporations. These corporations are adapting and changing to convergence culture and finding that they have to take a much greater interest in consumer needs, current fashions and technological changes that are democratising media. Jenkins observes that: 'Convergence is both a top-down corporate-driven process and a bottom-up consumer driven process. Corporate convergence coexists with grassroots convergence' (Jenkins 2008: 18).

Jenkins and others have highlighted the intellectual dissonances around this debate. In this participatory culture as more content becomes available by different platforms so content finds its exclusivity, its revenue stream and its intellectual property rights are all compromised. From the consumer's perspective this is a freeing up of unwanted restrictions allowing greater possibilities for creativity, and expression. Jenkins thinks this individualisation is internal and external: 'Convergence does not occur through media appliances, however sophisticated they may become. Convergence occurs within the brains of individual consumers and through their social interactions with others' (Jenkins 2008: 3).

Global media institutions such as Time Warner, News International and Virgin are embracing the new technologies while still working out how to make money from them. Broadsheet-style newspapers are still making losses in the new convergent media landscape; their owners are looking for alternative revenue streams. News International's *The Times* and *Sunday Times* put up an online pay wall in 2010 making consumers pay to read the newspaper online as one way of stemming losses of over £1 million a week. This is just one way multimedia conglomerates will cross-finance their media activities.

SMART TELEVISION

Traditionally, developing technology has sustained the public's appetite for television, although not always living up to the hype (Curran 2010). Viewing increased dramatically when colour TV became affordable in the early 1970s, and then in the 1990s widescreen encouraged consumers to upgrade to new TV sets. Twenty years later the enhanced crystal clear picture quality of High Definition (HD) television, and the increase in the number of HD channels, has spurred consumers to upgrade their TV sets. In 2010, 22 per cent of people told Ofcom they had bought an HD-ready TV set in the last 12 months with over five million homes having access to HD channels (Ofcom 2010).

Technology has always been important in the relationship between viewers and television institutions. People watch content but own hardware. Viewers are prepared to pay to upgrade their hardware for the content and viewing experience to be enhanced. Just as HD is becoming the 'norm', especially for viewing drama, sport and movies, so the latest video technology of 3D appears. Ofcom reports: '3DTV became a reality as content and 3D-capable equipment began to appear in the UK market. In April 2010, BSkyB launched Europe's first dedicated 3D channel to selected pubs and clubs around the UK' (Ofcom 2011).

A significant technological advance in the second decade of the twenty-first century is the hybrid or smart television set that incorporates broadband connectivity. These sets offer access to a range of web content and applications as well as the ability to watch catch-up TV via online devices such as the BBC iPlayer. This connectivity is also available through Apple TV and video games consoles such as Xbox or by cable and satellite digital boxes. Sony has gone into partnership with Google to launch an HD smart TV set powered by Google's android search platform (Warman 2010). This allows viewers to search for television programmes in the same way they browse the internet and access the Google-owned YouTube in their living rooms. Sales of internet-enabled devices for television sets are predicted to reach 430 million by 2014. This revolution in the way consumers relate to content was forecast by Ashley Highfield, the director of BBC New Media and Technology, in October 2003:

> Future TV may be unrecognisable from today defined not just by linear TV channels, packaged and scheduled by television executives, but instead will resemble a kaleidoscope, thousands of streams of content . . . which will mix broadcasters' content and programmes and viewers contributions . . . The traditional 'monologue broadcaster' to 'grateful viewer' relationship will break down.
>
> (Jenkins 2008: 253)

This break down has already happened as viewers effectively create their own multi-platform schedules watching iPlayer on their computers as well as using catch-up TV DVRs such as Sky+ and Virgin Media's V to view programmes that they have missed. With hybrid TV sets viewers will be able to incorporate other video content from sites such as YouTube, and be able to respond to social networking sites while watching *Coronation Street.* This may put even more pressure on relationships around the family TV set; although young people relish texting on their BlackBerry and using their laptops while watching *Glee* on E4.

For some time now the traditional model of the whole family watching linear television programming around an agreed schedule has been in transition. Cable and satellite companies require viewers to buy a digibox for each TV set, but hybrid televisions which include FreesatHD decoders can also include Wi-Fi connectivity. In Germany the sale of hybrid TV sets has really taken off. One in five of all TV sets sold in Germany during 2010 was a connected TV set. Mathias Birkel of Gold Media is confident that this will not displace traditional television programmes: 'In the short term there will not be a revolution in the living room . . . With more hybrid TV content complementing TV programmes, the internet may increasingly become part of the daily TV routine' (Briel 2010). The broadcasting hardware industry is naturally upbeat. Gerry Kaufhold is a principal analyst for In-Stat: 'TV programmes have come to the Internet. Now, the internet is coming back to TV, and savvy software engineers and smart TV producers are finding ways to create new "hybrid" services that bring it all together' (Briel 2010).

Television and video producers will be able to pitch ideas that combine all the benefits of internet access with the strengths of traditional television programming. These convergent programmes will form the spearhead of new television formats that will excite young audiences brought up on always-on internet access rather than always-on broadcast television.

THE CONTENT CONUNDRUM

This democratisation has led in television, as in film and the music business, to the erroneous idea that the consumer can download significant media content, such as a whole TV programme, for nothing, and that this does not affect the industry or future media content. Writer Mal Peet, conscious of internet piracy, observes: 'We are raising a generation that makes the equation On the Net = Free. An idea whose toxic twin is that you need neither talent nor effort to be successful' (Peet 2010).

Moving and still images, and audio from any broadcaster can be accessed by digital video recorder or via YouTube, where it becomes the user's virtual property to engage with as they wish. Images can be altered, rearranged and included in the user's own creative content. The individual gains some of the power that institutions used to hold. The dilemma is that users' creative responses rarely feed back into institutional professional output, but Citizen Journalism in the form of alternative sites such as Wikileaks contribute to and can drive news agendas, for example the release of US embassy cables in late 2010 was in the headlines of news agencies for some weeks (Quinn 2011).

In the third edition of *The Television Handbook* we postulated that citizen journalism would be a driving force in mainstream television news. Television companies continue to seek out responses and involvement from consumers, typically via blogs, Twitter and forums, and they are all looking for stories that can be used on television news. Online visual media such as YouTube has an enormous audience for its created (mashed) videos, music clips and short slices of everyday life, especially humorous visual anecdotes. This is not a competitor to broadcast TV but an adjunct.

The continued popularity of Reality TV may also suggest to some audiences that success, and its concomitant celebrity, can be achieved with only a modicum of mediocre talent and a fancy haircut. The charge against broadcast television has often been that it is too populist. However, Reality TV has different forms and in its breadth of inclusion mirrors the rise of 2.0 media. Jenkins argues persuasively that convergence allows the individual to flourish in the media landscape and multimedia involvement is fuelled by gossip and ethical discussions stimulated by television: 'Reality Television provides consumers with a steady stream of ethical dramas, as contestants are forced to make choices about whom to trust and what limits to set on their own behaviour . . .' (Jenkins 2008: 84). Television programmes are a prime driver in online interaction.

YOUVIEW

Of all the terrestrial broadcasters the BBC has most enthusiastically embraced the possibilities of convergence, through its comprehensive website, iPlayer and now with YouView. YouView is a joint venture between the BBC and partners BT, ITV, Channel 4, Channel 5, Talk Talk and Arqiva. It allows digital terrestrial TV viewers with a broadband connection to watch on-demand services and other internet services without paying a subscription other than for broadband costs.

This development was originally called Project Canvas: 'Canvas involves the creation and development and promotion of a set of core technical specifications to enable delivery of on-demand, interactive and web-based content to a television via a broadband connected digital device' (BBC News 2010).

Like the UK's current free-to-air brands Freeview and FreesatHD, YouView will be licensed to device manufacturers and internet service providers. YouView integrates the broadcast and on-demand worlds via the television set. It allows third-party business models to thrive through an open platform, bringing the benefits of next-generation TV to approximately ten million people who do not wish to pay for subscription TV. The principle behind YouView is that it should make it easier for viewers to catch up with programmes from the BBC iPlayer, ITV.com and 4OD on their TV set, rather than on a laptop, desktop, or mobile phone. It incorporates a basic search and browse functionality for web and interactive content, and applications and settings, for example, for parental controls.

YouView creates an open internet-connected TV environment to offer viewers seamless access to broadcast television and video-on-demand, web-based audio and video content, High Definition channels, and interactive services over the internet direct to the TV. YouView's chairman, Kip Meek, emphasises the plurality of this service: 'YouView is key to ensuring that everyone in the UK benefits from next-generation TV' (BBC News 2010).

Youview has come in for some criticism mainly from commercial media conglomerates who argue that it is anti-competitive. Sky and Virgin Media asked Ofcom to investigate. Sky launched its own version, Sky Anytime +, offering video-on-demand to three million of its ten million subscribers who have a set-top box with internet connection. Virgin Media provides the BBC iPlayer to its cable subscribers as well as video-on-demand, and is launching an internet-enabled TV recorder.

The future for broadcast television looks stronger than it was at the turn of the century. The technology is in place to deliver a wealth of content to large audiences on different platforms. Institutionally, the BBC has a standardised license fee until 2017 providing security and continuity; ITV is at last making a profit as advertising revenues increase, and attracting large audiences of over ten million with the extremely popular reality talent show *The X Factor*. Channel 5 has been taken over by the owner of the *Express* newspaper which alarms some but will probably revitalise the profits of the channel. Channel 4 is finding new and larger audiences for its digital channel E4, with popular young adult series such as *Glee* and *Skins*; BSkyB is set to become the largest media company in the UK. At the beginning of 2011 the UK's foremost mainstream broadcasters appear to be in rude health.

REFERENCES AND FURTHER READING

BBC News, Technology. 'Project Canvas to become YouView', 16 September 2010: http//bbc.co.uk/1/hi/technology/8424677.stm.

Bignell, J. *An Introduction to Television Studies*, London: Routledge, 2004.

Briel, R. *Hybrid TVs conquer German households*, in Broadband TV News, 2010, http://www.broadbandtvnews.com/2010/08/12/.

Curran, J. 'Technology Foretold', in *New Media, Old News*, ed. N. Fenton, London: Sage, London 2010, pp. 19–33.

Gillan, J. *Television and New Media* London/New York: Routledge, 2011.

Glanfield, T. *A decade of decline?*, Beehivecity, January 2011, www.beehivecity.com/television/a-decade-of-decline-bbc-one-bbc-two-itv-1-channel-4-five-98191/.

Holland, P. *The Angry Buzz: This Week and Current Affairs Television*, London: I B Tauris, 2006.

Jenkins, H. *Convergence Culture*, New York: New York University Press, 2008.

Lee-Wright, P. 'Culture Shock: New Media and Organisational Change in the BBC', in *New Media, Old News*, ed. N. Fenton, London: Sage, 2010.

Ofcom, *Annual Communications Market Report*, 2010: www.ofcom.org.uk.

Peet, M. 2010, http://www.alcs.co.uk/news/parting_shot.html.

Plunkett, S. Red Bee Media interviewed at Broadcast Video Expo conference, 2010.

Quinn, B. 'Wikileaks: the latest developments', *Guardian*, 18 January 2011.

Redden, J. and Witschge, T. 'A new News Order? Online News Content Examined', in *New Media Old News*, ed. N. Fenton, London: Sage, 2010, p. 184.

Warman, M. 'Only connect: from study to sofa', *Telegraph* 4 September 2010.

CHAPTER 2

Television regulation

A basic tenet of a stable democracy is a free media with the expectation that media power will not be unlimited. Effective citizenship stems from the availability of censorship-free news and information, and citizens have a right to a media which is held in check by a regulatory framework that protects and balances conflicting interests (Feintuck 1999). The progress of democratic government and the flow of ideas across frontiers is aided by a free media: 'This process of democratisation was enormously strengthened by the development of modern mass media . . . (and that) the media struggled successfully to become free of government' (Curran 2002: 4). In the UK the quid pro quo for broadcasting being free of government interference is a form of regulation known as compliance, by an independent regulator – Ofcom.

Issues of broadcasting regulation have taken on greater significance to television producers and audiences since the 2004 Hutton Report heavily criticised the BBC over reporting issues to do with the Iraq War (Hutton Report 2004). The BBC editorial system, BBC management and the BBC governors were all criticised, leading eventually to an overhaul of BBC governance, and the replacement of the governors with the BBC Trust as the governing body of the BBC set out in the current BBC charter which runs until the end of 2016.

The fall out from the Hutton report means that all broadcast television companies are more aware, and more wary, of regulations and operational guidelines – compliance – especially in news and current affairs, and areas such as the regulations for phone-in competitions, and media ownership.

Discourses concerning media regulation in the past have often revolved around issues to do with television content and audience offence, media power and the way excesses of commercialisation can be curbed. Due to media convergence, regulation now has to cope with wider boundaries and issues, and considerably more content via, for example, nearly 1000 TV channels in the UK. Regulation is not fixed – it is dynamic and fluid especially in relation to media ownership and control, and it needs to be, as global media operators increase in size and continue to colonise the digital environment. Phillips, Couldry and Freedman argue that audiences must take more responsibility for compliance: 'With the development of web TV, PVRs and online news, regulators are re-evaluating their approach to content regulation and shifting responsibilities for content not just on to the industry but on to audiences themselves' (Phillips *et al.* 2010: 66).

The pressure on regulators is now more to do with ownership and the public interest, child protection online and intellectual property infringement. In early 2011, News Corporation filed to buy all the remaining shares in the satellite broadcaster BskyB in a £7.5 billion deal – it already owns just under 40 per cent. Many newspaper owners and television companies believed this takeover not to be in the public interest. Ofcom referred News Corporation's takeover bid back to the Secretary of State, and the Competition Commission sought an inquiry into whether this deal would restrict choice for British audiences. Ofcom also produces in-depth reports including two on Public Service Broadcasting – see Chapter 3.

Ofcom has not been without criticism. Some commercial media organisations pressing for less regulation in the changing global media environment criticised it for not being fit for purpose. In December 2009 the British Screen Advisory Council, an independent body funded by the media industry, called for 'lighter touch' media regulation in the UK concluding: 'Ofcom under its current structure . . . needs to be reconstituted in order to be able to deliver a rapid response to evolving markets as an economic regulator' (BSAC 2009).

OFCOM

Ofcom is the independent regulatory body for all communications and broadcasting. It employs 880 people. Ofcom's responsibilities and duties were laid down in the Communications Act 2003 which was driven in part by the possibilities offered by convergence (Barnett 2003). It aims to make the UK's media regulations more efficient and more user friendly to viewers. It combines the functions of the previous regulators: the Independent Television Commission (ITC), the Broadcasting Standards Commission (BSC), the Radio Authority, the Office of Telecommunications (Oftel), and the Radio-communications Agency. It replaced other broadcasting watchdogs including the Broadcasting Standards Commission (BSC), which dealt with taste and decency matters on TV and radio, and the Radio Authority. The Act says that Ofcom's general duties should be to further the interests of citizens and of consumers. Accountable to parliament, Ofcom is funded by fees from industry for regulating broadcasting and communications networks, and by the Government. It is involved in advising and setting some of the more technical aspects of regulation, and implementing and enforcing the law (Communications Act 2003).

Ofcom regulates terrestrial and satellite commercial television and radio, and the whole area of telecommunications. It regulates the use of commercials on television but not the content. It is concerned to protect viewers and listeners from harmful or offensive material and from being treated unfairly in television and radio programmes, or from having their privacy invaded. It has technical responsibility for managing the radio spectrum – that is the airwaves used by everyone from taxi firms and boat owners, to mobile-phone companies and broadcasters (Ofcom 2011).

There are some things that Ofcom does not do regarding television. It does not regulate the content of TV advertisements which is done by the Advertising Standards Authority, the independent regulator of advertising across all media (ASA 2011), and it does not deal with complaints about accuracy in BBC programmes, or regulate the BBC TV licence fee.

When Ofcom receives complaints from the public about television programmes it assesses them under the Broadcasting Code, revised in December 2010.

BROADCASTING CODE

The Broadcasting Code sets standards for television and radio shows that broadcasters have to follow. They can be fined if they breach the Code which not only covers harm and offence, but also other areas like impartiality and accuracy, sponsorship and commercial references as well as fairness and privacy (Ofcom Broadcasting Code 2010). For example, the Code has rules on what can be broadcast on TV before the 9.00 pm watershed. (Programme makers for the BBC also follow the BBC's editorial guidelines which are the BBC's values and standards, and apply to all the BBC's content, wherever and however it is received – see Chapter 3.)

There are many sections under the Code which detail exactly what broadcasters must not show in their TV programmes. For example, under the section 'Protecting the Under Eighteens' broadcasters are required not to show: 'Material that might seriously impair the physical, mental or moral development of people under eighteen' (Ofcom 2010). Ofcom has to be responsive to the mores of the time and the public consensus on sensitive issues as these change over time.

GENERALLY ACCEPTED STANDARDS

Ofcom is charged with looking after in all broadcasting that difficult territory known in the BBC Editorial Guidelines as harm and offence. This now includes BBC programmes that had previously been regulated in this area by the BBC governors, before the BBC Trust was set up. This now comes under 'generally accepted standards'. The Ofcom broadcasting code requires television broadcasters to be vigilant particularly in live programmes:

> In applying generally accepted standards broadcasters must ensure that material which may cause offence is justified by the context. Such material may include, but is not limited to, offensive language, violence, sex, sexual violence, humiliation, distress, violation of human dignity, discriminatory treatment or language for example on the grounds of age, disability, gender, race, religion, beliefs and sexual orientation.
>
> (Ofcom Broadcasting Code 2010)

BBC TRUST

The BBC Trust was set up to replace the BBC governors whom the Labour Government of Tony Blair considered were not sufficiently independent as a regulator of the BBC, in the wake of the 2004 Hutton Report. The Trust was established by Royal Charter and became effective from 1 January 2007.

The BBC Trust's stated aim is to represent the licence fee payers – that is the public who pay for the BBC. The Trust sets BBC strategy and top-level budgets and appoints the BBC's top executive, the Director-General, and it makes sure the BBC has the right standards and that its programmes live up to those standards. Also the Trust reviews all BBC services at least once every five years. There are twelve trustees whose main stated aim is to support the BBC, and, crucially, guard its independence (BBC Trust).

For example the Trust had to fully consider the involvement of the BBC in the exciting and technically challenging cross-media Project Canvas that became YouView. In June 2010 the Trust approved YouView which is a joint venture between the BBC and commercial partners to develop and promote a common standard that will allow viewers with a broadband connection to watch on-demand video services and other internet content as well as broadcast TV, through their television sets.

The performance of the BBC Trust by 2011 suggests that its governance has created more distance from BBC management than the governors were able to do. This has led to disagreements, and the first Chairman of the Trust Sir Michael Lyons stepped down after one term in May 2011. Sir Michael said the trust had 'taken openness and transparency to a new level' and helped to ensure the BBC operated 'within clear boundaries' (Channel 4 News).

Some politicians from the Coalition government are critical of the BBC Trust as being a 'regulator and cheerleader' and being too 'close' to BBC management, and say they would prefer another – so far unformulated – system that would be even more independent. Critics have a strong point when they argue that the Trust cannot both support the BBC and regulate it. There is unlikely to be any fundamental change until the current BBC charter expires in 2016.

HARM AND OFFENCE

The most controversial area of regulation that used to be called taste and decency is now under the more upfront title of harm and offence. It comes within the BBC's charter obligation to apply: 'Generally accepted standards so as to provide adequate protection for members of the public from the inclusion of offensive and harmful material' (BBC guidelines).

Ofcom regulations under generally accepted standards include similar sections on harm and offence.

> This area of harm and offence is qualitative, and will change according to the time and what is culturally acceptable. It can vary from place to place and from one part of society to another. It is difficult to define; as a programme maker it is something that becomes part of your make up; to be always aware of your audience, whether they are children or adults, and when are they viewing – prime time, afternoon, late night or during the school holidays. It spans cultures and generations. It is concerned with respect for the traditions, background and rituals of all people and their beliefs.
>
> (Ofcom 2010)

The emphasis has switched from questions of taste to asking if the programme is likely to cause harm or offence. Offence against decency is usually more serious. An offence against decency implies the concept of actual damage and offence to a member of the audience. Regulators will only condone such breaches if they feel the subject matter is justified by context, and is in the public interest. Ofcom is charged with making sure the public is protected from the inclusion of harmful or offensive material across all television.

Recent UK research (Ofcom 2010) suggests that while people have become more relaxed about the portrayal of sex on television, they remain concerned about the depiction of violence. The use of strong language affects some audiences more than others, and can be a particular source of offence before the watershed. Parents with children are naturally concerned about what appears on television. Most people expect to be given clear signals if they are about to see controversial material or hear strong language.

THE WATERSHED

In this area of harm and offence the cornerstone of British policy is the 9.00 pm watershed. All the major broadcasters have signed up to this policy. Before this time all programmes on available-to-all channels should be suitable for a general audience including children. The watershed period runs from 9.00 pm until 5.30 am the following morning.

Ofcom's guidelines for the broadcast of explicit violence or sexual material in post-watershed programming are open to some interpretation. There are no outright bans, but decisions on breaches of the guidelines are dependent on many factors. For example, there are guidelines, but no fixed broadcasting rules except the law of the land, for the treatment of sadistic and sexual violence. In fact, the legislation on the portrayal of the occult and paranormal on television is probably stricter than that governing violence. Taking all these guidelines into consideration, it is appropriate for a mature society that there is no fixed idea of exactly what is within the bounds of harm and offence – it is a subjective matter which can vary from programme to programme depending on the context, intended audience, and time of broadcast.

SEX AND VIOLENCE

Viewers have become more liberal in their acceptance of sexually explicit material post-watershed. There is still control over the use of some sexual language on television, and the showing of explicit sexual activity. Sensitive handling of the material can prevent causing widespread offence. The context of the scene, the intention of the production, and the expectations of the audience have to be taken into consideration when planning the use of sexually explicit material.

In news and current affairs, audiences are more likely to accept disturbing material so long as it has a clear moral context, and is recognised as being true to life. Research shows that violence on television can upset many people and, in excess, it can be accused of desensitising viewers. Trailers of violent programmes or movies with violent scenes shown before 9.00 pm must not include unsuitable material.

Scenes of domestic and sexual violence, especially where women and children are portrayed as victims, attempted suicide, and any scene that may give the impression of approving of violence has to be approached with extreme caution (Ofcom 2010).

BAD LANGUAGE

The use of bad language on television used to generate the most letters and telephone complaints. In recent years viewers appear to be less concerned about swearing than they used to be. Audiences are most likely to complain if they are taken by surprise by the use of swear-words, or if the use of bad language feels gratuitous, or swear-words are used in a programme that is contrary to the expectations of the viewers of that programme. Bad language on *Animal Hospital* would not be tolerated, but on a late night chat show it would be acceptable.

Terms of racist abuse are considered to be offensive by all sections of the audience, may be against the law, and must be avoided at all times. Abusive names relating to disabilities are not acceptable.

All complaints and comments about harm and offence on available-to-all television channels go to Ofcom. Of all the complaints upheld by Ofcom most dealt with unsuitable behaviour broadcast before the watershed. Complaints received about adult-oriented programmes tended not to be upheld or were resolved, especially where the broadcaster in question had taken steps to deal with the problem promptly (Ofcom 2010).

COMPLAINTS

Anyone can complain to Ofcom if they think the Broadcasting Code has been infringed on any television channel available in the UK. If after a complaint Ofcom finds a programme has broken the rules, then it will be found in breach of the Code and Ofcom makes a decision about what will happen, which may be a warning or a fine. Ofcom assesses all the broadcast complaints it receives, but only investigates those which may raise issues under the Code. The Broadcasting Code (December 2010) may be visited at: www.ofcom.org.uk under the 'stakeholders' heading.

One of the most contentious issues that Ofcom deals with is complaints about bias in television programmes. Every fortnight Ofcom publishes its Broadcast Bulletin which includes the latest decisions about the complaints they have received. The Broadcast Bulletin reports on the outcome of investigations into alleged breaches of Ofcom codes.

An example of how Ofcom operates and how seriously it takes complaints comes from a complaint about a programme called *Remember Palestine* broadcast on Press TV, 5 June 2010, 11.30 am. In this case Ofcom had a difficult decision to do with possible political bias and freedom of speech. Press TV is an Iranian international news network broadcasting in English, and receives funding from the Iranian government. *Remember Palestine* was a current affairs programme presented by the journalist Lauren Booth, which discussed the events during and following the interception by Israeli military forces of a pro-Palestinian aid convoy in international waters in the Mediterranean Sea on 31 May 2010. In the incident Israeli commandoes killed nine of the people aboard the convoy. Ofcom received a complaint that the programme criticised the actions of the Israeli military forces, and failed to air alternative views. The detailed Ofcom report, including quotes from the programme gives this judgement:

> In assessing whether due impartiality has been applied in this case, the term 'due' is important. Under the Code, it means adequate or appropriate to the subject and nature of the programme. Therefore, 'due impartiality' does not mean an equal division of time has to be given to every view, or that every

argument and every facet of every argument has to be represented . . . In this case, Ofcom considered that the programme included a number of viewpoints, but all of them could be portrayed as being critical of the Israeli state's policy in this case to use military force against the aid convoy which led to nine deaths . . . We considered that the programme did not contain any alternative views . . .

(Ofcom Broadcast Bulletin, August 2010)

Ofcom's verdict was that the programme was in breach of Rule 5.5 of the Broadcasting Code which states: 'Due impartiality on matters of political or industrial controversy and matters relating to current public policy must be preserved . . . this may be achieved within a programme or over a series of programmes taken as a whole' (Ofcom Broadcast Bulletin, August 2010).

This is an interesting judgement. The regulator is quite clear that to observe due impartiality within a fiercely political one-off programme such as this, alternative views to the mainstream argument must be contained within the programme. Mainstream broadcasters can argue that impartiality is balanced over a period of time because they have a mixed schedule of political/topical programmes. A non-mainstream channel such as Press TV that just makes one programme on a contentious topic needs to be balanced with either another programme presenting the alternative views or within the same programme. Libertarian commentators might argue that this is a form of censorship as it restricts non-mainstream channels from airing one-off political programmes, as it is not financially viable to always provide an alternative programme observing 'due impartiality'. Others might take the position that it is this regulated balance that gives broadcasting in the UK its reputation for being truthful and impartial.

TELEVISION ADVERTISING

The only area of commercial television not regulated by Ofcom is the content of advertisements. This is covered by an independent body, the Advertising Standards Authority (ASA) which regulates all advertising across all media including internet, sales promotions and direct marketing. The ASA ensures all advertising is legal, decent, honest and truthful by applying the Advertising Codes. Its website details the rules for advertising, accepts complaints online, and explains how the ASA works to keep UK advertising standards as high as possible. See www. asa.org.uk/. The key regulation is that a television commercial should be **legal** – within all the laws of the land; **decent**, which means it does not offend anybody; **honest**, which means that it must be free of dishonest fakery; **truthful**, which means it must not make claims about the efficacy of a product that has not been proved (ASA 2011).

The Advertising Codes lay down rules that advertisers, agencies and media owners must follow. There is an Advertising Standards Code for TV and radio and one for non-broadcasting which includes cinema advertising. The ASA is not responsible for writing the rules, just making sure they are observed. The Broadcast Committee of Advertising Practice (BCAP) is responsible for writing and maintaining the TV and Radio Advertising Standards Codes. The members of this committee comprise the main industry bodies representing advertisers, agencies and media owners including individual broadcasters.

The ASA Code's wide-ranging rules are designed to protect the consumer and ensure that advertising does not mislead, harm or offend, and is socially responsible across all advertising. The Code also contains specific rules for alcoholic drinks, health and beauty claims, children, medicines, financial products, environmental claims, gambling, direct marketing and prize promotions. These rules add an extra layer of consumer protection and aim to ensure that UK advertising is responsible.

NB: The print press is self-regulated by the non-governmental Press Complaints Commission (PCC) which deals with complaints from the public about editorial content of newspapers and magazines. Complaints are investigated under the editors' Code of Practice, which binds all national and regional newspapers and magazines, and was drawn up by editors themselves. The Code covers the way news is gathered and reported, and provides special protection to particularly vulnerable people such as children, hospital patients and those at risk of discrimination (PCC 2010).

REFERENCES AND FURTHER READING

Advertising Standards Authority: www.asa.org.uk.
Barnett, S. http://www.mediaed.org.uk/posted_documents/
    The_2003_Communications_Act.htm.
BBC Editorial guidelines: www.bbc.co.uk/guidelines/editorialguidelines/guidelines/.
BBC News: http://www.bbc.co.uk/news/business-12185875.
BBC Trust, The: www.bbc.co.uk/bbctrust/about/how_we_govern/
    charter_and_agreement/.
British Screen Advisory Council report: Creativity, competitiveness and enterprise
    in Uk audiovisual: new vision new politics. December 2009: http://www.bsac.
    uk.com/files/creativity_competitiveness_and_enterprise_report_dec_2009.pdf.
Channel 4 News: http://www.channel4.com/news/articles/arts_entertainment/
    bbc%2Btrust%2Bchairman%2Bsir%2Bmichael%2Blyons%2Bto%2Bstep%
    2Bdown/3766487.html.
Communications Act 2003: http://www.legislation.gov.uk/ukpga/2003/21/contents.
Curran, J. *Media and Power*, London: Routledge, 2002.
Curran, J. (ed.). *Media and Society*, 5th ed, London: Bloomsbury, 2010
Feintuck, M. *Media Regulation, Public Interest and the Law*, Edinburgh: EUP, 1999.
Foster, R. *Future of Broadcasting Regulation*, London: Department for Culture,
    Media and Sport, 2007.
Frost, C. *Media Ethics and Self-regulation*, London: Pearson Education, 2000.

Hutton Report, The: in full, 28 January 2004: http://news.bbc.co.uk/1/
     shared/spl/hi/uk/03/hutton_inquiry/hutton_report/html/chapter12.stm#a90.
Ofcom: www.ofcom.org.uk/.
Ofcom Broadcast Bulletin, August 2010:
     http://stakeholders.ofcom.org.uk/binaries/enforcement/broadcast-bulletins/
     0bb163/issue163.pdf.
Ofcom Broadcasting Code: http://stakeholders.ofcom.org.uk/broadcasting/
     broadcast-codes/broadcast-code/.
Phillips, A., Couldry, N. and Freedman, D. 'An Ethical Deficit? Accountability,
     Norms and the Material Conditions of Contemporary Journalism' in *New
     Media*, *Old News*, (ed. N. Fenton), London: Sage, 2010.
Press Complaints Commission: www.pcc.org.uk/cop/practice.html.
Reynolds, J. Mediaweek 2009: www.mediaweek.co.uk.

CHAPTER 3

Public service broadcasting

The concept of public service broadcasting (PSB) in relation to television is a constant subject for discussion and debate in the media industry and in academic discourses. What is PSB for and how should it be funded in a less regulated digital media environment? PSB is a publicly funded not-for-profit broadcasting service for the benefit of everyone. Most developed countries have some degree of public service television funded by a form of licence fee and usually some advertising. PSB is seen by the public, as reported by a 2009 Ofcom report, as being both desirable and beneficial, and particularly in its independence: 'The ultimate safeguard of broadcasting independence is that it has generally the support of the public' (Curran 2002: 223).

Critics of PSB cite the distortion of the commercial media market in the UK and the size and power of the BBC: 'We seem to have decided to let independence and plurality wither. To let the BBC throttle the news market, and get bigger to compensate' (James Murdock 2009). In the UK PSB is synonymous with the BBC although all five free-to-air mainstream television channels BBC1, BBC2, ITV, Channel 4 and Channel 5 must provide some public service scheduling. PSB services include news and current affairs programmes and other programming that enlivens the cultural climate: 'The public service ideal has acted as a sort of "conceptual glue" which has enabled sometimes contradictory forces to co-exist in an interrelated system' (Holland 2003).

A major rationale for PSB is that it helps citizens to be better informed about society and their own communities. It is in the news arena that PSB is most supported, especially the impartiality and accuracy strenuously embraced by the BBC: 'We need to understand the world we act in: elite understanding is never a substitute for public knowledge. It is the BBC's duty to explain the world to publics that adds diversity and value to its news gathering . . . the BBC has the capacity to speak with authority on behalf of accuracy' (Seaton 2008: 123).

For the UK's mainstream commercial channels, ITV, Channel 4 and Channel 5, there is an obligation to provide a regular, quality news service throughout the day. There are other requirements to do with programming for minorities. A bone of contention for ITV 1 is that it is required to broadcast regular religious programming, and Ofcom has indicated that it may drop this requirement in the future.

Ofcom instigated a second comprehensive review of PSB, which reported in 2009, entitled Putting Viewers First: 'The recommendations . . . set out what we believe is required to fulfill a vision of diverse, vibrant and engaging public service content enjoyed across a range of digital media, which complements a flourishing and expansive market sector.' Their recommendations, that have been largely taken up by the Coalition government, include: 'Maintaining the BBC's role and funding, supporting investment in ITV1 and Channel 5 services as commercial networks with a limited public service commitment . . . and to ensure the supply of a choice of high quality news alongside the BBC in the devolved nations and English regions' (Ofcom report 2009).

THE BBC

The BBC is solely a public service broadcaster providing sophisticated and comprehensive broadcast television, radio, and interactive website services to UK citizens. It has to keep up with and in some cases lead the way (e.g. iPlayer) in technological developments. The BBC is an entirely independent organisation governed by the BBC Trust. It is run in the interests of its viewers and listeners. The BBC Trust safeguards its independence, sets its principal objectives, and approves strategy and policy as well as monitoring the BBC's performance, and publishing an annual report.

Stable funding is at the heart of any PSB service. The BBC derives its income from the licence fee (£145.50 per annum for a colour television set). This generates an annual income of about £3.7 billion to pay for all BBC services (BBC Trust). The advantage of this form of financing is that the BBC can concentrate on providing high-quality programmes, and interactive services, catering for everyone, including minority groups and organisations, without having to satisfy shareholders looking for profits. All households with a television receiver are required by law to pay the licence fee. Critics complain that the licence fee is a compulsory tax that no one can avoid which distorts the market. However, this has not stopped commercial competitors and critics, such as satellite broadcaster BSkyB, from making substantial profits: 'Sky has an annual turnover of £5.9bn, of which £4.8bn is from its core retail subscription business. That revenue line alone is £1.1 billion more than the

FIGURE 3.1
Broadcasting House

BBC's UK public service turnover . . . Sky's marketing budget is larger than the entire programme budget of ITV1' (Thomson 2010). Compared to the cost of digital channels provided by non-PSB broadcasters such as BSkyB and Virgin the BBC provides value for money. It provides an available-to-all (via Freeview and FreesatHD) comprehensive broadcasting service in television and radio and one of the most successful and well-used websites in the world. The licence fee pays for:

- Nine television channels: BBC 1, BBC 2, BBC 3, BBC 4, BBC News, BBC Parliament, CBBC and CBeebies.
- Five network radio services, and several digital radio services: Radio 1, 2, 3, 4 and 5; BBC Radio 5 Live Sports Extra, BBC Radio 1Xtra, BBC Radio 4Extra, BBC 6 Music and BBC Asian Network (although this is under review and will probably be axed).
- Regional television programmes and local radio services in England.
- National radio and television in Scotland, Wales and Northern Ireland.
- Interactive and online services: BBC Red Button, BBC Mobile, BBC iPlayer and the BBC website www.bbc.co.uk and it has initiated the online broadcasting service YouView.
- The BBC is also an important provider of broadcasting and media training. It supports British production skills and talent in music, drama, film, radio and television. (BBC Licensing 2011).

In October 2010 the coalition government agreed a deal with the BBC to freeze the licence fee at its current level of £145.50 until 2017. The BBC will have extra responsibilities including the cost of the World Service (previously Foreign Office-funded), BBC Monitoring and some of the costs of Welsh language TV channel S4C. Director general Mark Thompson said it was 'a realistic deal in exceptional circumstances securing a strong independent BBC' (BBC 2010).

This can be seen as a strengthening of PSB as it secures the funding of the BBC until after the next general election even if it means a cut in real terms of 16 per cent over the time period. PSB needs to remain a strong player in UK broadcast television with the challenges of online TV services from Google, BT and Apple TV and the increasing size and influence of BSkyB currently with 10 million subscribers and an estimated turnover by 2017 of £6.9 billion – double that of the licence fee.

THE PSB FUNDING DEBATE

The main terrestrial television channels available in all homes are regulated by Ofcom. They have to provide elements of public service broadcasting out of their own commercial funding. Alternative methods of raising finance for PSB generally involve advertising or subscription fees or both. The BBC is the only public service broadcaster with no commercial funding. The licence fee upsets some people as it is seen as a retrogressive compulsory tax. Governments do not like taxes that do not come to the Treasury. There have been many attempts to invent an alternative source of funding for the BBC. Other countries such as New Zealand have scrapped the licence fee, and fund all channels with advertising. This has not led to a better service for New Zealand's viewers. Some European countries keep a smaller licence fee and allow some advertising for their public service channels. Most commentators agree that by accepting advertising the independence of the channels is compromised. A recent Ofcom review found that funding public service broadcasting by the licence fee was the best and most cost-effective method of maintaining the range and quality of the broadcasting provided by the BBC (Ofcom 2009). All the evidence is that the majority of the British public are willing to pay for BBC services with a licence fee, although there is a feeling that the present fee is the maximum that the public will pay.

Alternative suggestions for sources of funding include a subscription service. This is how some of the public service channels in the USA are funded, often woefully inadequately. Also subscription undermines the principle of universality, whereby the broadcaster's output is available to everyone. Most commentators believe that a subscription model based on say HBO in the USA would not be viable in the UK as the population is less than a third of the USA.

Another idea is to top slice the licence fee, and give some of the money to other broadcasters who have a public service remit (Elstein 2008). Many broadcasters oppose this as it would confuse the public's idea of what the licence fee is for, and add an intolerable level of extra bureaucracy. There is the risk that public money would benefit shareholders rather than licence payers.

Another idea that is often floated is that the BBC should accept some advertising. This would reduce the licence fee according to the amount of revenue generated by advertising. The main argument against this is that the revenues of the commercial broadcasters, particularly ITV, Channel 4 and Channel 5, would be severely reduced. Other suggestions include a form of government grant made to a Public Broadcasting Authority, rather like a grant to an arts institution such as the National Theatre. Elstein advocates a mix of this approach with other forms of funding: 'If voluntary subscription and advertising were used to fund the BBC's market content, its non market content could be financed most equitably (given the regressive nature of the licence fee) by a fund sourced from normal taxation' (Elstein 2008: 87).

With the change of government in 2010 the BBC came under renewed pressure to, at the very least, not raise the licence fee by even the value of inflation. A think tank the Adam Smith Institute produced a report suggesting that the growing use of the internet for viewing has made licensing TV sets outdated and their less than radical solution is to scrap the television licence fee and replace it with a voluntary subscription service for some BBC programming – such as drama and entertainment (Adam Smith Institute 2010). It can be argued that collecting the licence fee from everyone is technically outdated as many people consume the BBC through the internet where a licence is not required. It is, however, very difficult to devise a fairer scheme that is better than the present one.

The latest report from Ofcom (2009) shows that a large majority of people agree that because the licence fee is separate from general taxation, and is not a government grant, it reinforces the BBC's independence, and keeps it focused on serving the public and is good value. The licence fee is paid by all TV households, and so the BBC does not have to take a populist approach to programme making and scheduling. It does not have to please all of its audiences all of the time in order to stay in business. Populist programmes can be scheduled alongside pro-grammes for minority audiences. This is the Reithian approach of mixed programming and even in a multi-channel environment it still can work to introduce audiences to ideas, concepts and information that they might not expect. This has recently been true of the new popular approach to science and history by programmes on the BBC.

NEWS

News is the backbone of public service broadcasting. Issues of balance, impartiality and understanding are at the forefront of PSB news reporting on all channels. This does not mean news is either perfectly delivered in terms of meaning and context or that it is always doing its job to keep the public fully informed. Philo and Berry challenge assumptions about how news is absorbed by an audience in a complex arena like the Israeli–Palestinian conflict, where they argue reporting of the conflict tended to be 'enigmatic and brief', leaving audiences likely to 'switch off' (Philo and Berry 2004). They worry that what is reported can be incomprehensible to audiences, not properly contextualised and relying too much on visual imperatives and avoiding social and historical background. Audiences do need to take some responsibility for understanding, but PSB news services may need to do more in this area of contextualisation to fully achieve their public service remit.

Modern international newsrooms servicing domestic TV news and twenty-four-hour news channels require large amounts of video footage each day. A TV newsroom aims to get up-to-the-minute pictures on the air as soon as possible. This is an extremely competitive business as news channels compete for the first pictures of a breaking news story. The main BBC newsroom in west London currently receives about 300 hours of video every day. The news footage comes in to a digital newsroom, utilising the latest technology. Citizen journalism is already an innovative news provider throwing up serious news stories such as Wikileaks in 2010, or more celebrity-orientated stories through Twitter feeds. Twenty-four-hour rolling news channels, such as BBC News, and Sky News, are continually updating their newsroom technology, and providing faster and more sophisticated on-air and online services. Sky News has a particularly fast rolling graphics service.

There is no doubt that BBC news services are very popular, reaching over 98 per cent of the UK population every week. Surveys show that viewers prefer radio and television news programmes which are not interrupted by advertising. The BBC website with over two million pages is one of the most popular in the world, continually winning awards.

One important way commercial channels fulfil their public service objectives are by providing local news. This is costly for them and throughout the world local TV news is not commercially viable. In the UK the commercial PSB channels provide local/regional news to keep their top billing in the on-screen electronic programme guides. When a viewer presses the menu or guide button on the handset the top five PSB channels are always at the top BBC1, BBC2, ITV1, Channel 4 and Channel 5. The Coalition government believe that developing good local news coverage is essential to the progress of the 'big society' where people are more involved in all aspects of local life. In a survey, eight out of ten people considered local news stories important. The Culture Secretary Jeremy Hunt in a speech to the Royal Television Society in September 2010 said:

> My vision is of a landscape of local TV services broadcasting for as little as one hour a day ... I will begin the process of redefining public service broadcasting for the digital age by asking Ofcom to look at how we can ensure that enough emphasis is given to the delivery of local content.
>
> (Royal Television Society 2010)

To begin the process of financing this local initiative the government is removing the local cross-media ownership regulations which paves the way for local newspapers and local commercial radio stations to produce local TV news. It will be interesting to see if this really does provide the sort of news people in small localities want to see. Already BBC local radio successfully serves this role in many towns and counties, and local television news is both expensive and notoriously hard to sustain every day. The Culture Secretary suggested in January 2011 he would like to see 'expressions of interest' in running a new national Channel 6 for local news run by both the BBC and ITV and available on Freeview by 2013: 'Mr Hunt is determined to push these plans through, and his aims are laudable: to create popular local TV news services that will hold local authorities, NHS trusts, schools and the like to account' (Midgely 2011). There is no doubt that local TV news sustains the principle of public service broadcasting. It may be that the BBC has to share a small proportion of the licence fee as a form of subsidy to these burgeoning local TV commercial news services.

CHILDREN'S TV

Children's television in the UK is an important element in the public service broadcasting mix. Children are the television viewers of the future, and they are considered uniquely vulnerable to undue influences from television. Many studies have purported to show the effects that television viewing can have on children. The effects debate has a discordant history with no firm conclusions about any adverse effects on children of watching children's TV. The debate is mired in conflicts over research methodologies and how effects can be measured. Especially contentious has been the issue of violence in cartoons.

One research study by a British team set up on the island of St Helena, when broadcast television first reached the island, found that children did not mimic violence on TV. Psychologist Tony Charlton's study seems unequivocal: 'We have produced evidence that when broadcast television becomes available in a community it needn't necessarily produce harmful effects upon children's behaviour' (BBC News 1998). An ongoing current debate concerns the amount of television watched by children and the possible way it affects their lives. Parents have always been concerned that their offspring spend too much time in front of the TV set. Now they also spend a lot of time in front of the computer screen logging onto Facebook and YouTube or playing video games. A BBC *Panorama* programme in June 2007 explored the effects of removing the TV from the family home. It found that the parents engaged more with the children when there was no TV set. This might suggest that children should watch less television. The issue is that the quantity of television watched may be damaging and not the content; too much television precludes other more life-enhancing activities in the home (BBC *Panorama*).

My first job in television in the 1970s was working on a BBC children's TV programme with the wonderful title of *Why Don't You Just Switch Off Your Television Set and Go and Do Something Less Boring Instead?*, which encouraged viewers to be active and not simply passive viewers of packaged content. The series was the first on British television to be presented entirely by children giving further weight to the show's underlying message. *Why Don't You . . .* ran for many years, but watching television is very attractive to children even though it is challenged by video games and online social networking services: 'Children can no longer be considered simply as an audience of television, but rather as part of the production of a broader television environment' (Barnet-Weiser 2009).

In the past the mainstream TV channels scheduled children's TV for a preschool audience in the morning and for children after school in the afternoon up to the 6 o'clock news. This had two advantages: the amount of time dedicated to children's TV was limited, therefore limiting the amount of time children could watch television; second, the programmes could be easily seen by adults as they were on the main channels. Adults quickly got to know *Blue Peter* (BBC) and *Playschool* (BBC) or *Rainbow* (ITV). As soon as multi-channel TV became ubiquitous television schedulers moved virtually all children's television to dedicated channels such as CBBC. Most parents in the twenty-first century have no idea what sort of programmes their children watch. Who can name the current *Blue Peter* presenters or their dog?

Children's TV is now a ghetto where broadcasters have the full responsibility to ensure that the content of children's TV is ethical, suitable, entertaining and to a certain extent mildly educational. But it may not be stimulating or do much more than keep children watching. Ofcom monitors children's TV like all broadcast output but children's TV content has fallen off the agenda in terms of how it affects children. There is still plenty of refreshing debate about the amount of television watched by children, and this includes family friendly programmes such as *The X Factor*, and dedicated children's programming is still thought to be a valuable contribution to children's upbringing and well worth preserving which is another strong argument for a stable PSB service.

Preschool programming is one area that attracts universal acknowledgement for its value in involving, entertaining and educating preschool children. The BBC has an unequalled record in providing high-quality, distinctive preschool programming. It began on radio with *Listen with Mother* where post-war children were introduced to a wide range of inventive stories. Television adopted a less imaginative approach in my view using stories with puppets, such as *Muffin the Mule* and *The Flower Pot Men*, which limited the range of experiences. Preschool television really took off when *Playschool* (BBC) started in 1964. It ran for twenty-five years with its genuinely innovative approach of songs, stories and presenters who involved children by talking to them directly and at their level. *Playschool* delighted and relieved parents who knew their children were safe in front of these daily programmes that were funny, entertaining, musical and helped their young children do many things including how to tell the time.

Playschool was succeeded by *Teletubbies* to much parental anguish at these oddly shaped humanoids who made weird noises. They were, however, an immediate success with preschool children, and with broadcasters all over the world who invested in the format.

Parents expect a child's viewing to have 'added value', entertainment built around sound educational foundations. Other TV series picked up on the early years of childhood such as *Fireman Sam* and *Postman Pat* have become fond memories for grown ups with ironic references in TV advertisements. Children now have new challenges from Facebook, and easy to schedule cartoons, video games and wall to wall programming on children's TV channels. In a multi-format digital environment the value and quality of characters and stories from children's programmes is not as secure as it should be. The real loss is that children's TV no longer has a role as part of our shared social and cultural environment where bankers and bus drivers all knew who Bob the Builder was.

The main concern for regulators is the overall investment in children's programmes and the lack of it from commercial broadcasters. In October 2007, Ofcom reported that investment on children's TV by ITV1, GMTV, Channel 4 and Channel 5 had halved in real terms since 1998. It found that just one per cent of children's programming was made in the UK and being broadcast for the first time. And it found that in 2006 cartoons accounted for 61 per cent of children's programming (BBC News January 2008). In the future it is likely that only the BBC will provide a wide range of children's programmes from preschool up to secondary school. This must be a very strong reason for ensuring secure funding for public service broadcasting by the BBC.

REFERENCES AND FURTHER READING

Adam Smith Institute. 'Global Player or Subsidy Junkie? Decision Time for the BBC', Graham, D. Report 2 August 2010: http://adamsmith.org/files/BBCreport%281%29.pdf.

Barnet-Weiser, S. 'Home Is Where the Brand Is', in *Beyond Prime Time*, ed. A. Lotz, London, New York: Routledge, 2009.

BBC, 2010: http://www.bbc.co.uk/news/entrtainment-arts-11572171.

BBC Licensing 2011: http://www.tvlicensing.co.uk/.

BBC News, 1998: http://news.bbc.co.uk/1/hi/despatches/47792.stm.

BBC News, January 2008: http://news.bbc.co.uk/1/hi/entertainment/7194149.stm.

BBC *Panorama*: http://news.bbc.co.uk/1/hi/programmes/panorama/6748119.stm.

BBC Trust: www.bbc.co.uk/bbctrust/index.shtml.

Bignell, J. *An Introduction to Television Studies*, London: Routledge, 2004.

Branston, G. and Stafford, R. *The Media Student's Book*, 2nd edn, London: Routledge, 1999.

Burton, G. *Talking Television: An Introduction to the Study of Television*, London: Arnold, 2000.

Curran, J. *Media and Power*, London: Routledge, 2002.

Corner, J., *Television Form and Public Address*, London: Edward Arnold, 1995.

Corner, J. and Harvey, S. (eds). *Television Times: A Reader*, London: Arnold, 1996.

Corner, J. *Critical Ideas in Television Studies*, Oxford: Clarendon, 1999.

Creeber, G. (ed.). *The Television Genre Book*, London: BFI, 2001.

Digital Britain Final Report. June 2009: http://webarchive.nationalarchives. gov.uk/+/http://www.culture.gov.uk/images/publications/ digitalbritain-finalreport-jun09.pdf.

Elstein, D. 'How to fund Public Service Content in the Digital Age' in *The Price of Plurality*, London: Reuters Institute for the Study of Journalism, 2008: http://reutersinstitute.politics.ox.ac.uk/uploads/media/The_Price_of_ Plurality_01.pdf.

Fiske, J. *Television Culture*, London: Routledge, 1992.

Franklin, B. (ed.). *British Television Policy: A Reader*, London: Routledge, 2001.

Gaber, I. 'A History of the Concept of Public Service Broadcasting', in P. Collins, (ed.) *Culture or Anarchy? The Future of Public Service Broadcasting* London: Social Market Foundation, 2002.

Holland, P. *Conceptual Glue: Public service broadcasting as practice, system and ideology*, MIT3 Television in Transition Conference Cambridge, Massachusetts USA, 2003.

McQueen, D. *Television: A Media Student's Guide*, London: Arnold, 1998.

Midgley, N. 'TV news gets local touch with new channel', *Telegraph*: http://www.telegraph.co.uk/culture/tvandradio/8268291/TV-news-gets-local- touch-with-new-channel.html.

Murdoch, J. *The Absence of Trust*, 2009 Edinburgh International Television Festival MacTaggart Lecture, 28 August 2009.

Ofcom, 2009: http://stakeholders.ofcom.org.uk/binaries/consultations/ psb2_phase2/statement/psb2statement.pdf.

Ofcom report, 2009: http://stakeholders.ofcom.org.uk/consultations/ psb2_phase21-statement/.

Philo, G. and Berry, M. *Bad News From Israel*, London: Pluto Press, 2004.

Philo, G. and Miller, D. *Market Killing: What the Free Market Does and What Social Scientists Can Do About It*, Harlow, UK: Pearson, 2001.

Robinson, James. 'James Murdoch hits out at BBC and regulators at Edinburgh TV festival', *Guardian*: www.guardian.co.uk/media/2009/aug/28/james-murdoch- bbc-mactaggart-edinburgh-tv-festival.

Royal Television Society, 2010: www.rts.org.uk.

Scannell, P. 'Public Service Broadcasting: The History of a Concept' in A. Goodwin and G. Whannel (eds), *Understanding Television*, London: Routledge, 1990, pp. 11–29.

Seaton, J. 'A Diversity Of Understanding: The Increasing Importance Of Major PSB Institutions', in *The Price of Plurality*, Reuters Institute for the Study of Journalism, 2008.

Thomson, M. James MacTaggart Memorial Lecture at the Edinburgh International Television Festival, 2010.

Part 2

Key concepts

CHAPTER 4

Genre

WHERE GENRE COMES FROM

Genre derives from the French word meaning 'type', and can be defined as the sharing of expectations between audience and programme makers about the classification of a programme. Much television output can be regarded as generic in this sense, and there has been a proliferation of genre-specific channels in recent years, such as Comedy Central, Animal Planet, Syfy, History or Sky Arts. Generic television recognises and uses the expectations of the viewer, for, as the writer David Edgar has observed, genre 'involves a transfer of power. It is the viewer saying to the producer, I possess key elements of this event before it's begun . . . If foregrounding the customer is the end, genre is the means' (Edgar 2000: 75). Genre is in this respect a democratic concept, since it takes account of viewers' preconceptions, expectations and demands of television. Genre television (such as soap opera, police or hospital drama, or game shows) is attractive to television executives because a popular generic programme has a brand identity. In the same way as casting a known television personality or performer, the recognition of familiar genre conventions provides both security and appeal for the audience.

Genres allow for change. Programme makers try out forms and modes of address in one genre that are adopted from apparently different genres. In semiotic terminology (semiotics is the study of signs and their meaning), the mixing of genre elements is a form of intertextuality, consisting of the borrowing in one programme text of signs from another. Since each individual programme is surrounded by others in different genres before and after it in the schedule, and by competing programmes on other channels at the same time, it requires both **similarity and**

difference from these alternatives to establish its own identity. The process of borrowing across and between genres is part of a continual negotiation of identity for programmes, and leads to generic instability. Programme-makers and television institutions continually imagine audience needs and desires, and attempt to address these and target them. If particular programmes seem to catch an audience constituency that shows up in the ratings, or generates press coverage, items on radio phone-ins or on other television programmes like talk shows, they quickly acquire generic centrality, economic value and public visibility. Television genre is negotiated between texts, institutions and audiences in a radically flexible way that both suggests television's specificity and also its connection with other media and with culture in general.

Key point

Genre is a democratic concept, since it takes account of viewers' preconceptions, expectations and demands of television.

This chapter discusses selected television genres that have been relatively stable, then considers programmes where genre characteristics are mixed together. Some of the most established television genres derive from types found in other media. For example, soap opera began in radio, where continuing serials were created to address the mainly female daytime audience by focusing on emotional relationships. These serials were sponsored by companies producing domestic products such as soap. News and current affairs television share conceptions of news values, and the institutional structures of reporters and editors with newspapers and news radio. Sketch shows and situation comedy have roots in music hall and variety, which were adapted for radio and later for television.

The study of genre is based on the identification of the conventions and features that distinguish one kind of work from another. The study of genre allows theorists to link the conventions and norms found in a group of texts with the expectations and understandings of audiences. Genre studies explain how audiences classify television according to features of the text itself, such as cues that they identify in programme titles or aspects of form such as setting and narrative structure. As Steve Neale (Neale and Turner 2001: 1) notes: 'Most theorists of genre argue that generic norms and conventions are recognised and shared not only by theorists themselves, but also by audiences, readers and viewers.' Genre is also signalled by the supporting information about programmes in listings publications, trailers and advertising. The identification of genre may also be apparent through the prominent presence of writers or performers associated with a particular genre.

However, theorists of genre have struggled to pin down where genre resides. It can be argued that genre forms arise from the properties of texts, so that identifying genre means listing elements of a text that determine its membership in one genre rather than another. However, the listing of constituents is not always reliable. In news, for example, interviews are coded in the same ways as in sports programmes. The address to camera in news can also be seen in sports or quiz programmes. News programmes contain actuality footage accompanied by a voice-over, as in documentary, current affairs or wildlife programmes. One of the difficulties in television genre study is identifying unique genre features and the boundaries of a genre.

Genres are also categories used by the producers of programmes and in the institutional division of creative staff in television institutions. Large organisations like the BBC divide their staff into departments based on genres, like drama, light entertainment, news or sport. However, some kinds of programme, like sitcoms for instance, are clearly dramas but are made by the staff of light entertainment departments. Another possible means of deploying the concept of genre is to regard it as a category brought by audiences to the programmes they watch. Some viewers might regard *The Kumars at No.42* as a talk show, since it features celebrity interviews, while others might regard it as a variant of the sketch show genre because of its scripted ensemble comedy routines. Wherever we look, we find genre being used to categorise programmes, but when we look deeper into how genre is used it becomes clear that its meanings are complex and ambiguous.

CROSSING GENRE BOUNDARIES

The ideological functions of programmes cross genre boundaries. Television police series are structured around the opposition between legality and criminality. The central detective or policemen is a personal representative of legality, against whom the otherness of crime and its perpetrators are measured. The television audience is encouraged to identify with the central figure, whereas the criminal is established as an outsider responsible for disruption.

In television news, a similar opposition is established between the public, the news presenters and the institution of television news on one hand, versus the other nations, public institutions, perpetrators of crime and the impersonal forces of chance, the weather, and natural processes which produce the disruptions and disorder reported in the news. Although these are different genres, the ideological oppositions between order and disorder, continuity and disruption, structure both.

Theorists of genre have a particular interest in programmes which transgress the boundaries of genre, considering them to be more valuable and interesting because they draw attention to the conventional rules of television genre by breaking or blurring them. Programmes which are firmly within the boundaries of a genre tend to be regarded as formulaic and of lesser significance. Nevertheless, all texts participate in genre to some extent, and often several simultaneously. Programmes become interesting and pleasurable by working against genre conventions as well as with them.

GENRE: THE SOAP OPERA

Soap opera is a relatively stable and identifiable genre. Multiple storylines built around a large group of characters living in the same location produce an impression of rapidly occurring events. The scenes and sequences in an episode are likely to involve several different combinations of characters, and scenes involving different combinations of characters follow each other rapidly, producing forward movement in the storylines. But on the other hand, any one episode of a soap opera usually occurs in a very short space of represented time such as one day or even just a few hours. The exchange of information between characters through gossip and conversation, and the withholding of information which has been revealed to the audience also encourages the viewer to be aware of developments a long time in the past. Viewers speculate about future events, and experience pleasurable uncertainty about which of the numerous occurrences in any one episode will have effects on the relationships between the characters. But many of the features mentioned here are also evident in other programmes that are not squarely in the genre of soap opera. For example, hospital drama series such as *House*, *Casualty* or *ER* share many of the same features. The most significant difference between soap opera and television hospital drama is in the degree of narrative closure in individual episodes. Hospital drama and police drama are characterised by narratives in which transitional characters appear and produce a disruption to the social space, and at the end of an episode this storyline is completed.

GENRE: THE SITCOM

The sitcom has a history that spans most of the post-1945 period, and is one of the most popular and enduring of television genres. Not only do new sitcoms figure prominently in the schedules of terrestrial television, but 'old' examples of the form are a staple of cable and satellite channels as well. Nostalgia and familiarity have enabled 'classic' sitcoms to retain an important position in the schedules despite some outmoded and sometimes embarrassing assumptions in them about race or gender for instance. Indeed, certain sitcoms have such a hold over the popular imagination that they can still gather audiences in the millions some time after their first screening: a repeat showing on BBC1 of an episode of *Dad's Army* (1968–77) in 2001 attracted 6.6 million viewers (Nelson 2005). But both British and US sitcoms have recognised the need to engage with cultural change, especially the changing position of women (see Hallam 2005), if only as a response to broadcasters' need to deliver a new generation of affluent and confident women consumers to the advertisers who sponsor or support programmes.

Some components of sitcom can be identified as key elements of the genre, but even these are not exclusive to it. Sitcoms have a situation, like a house or workplace where the action happens and where characters seemed trapped together. Audience laughter provides cues for the audience about what is expected to be funny, such as jokes and comic actions or a contrast between what characters say and what they do. Yet some sketch shows, variety, and cartoons also have this feature. The genre of sitcom is a particular combination of elements such as scripted fictional narrative, self-conscious performance by actors, jokes and physical comedy, and studio audience laughter. Focusing on performance discourages the audience from judging speech and behaviour according to the norms of everyday behaviour. The violence of the BBC sitcom *Bottom*, for example, in which characters attack each other with furniture and domestic objects, is made safe by being performance rather than realistic narrative. The BBC sitcom *The Office* lacks the laughter of a studio audience on the soundtrack, normally a generic marker of sitcom, and also appears to be shot with a single camera, as if it were a docusoap. But it has a situation, jokes, physical comedy, and a script, so it is a variant of the sitcom genre.

Sitcom is a genre that has evolved with relatively rigid boundaries that are now blurred and transgressed in some programmes. The most interesting sitcoms exploit the constraints of genre by drawing attention to the circularity of narrative in them. By definition, the situation that gives a programme its setting and main characters must be preserved no matter what challenges are introduced in a particular episode, for example BBC1's *My Family*. So there are firm limits on the possibilities for change, and only limited narrative progression that would affect subsequent episodes. However, as Barry Langford (2005) points out, certain sitcoms such as *Steptoe and Son* (BBC 1962–65 and 1970–74), *Porridge* (BBC 1974–77) and *The Office* (BBC 2001–3) have made room for some narrative progression that reflects on and challenges the series' premise. When the circularity of narrative within the sitcom genre becomes part of the drama as well as a framework for it, sitcom is able to engage viewers at a very sophisticated level.

GENRE: THE POLICE SERIES

Narratives in the police and detective genre begin with a disturbance in the social world of the programme, such as a murder or a robbery. It is the task of the policemen or detective to restore the equilibrium of that world. This is achieved by a sequence of processes that usually occur in a fixed order. First, the police find the explanation for the disturbance by collecting evidence and interviewing witnesses and suspects. This enables them to remove the disruptive force, usually by arresting the person who has committed the crime. This provides the conditions for the restoration of order. However, the fictional world of the police genre is unstable. Conflicts within the central character, among the workers in the police institution, and conflicts between the upholders of the law and the criminals they pursue are often equally of interest, and reduce the cosiness and security of the fictional world. The central characters of police and detectives series often work in teams of two or more, to provide opportunities for explaining plot points, evaluating the behaviour of witnesses and suspects, and assessing evidence. The differences between one central character and another not only serve to create possible tension for the audience but also enable each character to make up for the insufficiencies of the other. Buddy teams in police series might be, for example, a younger and an older man, a man and a woman, the married woman and a single woman, a black man and a white man. Some recent programmes in the police genre use the audience's awareness of these genre conventions in order to question them.

World Productions' BBC series *The Cops* was overseen by the producer Tony Garnett, and his work for television over more than forty years has challenged conventions of television realism, genre and narrative form. *The Cops* not only signalled conventional expectations of the police genre, but also sought to manipulate these through negotiation with genre and the audience expectations which it mobilises. At the opening of the first episode, the main character Mel was introduced in plain clothes, with no indication that she was a policewoman, and was seen snorting cocaine and dancing the night away in a club. The distinctions between the upholders of the law and those whose criminal activities make them the object of police attention were blurred right from the beginning. As the series progressed, the young police officers learned more about the inhabitants of the local housing estate who they were often called upon to deal with. They developed increasingly caring attitudes to these people and greater understanding of their problems, and the easy identification of perpetrators and victims, heroes and villains, was made increasingly difficult. Scenes in *The Cops* were shot with a single camera, always following the police characters into action, rather than establishing a scene before their arrival. The single camera was often hand-held, moving with the police as they moved through the corridors of the police station, through the streets, and into houses, to give the impression of unrehearsed action occurring in real time. This camera convention is used in documentary, and its effect was to generate a sense of realism in following action as it occurs. It also deprived the audience of the dramatic contrasts which would structure narrative in conventional police drama, and the interpretive voice over that would be expected in documentary. The effect was to demand more active viewer attention. *The Cops* both signalled genre conventions but also blurred them. The series put into question any easy distinction between 'us' and 'them', police and perpetrator, and creatively pushed the boundaries of a very established television genre.

FORMAT

The term 'format' is more commonly used within the television business than in academic writing. It refers to the features of a programme that define its uniqueness, such as the premise, type of setting, range of characters or performers, and genre. For example, some of the key aspects of *Big Brother* include the house, the group of 'ordinary' contestants, the process of nomination and voting-out, the hidden cameras and the role of Big Brother as the unseen authority. Once a programme format has been defined, it can be traded like a product, and sold to another production company in another country for example. If another programme-maker produces a 'copycat' programme using the same format without permission, a format owner could take the issue to court and claim that the format has been 'stolen'. The concept of format is not only useful when making programmes, to lay down the basic components that the production team are going to use, but it also has a legal and commercial status. Both genre and format are ways of pinning down the essentials that make a programme what it is, but these two terms are used in rather different ways.

SHOT SELECTION AND GENRE

Television genres have their own codes which enable viewers to recognise and expect particular kinds of meaning and pleasure. While many genres use extreme long shots (ELS) at the beginning of scenes and sequences to establish a physical location, close-up (CU) is very often used to denote emotion signified by performers' facial expressions. In general, the greater a genre's emphasis on emotional reaction, the greater the proportion of close-up shots. But while close-up is a signifier of performance in television *mise-en-scène*, and seems highly dramatic, the shot-length in soap opera and other emotionally focused dramas is relatively long. Shots are held in order to observe characters' reactions to each other, whereas in action dramas such as police or hospital programmes, there is less close-up and shorter shot length. Action dramas also use codes of shot composition differently, since static composition allows space to contemplate performance in soap opera versus the dynamic moving shot composition in police and hospital dramas like *CSI* or *ER*, which focus on disorientation, disorder, and seem to capture action as it is 'naturally' occurring. Colour choices are also significant to *mise-en-scène*, for example the sitcom *My Family* connotes the warm and comfortable environment of middle-class suburbia with yellow, red, and brown, while other programmes (like *The X Files*) use the conventionally colder colours of blue, grey and black to signify a more threatening and uncertain environment.

REWORKING THE POLICE AND DETECTIVE GENRE

Some of this critical reworking of the police genre is already there in the confusions between legality and deviance that the genre already contains, even in its most conventional forms. The characters and actions of the perpetrators of crime can be very similar to those of the policemen or detective. Lying, casual violence and disrespect of authority are all found both in the central characters and the criminals they pursue. What distinguishes the policeman or detective from the criminal is the effectiveness of their methods, and the aim that justifies their behaviour. John Fiske and John Hartley (1978: 29) have argued that this similarity between police and

PROFILE

Tony Garnett

Mark Thomson, the Director General of the BBC, has described Tony Garnett as 'probably the finest drama producer British television has produced' (*Guardian*, 10 November 1997). Well known and applauded for his collaboration with directors such as Ken Loach on television dramas and films, he helped to create a loose, naturalistic, vérité style that used everyday speech and location filming with a deceptively documentary look. His television dramas reveal social injustices and explore political issues. He produced the influential *Cathy Come Home* (BBC 1966) which instigated the setting up of the homeless charity Shelter, and later *Days of Hope* (BBC 1975) a drama series spanning the First World War and the 1926 General Strike. Tony Garnett still produces television dramas which explore issues, and are filmed with a gritty sense of realism. His own production company World Productions have come up with some remarkable new dramas including *This Life, Cardiac Arrest, The Cops* and in 2004 *No Angels* for Channel 4. This series deals with the lives of four feisty nurses, uncovering their sexy and fast-living social life:

In my opinion television should be a bloody great circus with lots of acts. Many years ago at the BBC when we were asking ourselves what our function and role should be, I argued that our job was to tell the truth. Not The Truth, because only God, if he or she exists, knows The Truth, but our job should be to tell our truth, to bear witness, whether through a situation comedy, a news programme, or a drama. That's what the public expect of us. But my truth or anyone's truths is partial, in both senses of the word, so we need a whole range of truths on television all the time. I used to say that all drama is political, only some drama *knew* that it was. I have had a lot of fun trying to create good entertainment, but it's the political ones that are remembered because they created a controversy. The kind of television drama that should have a place, and I would like to be part of it, is the drama of social criticism, the drama of anger. I'd like to see a drama that, through the experience of the characters, invites the audience to imagine an alternative, politically, socially and in the way that institutions are run, as we did in *The Big Flame.* I think the action now is in the long running series. I turned to series partly because that is now the reality of the industry, but then I discovered I was really excited by the challenge. Series are enormously difficult to keep fresh. It's easy to be repetitive and formulaic and it's easy to turn them into a branch of manufacturing . . . The long series is the

PROFILE

natural form of television, the equivalent of the nineteenth-century episodic novel.

He has distinctive views on young television directors, and believes they should have more experience working with actors:

> The problem with the film schools is that new directors emerge with the technical stuff coming out of their ears, very interested in how the camera moves, but with virtually no interest in or experience with actors. Orson Welles said you can learn all you ever need to know about directing a film in an afternoon, and he was right.

On the future of television, Garnett was one of the first to embrace digital shooting and editing. He argues that technology tends to predicate social and cultural change:

> Forget the idea of the audience as the nation gathered together round the camp fire, listening to the same story. That was born of channel scarcity. Think publishing – anyone can do it, but a handful will end up being dominant. One thing is unchanging. We must adapt to these changes and ride them. The alternative is certain oblivion. We must continue to keep our ideas alive and use the screen to argue them.

criminal, and the value placed on efficiency, are means of presenting ideological conflicts – conflicts in the taken-for-granted political assumptions about everyday reality:

> What the police versus criminal conflict may enact symbolically, then, is the everyday conflict of a competitive society in which efficiency is crucial . . . The common concern that television police are becoming more and more like the criminals in their methods and morals means that the few factors that distinguish them take on crucial significance. Of these distinctive features, efficiency is the most marked.

The police and detective genre establishes some activities as criminal and excessive. Breaking the law is the misapplication of the principles which underlie a law-abiding society. The representation of crime on television is a means of defining the boundaries between the legal and the illegal in terms of the reasonable versus the excessive, though the desires and motivations behind legal and illegal behaviours may be exactly the same.

GENRE: THE TALK SHOW

Talk shows are a television version of public debate where issues of the day are picked up and discussed, on the assumption that the television audience are interested and potentially involved in the discussion. Of course 'issues' can be very varied, from problems of childhood obesity to the release of the latest celebrity's cookbook. But talk shows are part of television's creation of a 'public sphere' – a space for rational debate, using the shared assumptions about putting arguments and views in public that originated in ancient Roman cities. Television's public sphere simulates democratic debate, both keeping alive the sense of participation and also substituting for the absence of places to meet, talk and argue with strangers in highly developed societies.

Talk shows rose to prominence in the 1970s with American programmes such as the *Oprah Winfrey* show and *Donahue*. The format was exported to Britain, and hosted by television personalities including Esther Rantzen and Michael Parkinson.

In its original form, the talk show focused on individual guests who represented a larger minority constituency which sought a voice. For example, black single mothers, the disabled, or people struggling with drug addiction were able to individualise the problems of that group in person. This was a mechanism of empowerment and resistance. The contributions of experts on talk shows connected the experiences of the guests to institutional discourses such as those of medicine, psychoanalysis and civil rights. The translation of personal experience into institutional discourses was also a mechanism of empowerment, although it served to convert anger and protest into more socially acceptable forms.

But the talk show has shifted its generic identity, especially in US versions, and has become a form of light entertainment. Audience preferences lead to the creation of new genres, and the reshaping of old ones. Graeme Turner (Neale and Turner 2001: 6) notes that 'the cumulative effect of repeated tweaking of the format and content amounts to a change in genre' as 'more finely grained, and more readily available, viewing figures have the effect of influencing content, format and, ultimately, genre'. American television talk shows such as the *Jerry Springer* show and the *Morton Downey Junior* show had become by the 1990s as internationally successful as Oprah Winfrey had been, but with a very different and much more aggressive attitude to their guests. The hosts of these programmes are much more inclined to make accusations against the opinions and behaviour of their guests than to support them. The most commented-upon feature of these programmes is the prevalence of aggressive physical behaviour when guests confront each other in front of the cameras and the audience. The role of the host, who has always functioned both as a representative for social norms represented by the collective audience behind him or her as well as a mediator between the guest, the audience and experts, has become instead an orchestrator of confrontation and a ringleader encouraging the audience to vent its condemnation of one or more of the studio guests. The prominence of experts has diminished in parallel with this, so that the conversion of social exclusion and violent emotion into the rational terms of institutional discourses is much less evident. A remnant of the liberal discourse of empowerment remains at the end of the *Jerry Springer* show, however, when Jerry delivers his weekly three-minute address direct to camera, containing a more considered homily on the foibles of human nature. Nevertheless the ideology of talk shows has become increasingly focused on the reinforcement of social norms, where audiences (represented by the studio audience) close their ranks against perceived deviance. Dramatic conflict, staged forms of exaggerated behaviour, and reinforcement of social norms each draw the talk show genre towards light entertainment.

This development was particularly apparent in BBC 1's very popular *Friday Night with Jonathan Ross* which is not billed as a chat show but an 'entertaining show featuring comedy, celebrity chat and the latest music'. This long-running show began in 2001 and ended in July 2010 after eighteen series and 273 episodes. The show attempted to push back conservative boundaries of taste and decency with risqué jokes and a patter of sexual innuendo from the host. The show was taken off air not because of falling audiences, but due to Jonathan Ross's behaviour, alongside comedian Russell Brand, on a Radio 2 programme which the BBC and the public deemed to have been inordinately insensitive.

GENRE: REALITY TV

New genres emerge at the same time as old ones change. The genre that has most become the subject of viewers', reviewers' and academics' interest at the beginning of the twenty-first century is Reality TV. Reality TV is a generic hybrid: it adopts constructed situations (like holding the contestants in the specially built *Big Brother* house), and is thus like sitcom in being based on a particular setting and featuring characters who cannot escape from it. Reality TV is obviously like documentary, inasmuch as it is a factual form with an ostensible concern to investigate human behaviour and relationships using a 'fly-on-the-wall' camera style. It is also like drama in its sequential flow based around detailed exploration of character. It is like the game show in being based on competition, where contestants compete to stay on the show and usually compete for a prize. It is like the talk show in being a means for reflecting on social issues (like how contestants will react to someone of a different sexual orientation or someone with a very different social background) and usually foregrounds opportunities for the contestants' personal confession (as in *Big Brother*'s diary room). It is like lifestyle television in its emphasis on making and changing the persona, and showing that people can change and learn from their surroundings and from each other, and that social relations are changeable. Although *Big Brother* came to a natural end in 2010 with falling audiences and a tired format, Reality TV shows continue to appear in the schedules.

The most popular television shows in the twenty-first century come under the genre of Reality TV but can also be referred to as 'contestant TV' or 'talent TV' – for example *The X Factor* and *Britain's Got Talent.* These shows deliver large audiences and involve viewers interactively through the voting system.

Reality TV also has generic relationships beyond the television medium. The exhaustive observation of the contestants by hidden or ever-present cameras recalls the permanent surveillance that characterises contemporary public and private buildings and the public space of town centres. In making 'stars' of some of its contestants, Reality TV is part of the celebrity culture that shapes public under-standing of personalities such as film stars, football stars and pop music performers.

Reality TV has crystallised from being a variant on the documentary to becoming a recognised genre in its own right, and there are many debates about which of its constituent elements are the essential criteria for defining a programme in this very popular genre. Reality TV is significant as an example of how genres mix and develop, and how the expansion of an apparently marginal television form can give rise to the recognition of a new programme category.

In Reality TV, as well as in other programme formats involving live coverage, unpredictability and threats to the format are in themselves part of the format. For example, contestants on *I'm A Celebrity Get Me Out of Here* (series 2), led by the TV chef Antony Worrall Thompson, rebelled because of late and insufficient deliveries of food to the programme's jungle location. With eight episodes to go in the run of the series, the contestants threatened to leave all together as a group, which would stop the series. They confronted the producers on camera and were rewarded (after some heated and protracted negotiation) by being given steak for dinner. This conflict both threatened the show but also made more exciting television for the viewers, thus serving the ultimate interests of the producers, the contestants and the audience. In another case, the Irish television reality show *Cabin Fever* involved participants sailing a boat around Ireland and the unfortunate amateur sailors were caught up in an unforeseen storm, putting them in great danger. The boat later ran aground and broke up, and the contestant-crew had to be rescued by helicopter. Two weeks later, six of the nine contestants returned to the programme when a new boat was found and the run of episodes continued. In this example, developments that could not have been predicted by the producers or the contestants provided exceptionally dramatic 'real-life drama'. These kinds of memorable moments demonstrate how the constraints of format and genre in Reality TV are also founded on television's ability to witness events live (or almost live) and the risk that this involves to participants, programme-makers and audience expectations. Reality TV exploits the unpredictability and excitement that older genres have sometimes lost.

REFERENCES AND FURTHER READING

Bignell, J. 'Television and Genre', in *An Introduction to Television Studies*, London: Routledge, 2004, pp. 113–34.

Brunsdon, C. 'Structure of Anxiety: Recent British Television Crime Fiction', *Screen* 39: 3 (1998), pp. 223–43.

Clarke, A. '"You're Nicked!": Television Police Series and the Fictional Representation of Law and Order', in D. Strinati and S. Wagg (eds), *Come on Down?: Popular Media Culture in Post-War Britain*, London: Routledge, 1992, pp. 232–53.

Creeber, G. (ed.). *The Television Genre Book*, London: BFI, 2001.

Edgar, D. 'Playing Shops, Shopping Plays: The Effect of the Internal Market on Television Drama', in J. Bignell, S. Lacey and M. Macmurraugh-Kavanagh (eds), *British Television Drama: Past, Present and Future*, Basingstoke, UK: Palgrave Macmillan, 2000, pp. 73–7.

Feuer, J. 'Genre Study and Television', in R. Allen (ed.), *Channels of Discourse, Reassembled*, London: Routledge, 1992, pp. 138–60.

Fiske, J. and Hartley, J. *Reading Television*, London: Methuen, 1978.

Hallam, J. 'Remembering *Butterflies*: The Comic Art of Housework', in J. Bignell and S. Lacey (eds), *Popular Television Drama: Critical Perspectives*, Manchester: Manchester University Press, 2005.

Kidd-Hewitt, D. and Osborne, R. (eds). *Crime and the Media: The Postmodern Spectacle*, London: Pluto, 1995.

Lacey, N. *Narrative and Genre: Key Concepts in Media Studies*, Basingstoke, UK: Macmillan, 2000.

Langford, B. '"Our Usual Impasse": The Episodic Situation Comedy Revisited', in J. Bignell and S. Lacey (eds), *Popular Television Drama: Critical Perspectives*, Manchester: Manchester University Press, 2005.

Livingston, S. and Lunt, P. *Talk on Television: Audience Participation and Public Debate*, London: Routledge, 1994.

Neale, S. and Krutnik, F. *Popular Film and Television Comedy*, London: Routledge, 1990.

Neale, S. and Turner, G. 'Introduction: What is Genre?', in G. Creeber (ed.), *The Television Genre Book*, London: BFI, 2001, pp. 1–7.

Nelson, R. '"They Do Like it up 'Em": *Dad's Army* and Myths of Old England', in J. Bignell and S. Lacey (eds), *Popular Television Drama: Critical Perspectives*, Manchester: Manchester University Press, 2005.

Rose, B. (ed.). *TV Genres: A Handbook and Reference Guide*, Westport, Conn.: Greenwood, 1985.

Shattuc, J. *The Talking Cure: TV Talk Shows and Women*, London: Routledge, 1997.

Sparks, R., *Television and the Drama of Crime*, Buckingham, UK: Oxford University Press, 1992.

Wagg, S. (ed.). *Because I Tell a Joke or Two: Comedy, Politics and Social Difference*, London: Routledge, 1998.

CHAPTER 5

Approaches to narrative

DEFINING NARRATIVE

Analysing narrative requires the distinction between story and discourse. Story is the set of events that are represented. They could potentially be told in any order (chronologically, or in flashback for example) and with any emphasis. Discourse is the narrating process that puts story events in an order, with a shape and direction. In any medium, someone or something must be doing the storytelling, and this agency is the narrator, whether it is a voice, on-screen performer, or simply the agency which viewers reconstruct as the force which controls the arrangement of camera shots, sound and music that deliver the story. Some fictional and non-fictional programmes have voice-over narrators throughout, or in particular sequences. *Star Trek: The Next Generation* begins with the familiar scene-setting narration for the programme as a whole, beginning with the 'Captain's log' where a voice-over narrates the setting and situation at the start of each episode's story. This is followed by the narration at the start of the title sequence, beginning 'Space, the final frontier . . .'. Narration can sometimes be found in the title songs of programmes, as in *Fresh Prince of Bel-Air* and *One Foot in the Grave*. *Desperate Housewives* has a narrator who is apparently talking to us from beyond the grave. Series like *ER* may open with a voice-over reminding the audience of scenes in a previous programme. A few drama programmes include a voice-over narrator or an on-screen narrator within scenes, as in *Sex and the City*. Non-fiction programmes like wildlife programmes, history programmes like *Time Team*, commercials, cooking programmes, and Reality TV like *Big Brother* or *Survivor* have narrators. In each of these examples, the function of the narrator is to establish a link between the audience and the programme narrative, by inviting the viewer to involve himself or herself in the ongoing progress of the story.

Although some programmes make the function of narration explicit in these ways, all television narratives rely on the more complex narration made up of camera shots in a narrative progression, often with music linking shots together into sequences and giving them an emotional point of view. Sarah Kozloff (1992: 79) notes that: 'Music, in film and in television, is a key channel through which the voiceless narrating agency "speaks" to the viewer.' The viewer is aligned with point of view shots of characters or performers, alternating with apparently neutral shots that observe the represented space and the figures in it. The performers in television fiction behave as if the viewer is absent, making it more evident that the camera is the agency conveying their actions to the audience, whereas factual programmes perhaps make narration less obvious because the camera appears more to be a neutral observer. But in each case, there is an implied narrator composed from the different camera positions.

The significance of narration is partly that the viewer is necessarily positioned by the changing sequence of camera shots, the words of on-screen or off-screen narrators, and the accompanying music. The position of the viewer is the place to which all of them are directed and from where they can make sense as a coherent whole.

Television viewers make an identification with the audience position laid out for them. In other words, the television viewer has occupied the role laid out for him or her by television, which is doing the looking on his or her behalf. It is often hard to specify what this institutional narrator is, whether for instance it is the production team who made the programme, or the channel on which it is broadcast. Both of these vague collective agencies seem to make claims to be overall narrators by virtue of the credits and copyright ownership information in the end credits of programmes and by the narrating voice of off-screen announcers who connect programmes with each other, and by the channel idents and logos which appear between programmes and are sometimes superimposed in the corner of the screen. This narrating discourse hails an individual viewer to constitute himself of herself as part of an audience.

Key point

Story is the set of events that are represented which can be told in any order (chronologically, or in flashback for example) and with any emphasis. Discourse is the narrating process that puts story events in an order, with a shape and direction.

SEMIOTICS

Semiotics is a method of study that gets its name from the Greek word which means sign, and it analyses how signs communicate meanings (see Bignell 2002). Semiotics started by working on language, made up of signs (like words) which communicate meanings. More recently semioticians have turned their attention to all kinds of other things that communicate meanings and can be studied in the same way as linguistic signs, using the same methods of analysis.

In television, the images of people, places and things are termed iconic signs, which mean that they resemble what they represent. A TV image of a tree looks like the real tree. But of course the image is two-dimensional, in a frame, with a certain composition, colour, depth of focus and perspective. The way the image of the tree has been constructed can shape the viewer's understanding of its meaning. Perhaps the shot will make the tree seem beautiful, magical, mysterious or threatening, especially if music or sound effects have been added to the shot. Signs give form and meaning to thought and experience instead of just showing what is already there, so the study of television signs in semiotics is a crucial tool for explaining how meanings are made.

The key questions semiotics asks include how an image or sequence represents something. Showing something is called **denotation**, but TV images never simply show in a neutral way. They always suggest shades of meaning, as in the example of the tree above. These shades of meaning are called **connotations**, and semiotics concerns how these connotations appear in single shots and how they are connected with the connotations of the shots before and after, and in comparable shots, sequences, whole programmes or whole genres.

Key point

Signs give form and meaning to thought and experience instead of just showing what is already there, so the study of television signs in semiotics is a crucial tool for explaining how meanings are made.

CODES

The meanings conveyed by signs often have much to do with how they are used according to the rules or conventions of a code. The word code is used here in a similar way to the phrase 'dress codes', to refer to the appropriate choice to make in a certain situation. For example, a television sequence of a newsreader behind a desk gains its meanings by drawing on recognisable codes. The newsreader looks into the camera, and addresses the viewer. He or she normally wears formal clothing, and speaks in a controlled and unemotional way. These aspects of shot type, costume and mode of address are all signs that belong to the conventions of news TV, the codes of news television programmes. Different codes constrain the way we might shoot and understand a drama sequence that, for example, shows cowboys shooting at each other on the main street of a western town. Codes of camerawork, costume and language would be different from TV news, and looking closely at how the visual and aural signs in the programme are used will tell us how the meanings of the programme are made. The semiotic concept of code is useful in dividing signs into groups, and working out how their meaning depends on their membership of codes. Individual signs become meaningful because of their difference from the other signs that could have been chosen in any shot or sequence. But the role of signs as members of code groupings means that many signs are heavily loaded with a significance that comes from the code in which they are used.

When analysing television narrative, using semiotics is an essential starting-point that reminds us to identify exactly what choices have been made to communicate a meaning. Semiotic methods would involve asking why a certain shot was selected at this moment rather than another shot, and what the effects of the selection are. By thinking about whether a certain shot or sound conforms to the conventions of a code, it is possible to show how viewers are predisposed to interpret a shot, sound or sequence according to their knowledge of television codes. If you want to describe how a shot or sequence is funny, exciting, mysterious or boring, semiotics provides the means to do this. The meanings of television depend on the selection and combination of visual and aural signs, and how these signs connect with codes that viewers recognise.

Key point

When analysing television narrative, using semiotics is an essential starting-point that reminds us to identify exactly what choices have been made to communicate a meaning.

FLOW

The academic and novelist Raymond Williams was the television reviewer for the BBC magazine *The Listener* between 1968 and 1972. In 1973 he wrote about his first exposure to American television in the previous year (Williams 1990: 91–2). Williams claimed that:

> in all developed broadcasting systems the characteristic organisation, and therefore the characteristic experience, is one of sequence or flow. This phenomenon, of planned flow, is then perhaps the defining characteristic of broadcasting, simultaneously as a technology and as a cultural form.
>
> (Williams 1990: 86)

He was less interested in analysing specific programmes or forms of programme than in the experience of television itself. The flow of material constitutes the experience of television, and also carries a flow of meanings and values deriving from culture and expressing that culture's characteristic modes of thought.

Williams wrote about his experience of American television as if it were typical of all television, and this made some of his conclusions questionable. Rick Altman (1986) argues that flow is not a characteristic of television itself but part of a specific cultural practice of American commercial television, where audiences are measured and sold to advertisers, and flow is required to ensure that the television is switched on even if audiences are not watching it. Altman's critique of Williams's insight draws attention to the fact that programme flow does not illuminate anything about the texts that are part of the TV flow, or the ways in which audiences actually respond to them. Williams's concept of flow confuses a property of the text (the continuing flow of images) and a form of audience response (a flow of feelings and experiences). Williams regards the flow of television as irresponsible, and John Fiske (1987: 100) has argued that this is a result of Williams's background as a literary critic and academic, specialising in the analysis of the novel and drama. For Fiske, Williams was articulating a desire that a named author should take responsibility for a text and provide a principle of unity that organises it. John Ellis (1982: 112) also revisited Williams's concept of flow and argued that Williams regarded the individual programme as the basic unit of television and thereby underestimated the significance of the segment: 'small sequential unities of images and sounds whose maximum duration seems to be about five minutes'. The links between segments are not causal but instead they have relations of juxtaposition and sequence. Ellis emphasised the real and potential liveness of television broadcasting, and argued that television's direct address produces a relationship of intimacy where the separation and immersion of cinema is replaced by glancing and overhearing. So although Ellis's argument distances television from cinema and the novel, and clarifies the notion of flow to some extent, it also reduces the difference between the genres and forms of television, such as factual and fictional forms, in favour of the similarities between segments and the similar modes of attention and address in different kinds of programme.

Nevertheless, these examples of later writers pointing out errors and omissions in Williams's idea have not diminished the fundamental significance of the idea of flow in studying television. The idea is still very commonly thought of as a key way of distinguishing TV from other media like cinema. The concept of flow opened the way for numerous later studies of how television programmes follow each other in an unbroken schedule through the day, and how viewers experience TV as flow of images, sounds and meanings.

Key point

The flow of material constitutes the experience of television, and carries a flow of meanings and values deriving from culture and expressing that culture's characteristic modes of thought.

IDEOLOGY

Ideology refers to the 'natural' and common-sense values that keep civil society running. It was an idea most thoroughly developed by radical Marxist writers who looked for ways of explaining how social injustice can continue without people recognising it and changing things. What ideology does is to make ways of thinking about ourselves and others seem self-evidently right, whereas a more careful analysis of the way things are might reveal that there is much that should be changed. In relation to television, the study of ideology looks at how people and ideas are represented in programming, to identify whether such concerns as race, gender, age-group or ethnicity are being distorted in ways that need to be modified. It also considers how television is organised as a business, for example to determine whether it is controlled in the interests of the audience or for the benefit of an elite group of owners and shareholders.

The pattern of television broadcasting that dominated the twentieth century and continues today was neither natural nor necessary. But it suited modern societies characterised by democracy and citizenship, and participation in a consumer society where owning a television means also being the recipient of commercial advertising messages. The home is not only the location of private leisure and family life, but also the site where ideological meanings are consumed and expressed though watching television and desiring or buying the commercial products and services advertised on it. Television in the home provides access by government and industry to private space and private life. This ideological conception of the place of television in people's lives and homes focuses on television's cultural role: it emphasises how television has become embedded in people's lives, in the places they live, the social structures to which they belong, and how television forms and reinforces the expectations about home, work and leisure that they hold.

Key point

In relation to television, the study of ideology looks at how people and ideas are represented in programming, to identify whether race, gender, age-group or ethnicity are being distorted in ways that need to be modified.

NARRATIVE SUPPORTS IDEOLOGY

In the police series, the task of the policemen or detective is to assemble evidence and information into a narrative of the crime. So the narrative of the programme is occupied with the construction of this other narrative whose events occurred usually either before the beginning of the programme, or in its opening few minutes. The closure of the narrative and the resolution of the programme are achieved when the policeman or detective has completed the assembly of the narrative of the crime. This narrative of the crime is presented to the perpetrator, or perhaps to a court or to the detective's superior. The programme can end when this narrative of the crime is confirmed as true, most often by the confession of the criminal. At this point, the ideologically correct positions of the characters can be established: the criminal is captured, justice is done for the victims, the policeman or detective has done his or her job, and the superior officer is satisfied. The stability of society and the security of the positions occupied by the various characters are confirmed. For the ordered structure of the narrative, its movement from beginning to middle to end, is itself a kind of proof that the assumptions and actions of its central characters are justified. The world of the police show is set up so that the events in that world justify the behaviour of its central characters. The structure of the narrative supports the structure of ideology.

In an apparently very different example, *Big Brother* can be seen as a coded representation of the ideological conditions of contemporary society (like the fictional novel by George Orwell, *Nineteen Eighty-four*, from which its title derives). In *Big Brother* and other examples of Reality TV such as *The X Factor*, individuals pursue self-interest and try to win a prize, but to do this they have to participate in a community. There is a tension between self-interest and participation. A structure of rules is imposed on the contestants, devised and enforced by the producers who act as a ruling elite who possess the power to punish or exile contestants from the show. Participants are required to work at tasks or undergo challenges in order to receive essential supplies and gain rewards. These components of the programme are evidence that *Big Brother* and other competitive Reality TV formats such as *The X Factor* are variations on a metaphor for contemporary capitalist society. *Big Brother* substitutes the house for society at large, and sets up the tensions between freedom and restraint, individual and community, and work and pleasure, which characterise contemporary ideology. *Big Brother* is not a critique of the ideology that it reproduces, and ideological analysis demonstrates that Reality TV both shows and conceals, reflects and distorts, the realities which it represents.

Key point

Ideological analysis demonstrates that Reality TV both shows and conceals, reflects and distorts, the realities which it represents.

REALISM

As John Corner (1992: 98) notes, realism has been regarded as 'television's defining aesthetic and social project'. The notion of realism operates as a standard of value within television institutions and for audiences, since each of these regard the connection of television programmes with reality as a basis for judging the value of television programmes. Raymond Williams (1976, 1977) discriminates between different definitions of realism, and first notes that the term 'real' is used in contrast to 'imaginary', to refer to the material existence of something in contrast to an unreal or fantastical world. This first definition concerns a notion of representation as reflection.

Realism as reflection is connoted not only by what is represented, but also by the level of apparently redundant detail included in a programme's *mise-en-scène* (which means the choices of casting, lighting, sound, music and shot composition it uses). Redundancy consists of the inclusion in the narrative of a number of signs that have a contextual or supporting role, to provide texture and tone. Details of setting, costume, much of the detail of the dialogue, and some of the narrative action is likely to be redundant from the point of view of the story. But in programmes claiming to be realistic, redundancy has the crucial effect of embedding the story in a fully realised world. Furthermore, one of the ways that narratives can be most pleasurable and interesting is when the relationship between redundancy and functional narrative components is changed in the course of the story. In detective narratives and whodunits, for example, an apparently redundant detail that seemed simply to lend texture to the fictional world might turn out to be a crucial clue. In science fiction television, redundancy is crucial to establishing a futuristic environment as realistic, in the sense that it has the detail and texture for it to be believable.

Key point

One of the ways that narratives can be most pleasurable and interesting is when the relationship between redundancy and functional narrative components is changed in the course of the story.

In a second meaning of realism, Williams points out that 'real' contrasts with the 'apparent', and refers to a hidden truth that might be revealed beneath the surface of what is communicated. This meaning of realism refers to revelation or analysis. Nineteenth-century notions of representation assumed that the real world could be adequately explained, and could be satisfactorily represented. Williams argues that this produces three features in realism: it is contemporary, it is concerned with actions that can be explained and which take place in the material world, and thirdly it is socially extended in that it has an ambition to represent ordinary people. As a consequence, a fourth element of realism is its ambition to interpret the world in relation to a certain political viewpoint in order to produce understanding.

Williams was a literary critic, and noted that naturalism in literature is a descriptive method that observes the detail of reality, whereas in contrast, realism aims to produce the experience of dynamic struggle over what reality is like, in order to provide an understanding of contradiction and causality. So realisms are possible inasmuch as they admit that they are partial. Realist representations in this critical sense are not deceptive appearances or figments of someone's imagination; they take on the task of representing the real world and confront it without being able to resolve its contradictions. For television, detailed representations of a real-seeming world can be found in dramas such as literary adaptations, or in documentaries like *Blue Planet*, and these would be more naturalistic than realistic. The interest in competing world-views and how events are caused in programmes like *The Cops* or the drama-documentary *Dirty War* about a terrorist attack, make these examples realist.

Key point

Naturalism in literature is a descriptive method that observes the detail of reality, whereas realism aims to produce the experience of dynamic struggle over what reality is like, to provide an understanding of contradiction and causality.

IDENTIFICATION AND NARRATIVE

Narrative depends on a shifting pattern of identification between the viewer and the programme. Viewers can identify with both fictional and non-fictional performers but also distance themselves from a performer (in order to find him or her funny, for instance). In some genres, viewers can also identify with a studio audience, taking up a shared position in relation to what the studio audience and home audience have seen. Narrative requires the shifting of the viewer's position into and out of the television programme, and a rhythm of identification and disavowal of identification. Narrative lays out positions for its viewers, offering signs and codes that invite them to make sense of and enjoy what they see and hear. But whether or not viewers actually occupy the position of being-an-audience, and how they inhabit this position, depends on the many variables comprising each viewer's social and psychological identity. In consequence of this, television theory has drawn, sometimes with reluctance, on an account of identification developed by psychoanalytic criticism and used to discuss cinema (as well as other media).

The pleasure of seeing images on TV brings with it an awareness of absence, that 'I' am separate from what I see, and am not 'you', 'he' or 'she'. Narrative offers numerous images of other people, places and things, and keeps repeating the pleasurable moment of identifying with others who the viewer is not, and the displeasure of recognising otherness forever beyond him or her. Wanting to watch television is part of the viewer's desire for the other, which narrative keeps displacing onto the next moment in the succession of images and sounds that it presents. This psychoanalytic account of pleasure in watching television has therefore argued that there are several identifications which viewers make.

The first of these is an identification with the television medium, as something which delivers images that promise to satisfy viewers' desire to see and imagine themselves differently. There are also identifications with all the figures on the screen, the performers who stand in for the viewer and play out the roles which the viewer might desire to play. There are identifications with the fictional and non-fictional worlds presented in television, just as in a day-dream or fantasy we might imagine and place ourselves within fictional worlds. Narrative texts are constructed from a network of looks: relations between the looks of the figures, the look of the camera, and the viewer's look. The movement of television narrative in this way is analogous to fantasies that allow for mobile patterns of identification across different positions. All the possible roles in the narrative are available to the viewer: he or she can imagine being the one who looks or the one who is looked at, and can occupy a position outside the scene, looking on from a spectator's point of view. The disjuncture between these looks and positions is parallel to the cutting and juxtaposing of different views in TV narrative to defer complete knowledge and total vision to the viewer, thereby stimulating the desire to keep on looking. Television narratives work by offering, connecting and partially fulfilling the viewer's many divergent identifications and understandings of the programme, and binding them into coherence.

Key point

Narrative texts are constructed from a network of looks: relations between the looks of the figures, the look of the camera, and the viewer's look.

VIEWERS LOOK AT TV 'AS A GLANCE'

This psychoanalytic model offers a very complex understanding of the processes of watching television, whereby it can be understood in terms of mobile processes of making sense, experiencing pleasure and displeasure, and giving and withholding interest. The approach was developed for understanding film spectatorship, where film viewers are much more likely to be immersed in narratives. The dark space of the cinema, the large size of the screen, and the choice to place oneself in the position of a viewer among an audience of other viewers, all militate in favour of much greater involvement in film than viewers often experience watching television. John Ellis (1982: 137) pointed out this distinction by describing the viewer's look at television as a glance, rather than the concentrated gaze of the film spectator. In response to this distinction, television theorists have increasingly moved away from psychoanalytic accounts of television viewing, and instead examined how television narratives offer audience positions for viewers who may be often disengaged glancers rather than immersed spectators.

STRUCTURES IN TV NARRATIVES

The predominant structures used in television narrative are the series and the serial. Serials consist of a developing story divided into several parts, and television soap opera is a special case of the serial form where the end of the story is infinitely deferred. The series form denotes programmes in which the settings and characters do not change or develop, but where new stories involving the continuing characters and setting are presented in each episode. *Doctor Who* is a good example of the series form. Contemporary television programmes now frequently combine the series features of a single setting and new stories in each episode, with the developing characters and stories that occur in serials. Robin Nelson (1997) has coined the term 'flexi-narrative' to denote fiction like this which adopts the short sequences of action and rapid editing which occur in television advertisements, along with the developing characters and stories found in television soap opera, and the new stories which are found each episode in television series. The flexi-narrative form is a case of the combination of television structures.

HOSPITAL DRAMA NARRATIVES

The hospital drama series *Casualty* is a flexi-narrative, whose narrative is patterned to include periodic bursts of rapid action interspersed with more leisurely character development, and the programme as a whole is segmented into a large number of relatively short scenes. The longer and slower scenes of character interaction draw on the conventions of soap opera, in which reaction by one character to events in the life of another are represented by frequent close-up, emotional cues provided by music, and an emphasis on the viewer's memory of past events in the characters' lives to enrich what is happening in the narrative present. By contrast, the shorter scenes of rapid activity, usually scenes in which the doctors respond to the arrival of an injured person, use rapid hand-held camera shots and rapid editing. These action sequences use conventions deriving from observational documentary or news footage of action caught on the run by the camera, adding to this the uses of dramatic music and complex sound found in action drama series such as police shows.

The US hospital series *ER* does similar things in a more extreme way. Flexi-narratives such as *Casualty* or *ER* are borrowing conventions and narrative structures from other programme genres, a technique of allusion for which the theoretical term is intertextuality. Intertextuality is essential to television, and it is one of the means for programmes and advertisements to establish their similarity and difference from other programmes and advertisements, and from other media texts.

SITCOM NARRATIVES

Binary oppositions underlie the narrative structures of many television programmes, for example oppositions between masculine and feminine, or young and old. The tradition in British sitcom, for example, is to oppose: masculinity and femininity, work and domesticity, rationality and emotionalism, intolerance and tolerance. Humour derives from contrasting these values when they are each embodied in a character, and also from aligning a character who might be expected to represent one side of a binary with the other side. For example, Victor Meldrew in *One Foot in the Grave* was masculine and intolerant, but redundant from his work and in an enforced domestic setting that is conventionally regarded as feminine. This offered numerous occasions to create comedy from his sense of being 'out of place' in a situation. *Frasier* adds to this by setting up oppositions between sophistication and crudeness, youth and age, so that Frasier's and his brother Niles's sophistication and relative youth can be contrasted against their father's crudeness and elderliness, for example.

The simplified character-positions in sitcom are too excessive to be 'realistic' because it is important to the comedy for a character's place in a system of binary oppositions to be clear in contrast to another character. Sitcom narrative sets up oppositions and connections, which by the end of an episode have been laid to rest. The movement of sitcom narrative keeps repeating and developing incompatibilities and compatibilities, playing on the already established position of each character in the system of binaries. But the audience's pleasure partly derives from the anticipation that these conflicts will be resolved satisfactorily. The audience needs to recognise the narrative codes of sitcom and the stakes of the binary oppositions in order to accept the surprising reversals and conflicts in it. The interruption of laughter and close-ups on the performers' facial expressions are important narrative turning-points where the viewer is invited to recognise a conflict or reversal among the binary oppositions, and measure its effect on the characters by reading their expressions. The bursts of laughter in the narrative set out the rhythm and pattern in each scene, and punctuate the narrative with stopping-points. This rhythm of stops and starts keeps confirming the position laid out for the viewer to make sense of the narrative and find it funny.

SHOT COMPOSITION AND NARRATIVE

Shot composition allows the relationships between people, and between people and things, to be expressed in spatial terms. More interesting uses of shot composition contribute to narrative progression and the tone and meaning of television sequences. The distance between speakers in two-shots, for example, and the relative closeness of each of them to the camera, can be manipulated to signify the quality of their relationship and to generate dramatic tension between them. Similarly, positioning characters in frames within the camera frame (such as doorways, windows or mirrors) can create spatial relationships that connote entrapment, or produce a feeling of distance between the audience and the character.

Human vision is binocular. Having two eyes close to each other but in different positions provides two slightly different images of the world which the brain interprets as a three-dimensional image with depth and perspective. TV cameras mimic many features of human vision, but television pictures are noticeably flatter so that techniques of lighting, sound, and shot composition are used to produce the impression of depth and coherence. Programme-makers have in mind the relationships of one shot to another, and shots which 'will cut' are those where the point of view of the camera and the relationships that comprise the shot composition fit the conventions of editing. Shots which will not cut are those where conventions are not being followed and for the viewer there will appear to be a leap from one represented space to another, from one camera point of view to another. In drama, for example, the conventions of a shot reverse shot will allow alternations of point of view between speakers so long as the camera does not break the 180 degree rule. For example, *Attachments* was a BBC drama serial about a company constructing a website, seethru.co.uk (the website actually existed, and followed the fictional story of the programme). The camera style of *Attachments* evolved from decisions by Simon Heath (the producer) and Tony Garnett (head of World Productions) to match the static environment of the company office with no moving camera work, to emphasise the close attention to details on computer screens that the characters' work involved by using a lot of close-up shots, and to allude to the very wide shot size of webcams by including wide shots covering the entire office space. Simon Heath commented in an unpublished interview with Helen Quinney in 2001:

> The energy of the show would come from its cutting style, which itself was a product of having lots of different angles on a scene. We were going for big wide shots which would take in the whole of the office, and then an ordinary close-up, and then a much tighter close-up that would highlight eyes, or mouth – the sort of detail you don't necessarily get on television but that you sometimes get in cinema. And then by fast cutting between different sizes and different angles and different characters in the scene, we'd generate an energy in the same way that a panning camera gave us the energy in *This Life*. (World Productions' earlier hit drama serial)

The aesthetic of *Attachments* allows figures to be shot in profile, sometimes with objects masking them, and even shooting through window blinds. By breaking some of the rules of television camera technique, the drama found an aesthetic appropriate to the setting, characters and subject.

POV

Shot composition is inseparable from point of view (POV), where the camera's closeness to or separation from the action is extremely influential on the audience's relationship with the action and the characters. For instance, the sense of being involved in the action or kept separate from it, the sense of being given information transparently by the camera or being denied it, are produced by the interactions between shot composition and point of view, and the relationship between one shot and those before and after it. The tone and meaning of television sequences can be further enhanced by the use of lighting, sound and music. No single element of a shot or sequence carries an intrinsic meaning, but attains its meaning by its interaction with the other elements of the programme. Tone and meaning depend on all the elements that contribute to *mise-en-scène*: the lighting, music, sound, shot composition, props and objects in frame, costume and camera movement.

Sound adds dramatic perspective to images by providing a 'sound point of view' on the action: action in long shot can be accompanied by sound appearing to bring the action much closer to the audience by its volume and clarity, or on the other hand close-up action can be distanced from the audience by muting or blurring sound. In documentary, background sound will be captured by the sound recordist, as well as the speech or other sync sound, for use to cover edits, and provide a background soundscape for the programme. In drama, sound can subtly suggest off-screen intrigue, or provide a rhythmical foundation to the programme, as in the ticking of a clock or approaching footsteps. Contrasting sound and image provoke moods and tones that shape interpretation for the audience, while sound montage opens up a whole range of meanings when running parallel with montages of images.

REFERENCES AND FURTHER READING

Altman, R. 'Television Sound', in T. Modleski (ed.), *Studies in Entertainment: Critical Approaches to Mass Culture*, Bloomington, Ind.: Indiana University Press, 1986, pp. 39–54.

Bignell, J. *Media Semiotics: An Introduction*, 2nd edn, Manchester: Manchester University Press, 2002.

Bignell, J. 'Television Texts and Television Narratives', in *An Introduction to Television Studies*, London: Routledge, 2004, pp. 85–112.

Corner, J. 'Presumption as Theory: "Realism" in Television Studies', *Screen* 33: 1 (1992), 97–102.

Ellis, J. *Visible Fictions: Cinema, Television, Video*, London: Routledge and Kegan Paul, 1982.

Fairclough, N. *Media Discourse*, London: Arnold, 1995.

Fiske, J., *Television Culture*, London: Routledge, 1987.

Fiske, J. and Hartley, J. *Reading Television*, London: Methuen, 1978.

Hall, S. 'Encoding/Decoding', in S. Hall, D. Hobson, A. Lowe and P. Willis (eds), *Culture, Media, Language*, London: Hutchinson, 1980, pp. 128–38.

Kozloff, S. 'Narrative Theory and Television', in R. Allen (ed.), *Channels of Discourse, Reassembled: Television and Contemporary Criticism*, London: Routledge, 1992, pp. 67–100.

Lacey, N. *Narrative and Genre: Key Concepts in Media Studies*, Basingstoke, UK: Macmillan, 2000.

Nelson, R., *TV Drama in Transition: Forms, Values and Cultural Change*, Basingstoke, UK: Macmillan, 1997.

Seiter, E. 'Semiotics, Structuralism, and Television', in R. Allen (ed.), *Channels of Discourse, Reassembled: Television and Contemporary Criticism*, London: Routledge, 1992, pp. 31–66.

Tolson, A. *Mediations: Text and Discourse in Media Studies*, London: Arnold, 1996.

Williams, R. 'A Lecture on Realism', *Screen* 18: 1 (1977), 61–74.

Williams, R. *Keywords: A Vocabulary of Culture and Society*, London: Fontana, 1976.

Williams, R. *Television, Technology and Cultural Form*, London: Routledge, 1990.

CHAPTER 6

Music television and postmodernism

INTRODUCTION

Work on postmodernism in discussing television has been part of a shift from structure to agency. **Structure** refers to the institutions, networks of relationships and professional practices that condition the ways that television is produced and broadcast. It includes theories of ideology and globalisation for example, which seek to explain audience responses and preferences, and also addresses the features of television programme texts, as the result of these structural conditions. **Agency** refers to a new value attributed to viewer choice, and the ways that audiences engage in negotiations with television texts and media structures in order to define themselves and empower themselves as individuals. Arguments about post-modernism address the political impact of the mass media.

The increased significance of the mass media is part of postmodernism and includes the liberating effects of the widespread distribution of information and ideas around the globe. On one hand, this provides unprecedented access to information, ideas, and creative possibilities. On the other hand, it reduces the uniqueness of each individual and the specific cultures to which individuals belong, so that places and people become virtually the same and are all affected by the same assumptions, desires and fears presented by multinational commercial broadcasters.

Stephen Hill defines postmodernism as the collapse of the distinction between the real and simulated and the blurring of boundaries between the physical world and its signification in society and culture:

> Post-modernism can be seen in the way in which media texts play with their own status and conventions. In this sense, they acknowledge the arbitrary

FIGURE 6.1
Television studio

nature of the meaning that is being communicated. A key convention of post-modern texts is **intertextuality**. This is the way post-modern texts borrow, re-work and parody the conventions of other texts.

(Hill 2010)

POSTMODERN MUSIC TELEVISION

Music television seems to be a perfect example of postmodernism: the material it broadcasts appears to be shallow, based around commodity images with no 'message' except the injunction to buy, it broadcasts a flow of short videos producing an endless present or perpetual flow in which the day parts and fixed points of conventional terrestrial television schedules are largely absent. It was these charac-teristics that drew the attention of television theorists to the MTV channel (and others that share similar features), and encouraged the American theorist E. Ann Kaplan (1987) to write the first major academic book that analysed the MTV channel as a postmodern form. The ideas about music video that Kaplan and other theorists put forward in the 1980s can be challenged however, both on the basis that they misunderstand some of the fundamental properties of music channels, and also that some of their wide-ranging theoretical ideas are problematic in themselves.

Key point

A key convention of postmodern texts is **intertextuality**. This is the way postmodern texts borrow, re-work and parody the conventions of other texts.

POSTMODERNISM AND THE MUSIC VIDEO AESTHETIC

Music television provides a twenty-four-hour soundtrack to the lives of its viewers, in which the repeated sequences of music videos work in combination with a restricted repertoire of imagery presenting the pop celebrities who make and appear in them. Although the means of delivery – the platform – has changed, YouTube online videos now have a greater audience reach than scheduled music television channels.

The conceptual basis of music videos on both YouTube and on music television channels remains the same. The celebrity pop performer on television – or YouTube music videos – is constructed out of a cluster of signs which can mutate and change according to context and over time, rather than being an 'objective' representation of a real personality who precedes the images seen on music TV. Kaplan (1987: 44) argued that this is a development that matches postmodern versions of identity:

> Perhaps most relevant to our discussion of the postmodernist devices in MTV videos generally is the blurring of distinctions between a 'subject' and an 'image'. What seems to be happening in the play with the image of the various kinds discussed is the reduction of the 'self' to an 'image' merely.

In other words, pop performers have their being in a world of images that are dissociated from an idea of their 'real' selves. It makes little sense to ask what Lady Gaga is really like; she is known to her viewers and fans only through the cluster of images and meanings transmitted by the media. Madonna's manipulation of her persona is a famous example of this, and performers such as Kylie Minogue and Britney Spears have transformed their images from girlish innocence to more sexual personas.

Celebrity pop performers' images change, producing changes in what they mean to their audiences, thus demonstrating that there is no stable self that holds their identities together coherently. While Kaplan was referring specifically to pop performers in making this point, she also wanted to argue that the same mutability of identity could be seen more generally in contemporary culture. Through fashion and consumer choices, everyone in developed Western cultures could define themselves through the images they project to others, marking a fundamental change in how ideas about the self and individual identity are produced and experienced.

This kind of change is one of the features that leads cultural theorists to adopt the term postmodernism to label such a state of affairs.

Key point

Celebrity pop performers' images change, producing changes in what they mean to their audiences, thus demonstrating that there is no stable self that holds their identities together coherently.

CELEBRITY CULTURE

Music television is a key part of a much wider culture of celebrity which involves the music industry, the Internet, newspapers, magazines and radio. It is notable that the notion of an identity being constructed out of changeable appearances, changing fashions of self-presentation, and thinking of the self as an image put on display to other people, are all conventionally associated with femininity. The examples of celebrities changing their image given above are all women. When men change their image in the same way (as David Bowie has done, for example), this is regarded as the adoption by male performers of a feminine emphasis on style, fashion and narcissism. One of the consequences of the argument that postmodern culture is an image culture is that it is also a feminised culture.

As well as connecting music television to what she believed were dominant characteristics of celebrity culture and consumerism, Kaplan (1987: 44) used her analysis of MTV to make a claim that contemporary television, and culture in general, had developed into a new phase: 'Television in this way seems to be at the end of a whole series of changes begun at the turn of the century with the development of modern forms of advertising and the department store window.' Television is closely connected to consumer culture, the desire for commodities, virtual tourism and the representation of the exotic. Whereas shopping and experiencing the exotic used to take place outside the home (on tours and in shopping malls), these experiences can be indulged in at home, by watching television and interacting via a remote control. Leisure and consumption have always historically been associated with women, with femininity, and television too as the medium belonging in the home, in domestic space, has also been regarded as feminine. For Andreas Huyssen (1986), postmodernism's celebration of mass culture is a celebration of feminisation, and the aesthetic of music television has contributed to this. These ways of recognising the changing patterns of difference, especially gender difference, in music television performance, have enabled voices representing diverse audiences and identity groups to celebrate music television performance as a force for unsettling restrictive definitions of gender, race, age group, and other ways of conceptualising identity. Music television and postmodern culture in general could be seen as a threat to patriarchy and the established masculine dominance over cultural life.

Key point

One of the consequences of the argument that postmodern culture is an image culture is that it is also a feminised culture.

The performers and videos featured on music television are surrounded by other kinds of text in media other than television that also refract and multiply their meanings. The meanings of celebrities depend not only on their construction and form within music television but also the other discourses generated around them. The stories about pop stars in newspapers and magazines offer information and advertise performers and music commodities like downloads, CDs, and videos in ways that support the personas established by the forms of the music videos themselves. The pop stars are represented as entirely familiar; articles and interviews profiling them presuppose familiarity with their identities, musical careers and influences, and major events in their lives. As a discourse that advertises both the star and his or her newest products, the underlying assumption in the codes of this discourse is the fascination with what products are about to become available for purchase.

The popular press compare and test this discourse of commodification and advertising against reality, running articles on the 'real' lives of the celebrities and on the differences between the marketing persona and the flaws, heartbreaks and scandals that they are involved in. The exaggerated coding of pop profiles and marketing images (their use of romantic or exotic biographical information, for instance) play against the down-to-earth and often sordid details of the performers 'real' lives. So the viewer's pleasure in music television must therefore partly depend on his or her recognition of the mediation of the pop star persona by other television forms and other media discourses. The back and forth movement between the star as ideal and the star as a 'real' person in these discourses maintains both their separation from each other and shows how interdependent they are, testifying to the unstable border between the star as just another person on one hand, and the idealised performance or image on the other.

Key point

The viewer's pleasure in music television must partly depend on his or her recognition of the mediation of the pop star persona by other television forms and other media discourses.

FEATURES OF POSTMODERN TELEVISION IMAGES

The characteristic styles of postmodernist television and many music videos is explored by Goodwin (in Frith *et al.* 1993: 46), who suggests that postmodern images especially in music videos can be seen as:

- the collapse of boundaries between high art and popular culture
- the abandonment of conventionally realist representations and narratives
- a variety of modes of address to viewers without a stable viewing position
- intertextual references and pastiches of earlier videos and rock styles
- a flattening out of the past into a continuous present
- an abandonment of any kind of political engagement, comment or analysis.

This list concentrates on the visual elements, and ignores the soundtrack. The music is often conservative within standard pop traditions, although hip-hop culture has given popular music an aggressive postmodernist characteristic.

ORIGINS OF POSTMODERN TELEVISION STYLES

Music television and other forms of postmodern TV not only draw on the resources of contemporary popular culture, but also on aesthetic forms that derive from the experimentation carried out by artists and filmmakers in the Modernist period of the early twentieth century. Music video uses surprising montage combinations of images, often lacks conventional narrative progression, and uses colour, special effects and lighting differently from other television programmes or mainstream cinema films. Many of these techniques derive from the experimental film forms developed in the early twentieth century by directors such as Sergei Eisenstein and Dziga-Vertov. (There is a fascinating postmodern clip from his epic film *The Man with a Movie Camera* on YouTube at http://www.youtube.com/watch?v= KytJFyMHZl0.) Music television's mixing of Modernist experimental forms with commercial culture questions the hierarchies of taste and style in media dissemination and consumption that are associated with modernity. Since MTV is clearly a mass audience television form, and television is itself part of mass-media culture, the co-option of Modernist aesthetic forms represents the democratisation of what were once elite artistic techniques and ideas. Postmodernist theory values music television in part because it seems to undo the notion of culture as a hierarchy of taste with an elite at the top and a mass popular audience at the bottom, with distinct cultural forms offered respectively to the elite and the mass audience.

VIDEO ART

The ways that the music television aesthetic has been explained here are not significantly different from how media theorists have discussed video art, made for gallery exhibition and not for broadcast, usually with an emphasis on experimental techniques and challenging ways of addressing the viewer. The American theorist Fredric Jameson (1987) uses the term 'video-text' to refer to commercial television and video art, and argues that video is postmodern. Video, 'closely related to the dominant computer and information technology of the late or third stage of capitalism' (1987: 207) is 'a sign-flow which resists meaning, whose fundamental inner logic is the exclusion of the emergence of themes as such in that sense, and which therefore systematically sets out to short circuit traditional interpretive temptations' (1987: 219). Because video enables the manipulation of time, cutting it up and slowing it down by using the capabilities of electronic technology, it can contrast with the ordered control of time, pacing and narrative, which television and film have customarily used. Jameson's conception of video and television is much closer to video art than to network television programmes and the aesthetic conventions and scheduling practices which they involve, but it is quite an effective description of how music television works.

Music video can therefore be paralleled with video art, at the same time as it belongs securely to mainstream commercial culture. Kaplan (1987: 47) refers to the makers of music video as 'artists', and explicitly regards their borrowing of ideas and forms from European and American art as well as popular commercial culture as a radical deconstruction of the boundaries between art and popular culture: 'video artists are often playing with standard high art and popular culture images in a self-conscious manner, creating a liberating sense by the very defiance of traditional boundaries'. Postmodernism involves mixing the hitherto experimental and innovative methods of the Modernists with commercially distributed mass commercial culture, and the theorist Andreas Huyssen wrote (1986: 57), 'it is by the distance we have travelled from this "great divide" between mass culture and modernism that we can measure our own cultural postmodernity'. In other words, postmodernism breaks down the division between culture for a small elite group and culture for a mass audience. Television has been a crucial contributor to this process, and music television has been used as a key example in explaining and promoting this insight.

Key point

Postmodernism breaks down the division between culture for a small elite group and culture for a mass audience.

POLITICS, GENDER AND PERFORMANCE

The arguments about MTV in postmodern theory in the 1980s were also carried through in relation to the performances, especially MTV music video performances, of Madonna. Madonna offers radical challenges to conventional norms. She has challenged the representation of femininity by the repeated changes to her celebrity persona, suggesting a freedom of self-expression and pleasure for women. She has been critical of the Catholic Church, especially in its condemnation of sexual pleasure and homosexuality. She has confronted the limits of mass-media representation, especially of sexuality, by producing pop videos and other commodities that have generated controversy and occasionally censorship because of their explicit sexual imagery and promotion of sexual pleasure for its own sake. Madonna's economic success on music television, and the financial assistance for her career provided by her associations with major corporations can be seen as ways of using the capitalist media system against itself. Perhaps by drawing on the global media presence of music television to get her messages across, and by drawing on connections with other globally recognised brands which keep her own celebrity image to the forefront, Madonna is able to disturb the very structures and ideologies which underlie contemporary television. The most interesting characteristic of postmodern theory, and of postmodern media culture, is the way in which contrasting ideas can be shown to be two sides of the same coin. The complexity and confusion which this produces in theories of television mirrors the complexity and confusion that postmodern theorists see around them in television itself.

Just as Madonna has been presented as an icon who can manipulate the creation of her own image by the media, and by music videos in particular, the play, reflexivity and multiple meanings identified in postmodern television texts are also available to audiences. As Robin Nelson (1997: 246) suggests: 'Postmodern texts might be summarily characterized by a formal openness, a strategic refusal to close down meaning. They create space for play between discourses allegedly empowering the reader to negotiate or construct her own meanings.'

Television viewers construct sense from the diverse fragments of narrative, character, visual pleasure and intertextual reference which postmodern television offers. While there are moments of stability and involvement in television, the role of fragmentary signification, the withholding of resolution and the sense of being suspended in a perpetual middle is what makes the term postmodern useful for describing television now.

Key point

The most interesting characteristic of postmodern theory, and of postmodern media culture, is the way in which contrasting ideas can be shown to be two sides of the same coin.

If television viewers construct sense out of the postmodern fragments that MTV and postmodern television in general offer to them, the fragmentation and multiplicity of the text must be reflected in the fragmentation and multiplicity of identity, inasmuch as television is one of the resources for constructing that identity. Identifying postmodern style and form leads to the argument that television is changing subjectivity.

Theories of viewer positioning adapted from analyses of classical Hollywood cinema, like those that Kaplan drew on in her work on MTV, would no longer be appropriate (as she argues herself) to MTV because the texts of music video are so different from those of cinema. The involving narratives with beginnings, middles and ends, and psychologically realistic characters in conventional cinema lay out a secure spectator position for the spectator, and stabilise him or her in the identity of an audience member for the film in question. This kind of stable audience position seems inappropriate for the reflexive, intertextual and ironic processes of meaning in contemporary television and in music television especially. Features of television programmes match descriptions of identity as mobile, fluid, and fragmentary, and this is one of the aspects of a political reading of music television.

If music television textuality both reflects and produces fluid and fragmentary identity, this can be seen as a resource for the reworking of the conceptual category of the individual subject in Western capitalist society. The ideological function of stabilised subjectivity is to hold the subject in a position in a social hierarchy and a gender role. If that stability is questioned, new configurations of social role and gender identity could be the result. Watching music television would then be a means to unsettle and advance the role of the individual subject in contemporary society. It is that possibility that has attracted television theorists to both studies of music television and of postmodernism, since television culture of that kind matches the radical or even revolutionary politics of many theorists in the field.

Key point

While there are moments of stability and involvement in television, the role of fragmentary signification, the withholding of resolution and the sense of being suspended in a perpetual middle is what makes the term postmodern useful for describing television now.

MUSIC TV AND GLOBALISATION

Celebrity is the commodification of personality, and not only does music television further this process but it also advertises itself as a commodity which is purchased by multi-channel audiences. In order to achieve this, a music channel needs to present its own personality attractively. This is achieved by simultaneously marketing the channel's global engagement with the global music and entertainment industry, and also by addressing local and regional audiences. In contemporary television culture there is no such thing as a common culture, a national culture, or an international culture. Instead there are numerous overlapping and competing cultures at local and regional levels, which co-exist with a multinational and global culture.

MTV, for example, is programmed differently in each territory to which it is broadcast, though the formats remain largely the same and many of the products advertised on MTV are also global brands appearing in different languages and different territories. MTV is owned by an American media corporation. It can be argued that MTV is a vehicle for the global spread of American capitalist values, expressed through the international pop music market which sells products with no intrinsic value. In its early years, MTV advertising seemed to proclaim this in the slogan, 'One world, one image, one channel: MTV', which celebrated the erosion of local differences by the global channel.

Connections between the MTV channel and global consumer culture could be seen in the deals made between pop stars and the soft drink industry, such as the association of Madonna and Michael Jackson with Pepsi Cola. Commercials featuring the performers and the soft drinks appeared on MTV, making a vicious circle of advertising that encompassed American performers, American television, American soft drinks and American record companies.

For these reasons, some cultures and nations have attempted to block the broadcasting of MTV within the regions they control. The processes of globalisation are open to regulation by individual nations, rather than being an autonomous and unstoppable process, and global markets are regulated by contracts and by international and national laws. But the world organisations that oversee international television agreements generally support the lowering of national restrictions and quotas, because they seek to create a global free market economy in communications.

The World Trade Organization, the International Monetary Fund, and regional agreements such as the North American Free Trade Agreement and the European Free Trade Association provide support for cross-border television exchanges which are based on the principles of unrestricted commercial exchange. The apparently free and uncontrollable television market is not a natural fact and depends on the taking of political decisions about deregulation and competition in television by nation-states and groupings of states. Countries and regional groupings tend both to deregulate and encourage globalisation, but also to introduce further regulation to protect their societies against it.

Key point

In contemporary television culture there is no such thing as a common culture, a national culture, or an international culture. Instead there are numerous overlapping and competing cultures at local and regional levels, which co-exist with a multinational and global culture.

MEDIA IMPERIALISM

The case of MTV is therefore an interesting location to consider the analytical purchase of the media imperialism thesis, discussed by Herman and McChesney (1997), for example. The legacy of the media imperialism argument is that it is not American programmes or American television owners that perpetuate regressive kinds of television organisation. American programmes do not always dominate the schedules of countries with less-developed television cultures, and even if they did, it is not proven that these programmes simply transmit American values to their audiences. Similarly, many American television producers are not owned solely or at all by American individuals or companies, and the ownership of television broadcasting institutions in other parts of the world is more likely to be through a combined deal between global media corporations and local or regional interests.

But the aspect of the media imperialism thesis that does remain valid is that the American system of television organisation has been successfully exported to very many of the world's national broadcasters. This trend tends to increase as deregulation and liberalisation of television markets advances with the collapse of rigid state broadcasting controls in former authoritarian societies. The financing of television by advertising, where audiences are targeted by particular programme types in order to deliver them to advertisers, is an American model which has become increasingly common. The American model of the competition between broadcasting channels affiliated to major network or cable and satellite providers is also adopted in nations that have their own indigenous television production bases.

HISTORY AND THE MTV DEBATE

The first academic writing on MTV was published in the late 1980s and early 1990s, and MTV has changed considerably since then. Rather than one channel, MTV now has many channels and a formidable online presence. As well as MTV itself which is a general pop music channel, there are a further eight MTV channels in music genres such as Dance, Classic and Base, as well as a High Definition channel MTVNHD. Online MTV streams all its TV channels and has an archive of 20,000 music videos. There are other accessible music channels that compete with it. This raises an interesting theoretical question about how MTV could have been postmodern in the 1980s, but now may be a relic of a previous phase in television. If MTV is no longer postmodern in the sense that its aesthetic and organisation are not of the present, is postmodernism itself an historical phase that has now passed, or must MTV be re-categorised as modern rather than postmodern? How does postmodernism relate to the idea of history?

The French philosopher Jean-François Lyotard (1993: 44) argued that something is 'modern only if it is first postmodern'. He uses the term 'postmodern' as an adjective to describes cultural artefacts for which the criteria for aesthetic judgments about value and artistic success cannot be straightforwardly applied. This insight is clearly relevant to the debates about MTV discussed in this chapter (and also to other debates about television and value considered elsewhere in this book). For television theorists, analysis of MTV has led both to the condemnation of its aesthetic features as repetitive, manipulative and conventionalised, but also to the judgement that it represents a fluid, discontinuous and experimental representation of emotion, time and space that could provide a template for other innovative television forms. A further aspect of this problem of judgment is that the categorisation of the material is problematic, and therefore the critical approach that should be adopted for it is impossible to decide on. Kaplan, for example, drew on film theory to show how MTV refuses the conventions of point of view and identification that audio-visual sequences in cinema have used. On the other hand, Andrew Goodwin (1996) argued that this categorisation of MTV in relation to cinema was inappropriate, and that music video should be aligned with the aesthetic of the live pop performance or rock concert. Decisions about which category MTV video should be placed in determined the criteria of judgment brought to the problem by different analysts, and sometimes these criteria were incompatible.

It is this very incompatibility of criteria, and undecidability about value, that Lyotard cited as evidence that a cultural form is postmodern. What we think of as modern, as appropriate to our current state of culture has to pass through this postmodern state of ambiguity and confusion. The condition of being postmodern is a state that can be recognised only after the event, once categories and criteria have been applied to MTV and it has become comprehensible by means of them. Once this has happened, the initial confusion about what MTV is can be resolved. But the resolution of ambiguity and the dispersal of the problem of judgment remove MTV from the category of the postmodern by definition. MTV is relegated to the epoch or style that preceded the postmodern, and which would therefore be called modern. But there was a time (probably the 1980s when the first attempts were made to categorise and evaluate MTV) when critical discourse could not gain a grip on the channel and its significance. MTV is modern, but that state of confusion in which it first appeared was a postmodern moment. This theoretically complex but very persuasive work on the definition of postmodernism has three main planks: first, that the term postmodern is retrospectively attributed. Second, the postmodern is a momentary condition which lasts for the short time in which new cultural forms are not yet assimilated into discourse and ideology. Finally, as a result of the first two arguments, the postmodern is not an epoch or period but is a characteristic of how cultural forms appear and are perceived. The positive contribution that postmodern forms such as MTV make to television culture is that they problematise categories and assumptions that are taken for granted in the perception and study of the medium. Once this radical postmodern moment has passed, and MTV can be explained, judged and categorised, its creative challenge and artistic interest reduce.

NEW DEVELOPMENTS IN MUSIC TELEVISION

Music television may appear to be losing its iconic status as a beacon for youth. The BBC blamed year-on-year declining audiences for axing the long running weekly *Top Of The Pops* leaving the UK's two main television channels BBC1 and ITV without any regular popular music programming. ITV argues that popular music is present in its talent shows such as *The X Factor* but these shows are aimed at family audiences and not specifically at young people.

Live popular music is well served on BBC2 with the excellent *Later . . .* and *Later Live with Jools Holland* which is in its thirty-seventh series. It has an average audience of 600,000 for each of its two weekly broadcasts and brings to a television audience the best popular music acts. It sets out to be professionally musical rather than popularly fashionable. The BBC also has a good track record in broadcasting the Glastonbury festival and other live music events.

However, the MTV aesthetic that caused a so called 'youthquake' when MTV erupted in 1981 no longer carries the charisma that 'yoof' music television once had. Inevitably MTV is no longer iconoclastic nor does it dictate trends in fashion and music video production, even though the MTV brand is still popular. MTV's role in promoting million selling artists from Michael Jackson to Madonna has not been equalled by any online music service.

It initially appears that the video clip websites such as YouTube and MySpace have made music television obsolete. Millions click on YouTube to see Lady Gaga or Lily Allen but these sites merely provide a platform to watch what you want to see. These sites do not thrust talent into our front rooms – they do not direct the viewer towards a new act or put any editorial comment into premiering a new band. Broadcast television still has the power to do this – to shape what we see, hear and experience especially in the continually changing world of popular music.

Television brings the shape shifting images – Lady Gaga in a meat dress, Robbie Williams reuniting with Gary Barlow. Broadcast television can take the lead and bring the energy and iconoclasm of ground-breaking popular music directly to teenagers. The BBC is trying to discover what it needs to do to develop a stylish 'cool' music policy. It is important in a time when amateurs can demand media attention so easily that a trusted organisation like the BBC can use its authority to uncover and promote the best professional acts. It already does this with classical music through the *Young Musician of the Year* show and by televising world-class performances from the Proms every year.

Channel 4, tasked with the job of creating alternative programming, is coming to popular music television from a different angle – drama – albeit through a very successful US import on its E4 channel. *Glee* is the creation of music guru Ryan Murphy, and on the face of it is a hybrid genre youth sitcom spin-off from *High School Musical* and *Fame*, using retro music and a talented young cast of wannabees. *Glee* has won twenty Emmy nominations and a golden globe for Best Television Series after its first series in 2009. The most important statistic for producers and parent institution Fox is that half the twelve and a half million viewers in the US are aged eighteen to thirty-four. Youth music TV is back. *Glee* has changed the way television presents music. In the show a racially mixed and diversely abled cast perform covers of a wide range of songs as members of their Glee club at college. There is romance, competition and heartache, and there are these high energy, well mixed, stylishly produced performances of hit songs. Some episodes are themed on one artist such as Madonna. Where *Glee* really scores is in the original unadorned interpretation of classic songs, usually sung with 'as live' instrumental backing in the Glee rehearsal room – no fancy postmodern music video styles here. Crucially, all the songs are available to download. After one US TV show there were 410,000 downloads of the five songs featured, and five million albums have been sold world wide after the first series.

The format is simple and very flexible. The core cast can invite guests to join them such as Gwyneth Paltrow or Paul McCartney, and the songs from any genre can be geared to the competition with other Glee clubs, or to expose teenage issues or emulate the feelings of a love affair. As well as contemporary hits by Jay-Z or Lady Gaga, the cast sing songs from Broadway musicals, and hits from pop music's heritage that they and the audience are unlikely to have heard before.

Watching *Glee* is more like going to a west-end rock musical than watching television. The feel and tone are of a live performance. The characters are varied and talented enough to appeal to a wide range of viewers without being glamorised in the way that talent TV bigs up the contestants. Throughout the history of pop music previous hits have been dusted off and presented in a cool way as if the current generation were discovering them for the first time. In these postmodern times the cover version sells and then, through the internet, young people seek out the original version from say Neil Diamond or the Beatles and see that video on YouTube. Then they buy the download of the original. Broadcast television is cross-fertilising the back catalogue of the music industry with those young people who have come in from their video games and do not regularly watch television. Ryan Murphy says: 'the show is about reaching out'.

Glee reflects postmodern intertextuality not through images but through music. The conscious unambiguous Glee club presentation references both the panoply of past musical golden moments, and the present generation's unconscious bricolage of style, music, ideas, ethics and iconoclasm. Once again television and popular music have achieved a pluralistic continuum to excite modern young people.

REFERENCES AND FURTHER READING

Attridge, D. and Fabb, N. (eds). *The Linguistics of Writing: Arguments between Language and Literature*, Manchester: Manchester University Press, 1987, pp. 199–233.

Barker, C. *Global Television: An Introduction*, Oxford: Blackwell, 1997.

Bignell, J. *Postmodern Media Culture*, Edinburgh: Edinburgh University Press, 2000.

Brooker, P. and Brooker, W. (eds). *Postmodern After-Images: A Reader in Film, Television and Video*, London: Arnold, 1997.

Dowmunt, T. (ed.). *Channels of Resistance: Global Television and Local Empowerment*, London: BFI, 1993.

Frith, S., Goodwin, A. and Grossberg, L. (eds). *Sound and Vision The Music Video Reader*, London: Routledge, 1993.

Goodwin, A. *Dancing in the Distraction Factory: Music, Television and Popular Culture*, London: Routledge, 1993.

Goodwin, A. 'MTV', in J. Corner and S. Harvey (eds), *Television Times: A Reader*, London: Arnold, 1996, pp. 75–87.

Hill, Stephen, 2010. www.mediaedu.co.uk.

Herman, E. and McChesney, R. *The Global Media: The New Missionaries of Global Capitalism*, London: Cassell, 1997.

Huyssen, A. *After the Great Divide: Modernism, Mass Culture and Postmodernism*, London: Macmillan, 1986.

Jameson, F. 'Reading without Interpretation: Postmodernism and the Video-text', in D. Attridge and N. Fabb (eds) *The Linguistics of Writing: Arguments between Language and Literature*, Manchester: Manchester University Press, 1987, pp. 199–233.

Kaplan, E.A. *Rocking Around the Clock: Music Television, Postmodernism and Consumer Culture*, London: Methuen, 1987.

Kellner, D. *Media Culture: Cultural Studies, Identity and Politics Between the Modern and the Postmodern*, London: Routledge, 1995.

Lewis, L. *Gender Politics and MTV: Voicing the Difference*, Philadelphia, Penn.: Temple University Press, 1990.

Lull, J. (ed.). *World Families Watch Television*, London: Sage, 1988.

Lyotard, J.-F. 'Answering the Question: What is Postmodernism?', in T. Docherty (ed.), *Postmodernism: A Reader*, Hemel Hempstead, UK: Harvester Wheatsheaf, 1993, pp. 38–46.

Mclean, Craig. 'The show every singer wants to star in', *The Times* 1 October 2010

Mundy, J. *Popular Music on Screen: From Hollywood Musical to Music Video*, Manchester: Manchester University Press, 1999.

Nelson, R. *TV Drama in Transition: Forms, Values and Cultural Change*, Basingstoke, UK: Macmillan, 1997.

Woods, T. *Beginning Postmodernism*, Manchester: Manchester University Press, 1999.

CHAPTER 7

Schedule and audience

TELEVISION IN EVERYDAY LIFE

The emphasis in this chapter is on the ways that the scheduling of programmes in British television attempts to match the perceived interests and demands of the audience. As well as explaining how scheduling can be approached critically as a mechanism for shaping audiences and the ways that audiences watch television, the chapter also debates how audiences may be incompletely understood, and how audiences may evade or resist the attempts by television institutions to determine how the meanings of programmes are perceived and used.

Before beginning this discussion of audience and schedules, it is worth noting that television is not only a delivery system for television content, but also a physical object that is embedded in the domestic household. It is important to consider not only what people watch, or even which organisations bring television to the viewer, but also what the physical presence of a television within a household means. Television viewers' experience of television is partly determined by their social positions in society, and differences between individual viewers and household audiences are significant within cultures and nations as well as between them. The uses of the television in the household, and the programmes watched on it, are affected by and have effects on the sense of social identity constructed by individual viewers and their fellow viewers. Keeping wedding photographs on top of the television, placing it prominently as a symbol of affluence, or concealing it inside a piece of furniture, might each tell us a lot about the household and how television supports or conflicts with that household's self-image and self-presentation to visitors and other family members. The television set, its programmes, and the objects around it, form a complex set of negotiations with the past and the present, public and private life, technology and everyday routines of behaviour, and the household's family members and their absent relatives and friends. The study of television in this anthropological sense shows that it is not just programmes which are significant to television's place in culture, but also the embedding of TV in everyday life as a way of understanding identity and community.

SCHEDULING PRACTICES

Scheduling comprises selection and combination. John Ellis (2000: 25) has argued that the composition of a television schedule is parallel to the operations involved in editing:

> Instead of combining shots and sounds into a sequence and sequences into a programme, as an editor does, the scheduler combines whole programme units into an evening's flow, whole evenings into a week, whole weeks into a season, and whole seasons into a year.

Some programmes have connections between them while others are placed next to programmes that have a quite different genre and format. While in the early years of television production the lengths of programmes and their interrelationships with each other were subject to little overall planning, by the 1980s standard programme lengths such as thirty minutes and one hour had produced grids of time slots such as were already common in the United States.

The problem of placing new programmes arises in part from a vicious circle that affects schedulers' use of audience data from the Broadcasters Audience Research Bureau (BARB):

> The success or failure of a particular scheduling strategy is measured by the same methodology that suggested it in the first place. A problem with audience size or composition produced by a particular programming policy is identified through using the BARB figures. This leads to changes in that policy, whose success is measured by using the same BARB data.
>
> (Ellis 2000: 35)

This makes television schedulers wary of taking risks by making decisions that run counter to their expectations about time-slots and the positions of programmes within television seasons.

One way of deciding on the scheduling of a new programme is to test the idea for the format, or a completed sequence or whole programme by setting up focus group discussions. For example, focus group participants might be asked whether they would prefer to watch the new programme at 7.00 pm or 8.00 pm, and whether it would be best placed on a weekday or at the weekend. Finding out whether viewers might prefer the new programme to a competitor on another channel can enable schedulers to make decisions about whether the new programme should aim to inherit the same audience as a competitor, and whether to place the new programme directly against the competitor. Since the majority of viewers watch television accompanied by other members of their household, the focus group might also be asked whether they would be embarrassed to watch with their children, their parents, or their spouse. Clearly, focus groups represent very small samples of the total viewing audience, and the results can be unreliable. Viewers tend to make judgments based on what they already know, which is why television broadcasters are criticised for producing a diet of television that seems always the same. However, surprising successes can result from placing programmes in unexpected ways. The scheduling of *Big Brother* in the summer, for example, was successful for Channel 4, and gathered large and young audiences. Its placing in the summer period is surprising since summer programming is usually made at low cost per hour and the schedule involves numerous repeats. When, however, the audience tired of *Big Brother* as it did by 2010 no amount of rescheduling could lure back large audiences.

PRE-ECHOES AND ECHOES

By re-evaluating audience figures, channel controllers and schedulers identify patterns of audience movement. For example, a 'pre-echo' is an audience group intending to watch a programme starting shortly, thus increasing the audience for the programme scheduled just before the one they are interested in. 'Echoes' are audiences inherited from a programme that has just been broadcast. Now that British programmes tend to fit into the grid of half hour and hour-long slots, there are more 'junction points' at which large numbers of viewers may switch from one channel to another. For example, at 10.00 pm, news is broadcast on both BBC1 and ITV1. The 9.00 pm watershed is a point at which programmes aimed at a more adult audience can begin, so there is a tendency for all channels to change the kinds of programme available at 9.00 pm or 10.00 pm, thus producing a junction where audiences may choose to move to one channel or another. 'Tent pole' programmes are those that can be relied on to gain a large audience, thus lifting up the trend line showing audience size, like the ridge pole of a tent. Schedulers might also position a programme with a relatively small audience between two popular ones, hoping to inherit audiences from the preceding programme and to pick up audiences expecting to see the following one. This is called 'hammocking', whereby a less popular programme is held up by those on either side.

THE VIEWER AS SCHEDULER

The arrival of the personal video recorder such as Sky+, and particularly the BBC iPlayer and its equivalent on ITV and Channel 4, signals the possible demise of this kind of planned scheduling. Television programmes can now be viewed on a computer or laptop via iPlayer technology where and when the viewer wishes. From 2011 hybrid flat LCD television sets offer full access to websites, and iPlayer technologies. The internet can now be the personal video recorder streaming programmes to a self-scheduled audience on their home television sets, as well as their mobile phones or iPads.

Internet-enabled televisions make it easy to view a programme at a variety of different starting times. The viewer's chance to catch a programme is greatly increased. Correspondingly, the power of television schedulers to control what audiences watch and when diminishes as television viewers become schedulers themselves. With digital television viewers can call up additional information about programmes, and access brief television segments that support the programme they are watching. Wildlife programmes, for example, may have supporting material giving further information about the animals seen in the programme, or providing further footage that was not included in the broadcast version. The technology of picture in picture allows this material to appear in smaller windows within the television screen, or for the viewer to see what is being broadcast on another channel.

Simon Nelson, the BBC's controller of multi-platform services, thinks we have not yet seen the full power of online television: 'The arrival of the internet has deepened viewers' relationship with programmes, and the most committed fans now want even more.' He is talking about new ideas that broadcasters are working on where special episodes, or 'extras', of a popular series like *Top Gear* or *Doctor Who* are made available online. Nelson wants to extend this idea at the BBC: 'From *Luther* [detective drama] to *Flog It* [antiques game show] there's interesting stuff you can do around every genre and every type of programme' (*Sunday Times*, 3 October 2010).

It is also possible for viewers to see alternative endings to drama programmes, or to change the relationship between narrative sequences, in a way that is already possible in retail DVD systems where the 'chapters' comprising the film can be viewed in any order.

According to a recent Ofcom report (2010) more than two-thirds of homes have broadband and nearly 40 per cent of the population watch television services online. As internet-enabled television sets become more popular the number of people watching online television services will increase. This does not mean people will stop watching broadcast TV; they will use the internet to enhance their viewing. With a range of more than 200 available channels, conventional schedule listings are difficult to use, and instead, electronic on-screen programme guides (EPGs) list all available programmes in a timeslot often with the ability to record programmes for future viewing. Electronic programme guides are easiest to use when programmes are of standard lengths, and digital television has produced greater standardisation of programme lengths for this reason.

Interactive and online television both challenges conventional scheduling, since viewers have more choices among and within programmes, and also standardises the lengths and formats in which programmes are produced.

Key point

The power of television schedulers to control what audiences watch and when diminishes as television viewers become schedulers themselves.

TELEVISION FOR THE FAMILY

Schedules are planned on the basis of assumptions about the nature of the television audience and the ways audiences watch. Television schedules have for a long time been planned around the ways that hypothetical family audiences organise their time. Television still often assumes that the audience is a family group with gender and family roles that are reinforced by TV programmes. So television's ideological effect is therefore to reinforce the family values on which capitalism is politically based. Children come home from school at the end of the afternoon, meals are usually eaten in the early or mid-evening, and children are expected to go to bed at around 9.00 pm. In general, the early evening contains shorter and more diverse programmes, while the later evening offers adult viewers longer and more complex forms and formats. Across the year as a whole, new programmes are traditionally introduced around September, when the holiday season has finished and family routines get back to normal as school time begins. In the summer, people watch less television because they are more likely to be outside in the warmer weather, so the summer period contains more repeated programmes and fewer high-profile programmes. At particular points during the year, expected events such as the football cup final, the Olympics or Christmas celebrations will require the schedule to be re-arranged and specially planned.

Different decodings are produced by viewers who occupy different social positions. Women in Western societies are expected to be emotional, caring, and community forming (as opposed to the masculine characteristics of adventurousness, aggression, and individualism). The negotiation of the meanings of television programmes is affected by the social status of the viewer. Audience responses are not only determined by the text, but also by the social environment in which talk about the programme among friends, workmates and family members takes place. Viewing context, such as watching television with other members of a family, or with friends, for instance, affects viewing experience. People watching with their families will often be persuaded to watch something they do not enjoy, whereas watching a favourite programme with a group of friends might help to confirm a person's shared relationships with members of that group. John Storey (1999: 114) summarises this social role of television viewing by arguing:

> Watching television is always so much more than a series of acts of interpretation; it is above all else a social practice. That is, it can be a means to isolate oneself . . . or to make contact with other family members . . . In these ways, the cultural consumption of television is as much about social relationships as it is about interpretations of individual programmes.

Key point

Audience responses are not only determined by the text, but also by the social environment in which talk about the programme among friends, workmates and family members takes place.

Rather than being passively positioned by the meanings of television programmes, watching television requires viewers to draw on their personal histories, their cultural, class, racial, economic or sexual identities, and to use their cultural competence, gained from media knowledge of comparable programmes and the various information sources available to them, to construct a relationship with the television programme in the context of their cultural lives.

John Ellis (2000: 26) goes as far as to say that the schedule is:

> the locus of power in television, the mechanism whereby demographic speculations are turned into a viewing experience. And it is more than that as well, for any schedule contains the distillation of the past history of a channel, of national broadcasting as a whole, and of the particular habits of national life.

For example, programmes about home improvement are likely to be shown at times when people are considering doing work on their houses, such as on Fridays and Saturdays when major DIY superstores will be open for people to purchase materials. ITV1 is unlikely to show DIY programmes on Sundays when viewers will already have completed their shopping for such items. This British situation is different from that in the USA, where programmes are generally scheduled in strips, for example, soap operas in the afternoon, sitcoms in prime time, drama in the late evening. Each American network channel's schedule is similar to its competitors, with much less variety and unexpectedness than in Britain.

Audience research about who talks about television, to whom, where and how reveals the different roles television can play in making, breaking and maintaining social relationships. Researchers have looked at how 'television viewing is generally a somewhat busy activity, interrupted by many other activities and routinely accompanied by talk, much of it having nothing to do with the programme being watched' (Storey 1999: 16). For the discipline of Television Studies in general, a shift of interest onto viewers and audiences rather than on television programmes as texts has focused on 'active' rather than 'passive' viewing, and provided good reasons to value kinds of viewing and kinds of programme which have been considered of low quality.

Key point

Watching television requires viewers to draw on their personal histories, their cultural, class, racial, economic or sexual identities, and to use their cultural competence.

FAMILY AND FEMINISATION

In as much as television audiences are regarded as domestic and members of a family, television is also a feminised medium in that it adopts this domestic tone and form. Television programmes are dominated much more than cinema, for example, by people talking and interacting in familiar situations, just as life for viewers at home is often centred around these activities. Much of the theoretical work carried out in the 1980s on the domestic context of ordinary viewing focused on women viewers, and on programmes attractive to female audiences. Indeed, the genre of soap opera in particular became a focus of attention because the textual characteristics of the genre were argued to map closely onto traits conventionally recognised as feminine. Soap opera works primarily through dialogue, both between the characters in the programme and between members of the audience who are invited to speculate about what will happen and to make judgments about the moral and emotional problems experienced by the characters. Talk and gossip are recognised by sociologists as an important component of women's lives, as ways of constructing community and shared experience. Soap operas provide both a representation of this community, and material that actual women can discuss with each other.

Furthermore, since narrative information is conveyed largely through dialogue in soap opera, it is possible to watch soaps with what Jeremy Tunstall (1983) called secondary involvement, getting on with other tasks and looking occasionally at the screen. Tunstall distinguished between primary, secondary and tertiary involvement with media. Primary involvement is close concentration to the exclusion of any other activity. The kind of attention where viewers are sometimes distracted is secondary involvement, where the viewer may also be doing something else at the same time. Tertiary involvement is only momentary attention while engaged in another activity, scarcely seeing any of the images on the screen and hearing only occasional sound.

Key point

The level of involvement makes a lot of difference to the meanings that viewers can make, and while some television programmes (like news) are constructed in order to attract primary involvement, soap opera and other genres aimed at female audiences can be satisfying with secondary or even tertiary involvement.

The production of viewer talk is encouraged and mirrored by talk in programmes themselves. Programmes as diverse as *EastEnders* and *The X Factor* consist largely of sequences of conversation between the performers or participants, representing familiar interaction and conversation which could then be talked about by viewers. The frequent use of close-up shots of faces in soap opera and in Reality TV, and on television in general, reinforces this sense of intimacy between the viewer and what is shown on television, and contributes to an apparent equivalence between the ordinary world of reality and the constructed worlds of television. This way of using and experiencing television gives the illusion of physical closeness, and invokes rules of social interaction which demand attention and create social proximity. Soap opera has been discussed in these terms for a long time.

Family audiences are no longer the only predominant audience addressed by schedulers and programme makers. For example, Reality TV shows focus much more on individuals in specially formed groups or in workplace groups. Contemporary audiences are watching increasingly in same-generational groupings rather than inter-generational family groupings, and are interested in programmes that are also about same-generational groups. This is particularly true of programmes for young people. Channel E4 is a no adults zone for young people especially with the edgy sitcom *The Inbetweeners*. This is *The Young Ones* for the postmodern generation, and it aims to shock parents with very bad language, drinking and plots based on sexual activity, just like its predecessor did. It is also quite sophisticated and polished.

Big audience Reality TV has morphed into Talent TV with *The X Factor*, and *Britain's Got Talent*. Some commentators even put the BBC's immensely popular Light Entertainment show *Strictly Come Dancing* into the Reality TV genre. In spite of the competitive element being more to the fore these shows still express virtual sociability. The sociability of Reality TV is what we might call 'parasociability', comprising temporary same-generational groupings that are often goal oriented, not communal, and not familial. If Reality TV is an image of contemporary society that would be a very unhappy situation. But in fact, it is a representation of broadcasters' imagination of the audience, not of society as a whole at all. Reality TV, like other contemporary programme forms, selectively represents the imaginary relationships between broadcasters and audiences.

Key point

The frequent use of close-up shots of faces in soap opera and in Reality TV, and on television in general, reinforces the sense of intimacy between the viewer and what is shown on television, and contributes to an apparent equivalence between the ordinary world of reality and the constructed worlds of television.

IMMEDIACY AND INTIMACY

Jostein Gripsrud (1998) writes about the opposing ways we might think of television. The first of these is immediacy versus intimacy. Television, in news for example or live broadcasting of sport, claims to bring immediately occurring events to its viewer, and obviously television's heritage of live broadcasting is crucial to this. Intimacy, on the other hand, has more to do with relationships of identification, with an exchange not only of information but also of feeling between viewers and what they see on screen. Television's intimacy is also based on a sense of closeness of connection between the viewer and what he or she is watching.

Gripsrud pursues this point by contrasting the two functions of the window and the mirror. Television can function as a window on the world, and again news, current affairs and documentary would be appropriate examples here. But television can also function as a mirror. Its representations of domesticity and the family, documenting ordinary life and the ways that culture functions in the present, all have to do with television's mirroring function. Factual genres like documentary have a special claim to presenting the world outside to the viewer, but television has also been significant in shaping the domestic space of the viewer simply by virtue of the presence of the television set in the room and the ways that TV affects domestic life.

TV has also been significant in representing the family, and particularly perhaps women and the notions of gender relations that circulate in culture. Reality TV is a subset of documentary, so it would be expected to emphasise immediacy, the function of the screen as a window, and representations of the world outside the viewing space. However, that is the opposite of what many Reality TV shows seem interested in. Reality TV emphasises intimacy, it mirrors aspects of the lives of some of its viewers, and it not only represents but also debates the meanings of domestic space and the interrelations of people who inhabit the same space.

Key point

Thinking about immediacy and intimacy, window and mirror, are useful ways of understanding what programme genres and formats do.

THE VIEWER AS INDIVIDUAL CONSUMER

Television is increasingly considered as a market in which providers of programmes give their publics what they seem to want. With multiple channels available to all after completion of digitisation in 2012 it is no longer necessary for each channel to expose the audience to the full range of both 'accessible' and 'difficult' programmes. This marks a change from a paternalistic notion of the viewer as a member of a collective national audience to the notion of the viewer as an individual consumer, offered multiple TV choices by a proliferating number of channels. Rather than leading the viewer towards 'better' taste and informed citizenship, television institutions increasingly offer either mixed programme schedules which attempt to satisfy perceived desires and capture audiences through entertainment, or diversify their offerings into themed channels which offer related programme types to small niche audiences.

The power to commission new programmes is in the hands of broadcasting executives, but schedulers have an important role to play in identifying programmes which are likely to gain audiences, based on information schedulers have about what audiences have watched in the past. So schedulers provide recommendations to commissioning executives and thus influence which programmes are made.

Different regulations affect the scheduling of programmes on non-terrestrial channels, as well as different strategies developed by broadcasting institutions to use them as add-ons, alternatives, or groundbreakers for their terrestrial free-to-air services. Terrestrial broadcasters have for a long time agreed on a 9.00 pm 'watershed' (see Chapter 2), before which programmes that could be offensive or disturbing to children will not be broadcast. The additional coverage of, for example, Reality TV programmes in non-free-to-air channels is not subject to the same watershed rules that are enshrined in the Ofcom guidelines on Family Viewing Policy which states: 'The decision to subscribe to a specialist channel available only to those who have specifically chosen it, carries with it an acceptance of a greater share of responsibility by parents for what is viewed and the watershed on such channels is set at 8pm rather than 9 pm' (Ofcom 2004).

The issue of taste and standards is closely connected to the imagining of television audiences, and the mechanisms of scheduling. Schedulers have to consider if any special 'sensitivities' in the real world surround the broadcasting slot, such as religious festivals, national anniversaries of major, possibly tragic, events. It could, for example, be considered insensitive to broadcast a documentary about the relative merits of fundamental religious beliefs in the same week as the anniversary of the 7 July 2005 London bombings.

Schedulers consider not just the content of a particular slot but also the 'pull-through audience', i.e. the nature of the preceding programme and what kind of audience it is likely to attract.

ACTIVE AUDIENCES

John Fiske (1987) made an important argument about how audiences make all kinds of meanings out of watching television, rather than just consuming what they are given. This suggests that attempts to regulate how audiences watch, and to determine what they get from what they see, will never wholly succeed. Fiske argued that the television text will exhibit resistances to coherence and internal contradictions, such that no single meaning can be imposed or received, and instead meaning is produced by programme-makers and understood by audiences in a wide range of ways. Viewers actively connect the separate shots and segments of a programme and bridge the gaps between them. They also remember and connect what they see with the previous episodes of a series or serial, or between the images on different channels as they zap from one to another. For Fiske (1987: 95) television offers a 'semiotic democracy', meaning that the signs and meanings in television's images and sounds are interpreted with a certain freedom by each viewer.

Furthermore, since television is not the property of a particular segment of the population, it escapes the control of elites and is sometimes incorporated into resistant subcultures by its viewers. Television Studies theorists began to regard the television audience not as a uniform mass but as a complex set of overlapping groups with different allegiances, backgrounds and interests. This shifted the object of study from the television programme as a text, to the television audience responding to this text. The key concepts of plurality and difference were applied not just to the many possible meanings of programmes, but to the different ways audiences might interpret them. By focusing on the audience, often by setting up situations in which researchers listen in person to the talk of actual viewers, Television Studies granted more power and authority to viewers, in particular viewers belonging to ethnic subcultures, women and children. Audience studies also provided an opportunity to find new sources of potential resistance to the ways that the television business is organised, and to the conventional and ideological meanings discovered by close analysis of programmes. Rather than just looking for instances of resistant programme texts that might make new and politically radical meanings, researchers looked for groups of resistant and radical viewers.

Landmark studies conducted by feminist Television Studies academics showed how programmes often regarded as of low quality (such as soap opera) could be central to the experience of women viewers, who themselves were in a position of relatively low social power (see Ang 1996, Geraghty 1991, for example). It became possible to see how viewers might actualise the many meanings in a television text. The primary emphasis of research on soap opera, and of much audience research by Television Studies academics in general, has been on the viewer's pleasure in television, and methodologies have been developed to engage viewers in talk and discussion about their everyday viewing experiences and their reasons for watching and enjoying particular programmes or genres.

Key point

Television Studies theorists apply the key concepts of plurality and difference not just to the many possible meanings of TV programmes, but to the different ways audiences might interpret them.

IMAGINARY COMMUNITIES

Ethnographic audiences studies ask how television functions in relationships between people, and affects the ways that daily lives and self-understandings are formed (see Geraghty 1998). Yet ethnographic audience studies are most often carried out by talking to respondents who have voluntarily put themselves forward, and are therefore likely to have something to say. The methods used to find respondents can give rise to a number of problems. Some researchers have used 'snowballing' in which one person finds another who will participate, then that person finds another, and so on. This methodology is less artificial than selecting a representative panel, but it inevitably produces a self-selected group. Other researchers have placed advertisements in magazines, for example, and reviewed the responses they receive. Those people who respond have something that they wish to communicate, and adopt the formalities of letters, such as politeness. Talking can present some of the same problems, when respondents give answers they think may be most interesting to the researcher, or that present them in the most interesting light. Nevertheless, interpreting audiences reveals the intricate, singular and different ways in which people make interpretations of their world and think about their own cultural behaviours.

Specific cultural groups, like the resistant television audience groups studied in media audience research, are imaginary communities. The theorist of fan cultures, Henry Jenkins (1992), conducted studies of the attitudes to *Star Trek* of a range of different groups including science students and members of the gay *Star Trek* fan group The Gaylaxians. Jenkins points out that MIT students largely share the ideological values of the programme, such as faith in science and human progress, and are hardly a resistant audience. In his study of The Gaylaxians, Jenkins (1995: 264) notes that:

> Resistant reading can sustain the Gaylaxians' own activism, can become a source of collective identity and mutual support, but precisely because it is a subcultural activity which is denied public visibility, resistant reading cannot change the political agenda, cannot challenge other constructions of gay identity, and cannot have an impact on the ways people outside the group think about the issues which matter to the Gaylaxians.

The more that an audience is identified by researchers as an emblem of resistance to the dominant norms of television and contemporary society, the less likely it is that this audience group will be able to exert any actual power to create change in either television or society.

In a discussion of some of the many studies of women viewers of soap opera, for example, Ien Ang and Joke Hermes (1996) have pointed out that researchers have a tendency to assume that the responses of particular research respondents are representative of the larger group made up of women viewers in general. The impetus behind much audience research is to value the voices of viewers in a dominant television broadcasting culture which largely excludes them, and thus to claim power for the audience. Since research is always carried out with an explicit or implicit research agenda, or set of research questions, there is a tendency for academic publication of audience research to find the answers that it has already aimed to find. This problem is the same as the one identified above in relation to broadcasters' audience research, where interpretation of ratings information or focus group responses tends to validate the decisions made in the television industry in the past, producing inertia and circularity rather than innovation.

REFERENCES AND FURTHER READING

Allen, R. 'Audience-oriented Criticism and Television', in R. Allen (ed.), *Channels of Discourse, Reassembled: Television and Contemporary Criticism*, London: Routledge, 1992, pp. 101–37.

Ang, I. *Watching Dallas: Soap Operas and the Melodramatic Imagination*, trans. D. Couling, rev. edn, London: Routledge, 1989.

Ang, I. *Desperately Seeking the Audience*, London: Routledge, 1991.

Ang, I. *Living Room Wars: Rethinking Audiences for a Postmodern World*, London: Routledge, 1996.

Ang, I. and Hermes, J. 'Gender and/in Media Consumption', in I. Ang, *Living Room Wars: Rethinking Audiences for a Postmodern World*, London: Routledge, 1996, pp. 108–29. 2002, pp. 127–39.

BBC Editorial Guidelines. www.bbc.co.uk/guidelines/editorialguidelines/edguide/.

Bignell, J. 'Writing the Child in Media Theory', *Yearbook of English Studies* 32.

Bignell, J. 'Shaping Audiences' and 'Television in Everyday Life', in *An Introduction to Television Studies*, London: Routledge, 2004, pp. 253–302.

Bruhn Jensen, K. (ed.). *News of the World: World Cultures Look at Television News*, London: Routledge, 1998.

Buckingham, D. *Public Secrets: EastEnders and its Audience*, London: BFI, 1987.

Buckingham, D. *Moving Images: Understanding Children's Emotional Responses to Television*, Manchester: Manchester University Press, 1996.

Dickinson, R., Harindranath, R. and Linné, O. (eds). *Approaches to Audiences: A Reader*, London: Arnold, 1998.

Dovey, J. *Freakshow*, Cambridge: Polity, 2000.

Drummond, P. and Patterson, R. (eds). *Television and its Audience: International Research Perspectives*, London: BFI, 1988.

Ellis, J. 'Scheduling: The Last Creative Act in Television', *Media, Culture & Society* 22: 1, 2000, pp. 25–38.

Fiske, J. *Television Culture*, London: Methuen, 1987.

Geraghty, C. 'Audiences and "Ethnography": Questions of Practice', in C. Geraghty and D. Lusted (eds). *The Television Studies Book*, London: Arnold 1998.

Geraghty, C. *Women and Soap Opera: A Study of Prime Time Soaps*, Cambridge: Polity Press, 1991.

Gray, A. *Video Playtime: The Gendering of a Leisure Technology*, London: Routledge, 1992.

Gripsrud, J. 'Television, Broadcasting, Flow: Key Metaphors in TV', in C. Geraghty and D. Lusted (eds), *The Television Studies Book*, London: Arnold 1998, pp. 141–57.

Hallam, J. and Marshment, M. 'Framing Experience: Case Studies in the Reception of *Oranges are Not the Only Fruit*', *Screen* 36: 1, 1995, pp. 1–15.

Jenkins, H. *Textual Poachers: Television Fans and Participatory Culture*, London: Routledge, 1992.

Lewis, L. (ed.). *The Adoring Audience: Fan Culture and Popular Media*, London: Routledge, 1991.

Liebes, T. and Katz, E. *The Export of Meaning: Cross-Cultural Readings of 'Dallas'*, New York: Oxford University Press, 1990.

Lull, J. (ed.). *World Families Watch Television*, London: Sage, 1988.

Morley, D. *Television, Audiences and Cultural Studies*, London: Routledge, 1992.

Petrie, D. and Willis, J. (eds). *Television and the Household: Reports from the BFI's Audience Tracking Study*, London: BFI, 1995.

Ruddock, A. *Understanding Audiences: Theory and Method*, London: Sage, 2001.

Storey, J. *Cultural Consumption and Everyday Life*, London: Arnold, 1999.

Tulloch, J. *Watching Television Audiences: Cultural Theories and Methods*, London: Arnold, 2000.

Tulloch, J. and Jenkins, H. *Science Fiction Audiences: Watching Doctor Who and Star Trek*, London: Routledge, 1995.

Tunstall, J. *The Media in Britain*, London: Constable, 1983.

Part 3

Factual television

CHAPTER 8

Documentaries

TRUST IN DOCUMENTARIES

Television documentaries have a reputation for being serious, reliable and objective in their reporting, with a commitment to truthfulness. There are documentary programmes with elements of comedy, Reality TV or drama, and the modern documentary uses elements from many programme types and entertainment programming techniques to attract audiences and be anything but dull and overtly discursive. A documentary seeks to 'document', or to make a record of, aspects of real life.

The British filmmaker John Grierson is credited with first using the word documentary in about 1926 to describe film making that involved real people, and not actors, and situations taken from real life. He described his approach to the films as 'the creative treatment of actuality' using 'fragments of reality'.

Grierson understood that he could not film 'reality', because the director or programme maker always had some input into the interpretation of any scene. In the celebrated documentary film *Night Mail* (GPO films) about the mail trains that took the post overnight from London to Edinburgh, Grierson recreated scenes in the studio that he was not able to film on the train. He used some of the actual postmen speaking the natural dialogue they had used on the train while sorting the mail. While technically a re-enactment, the authenticity – or truthfulness – of what is seen by the audience is not in doubt. Later Bill Nichols defined the documentary as 'representing reality'. This is usually taken to mean the act of representing the reality of a subject and includes reporting, observing, investigating, interpreting and reflecting on that subject.

The success of Reality TV, and the newer forms of factual programmes including make over shows and relocation programmes, has injected new vigour into the overall area of factual programme making. These programmes may not educate in quite the way John Grierson envisaged, but they do provide a social snap shot of the times and lead to trust in the overall contribution of television to daily life. Broadcast television has never had so many ordinary citizens as the main contributors to prime-time programming. Viewers feel they can trust ordinary people on their screens more than TV celebrities, or, for that matter, politicians.

Television is becoming democratised by the documentary, and not, as some may think, by the increasing nod to audience participation through emails, and online, or telephone, voting. Documentaries are bringing viewers in front of viewers.

Key point

The viewer is both in the armchair and in the frame.

NOTIONS OF REALITY

In a documentary programme we the audience interpret the reality of what we see on the screen, according to our own preoccupations and prejudices. We construct our own notion of reality. The freedom fighter on your screen is the terrorist on someone else's television. The viewer's interpretation of the programme is an integral part of the viewing experience.

Broadcasters believe that modern viewers will accept a programme labelled documentary as a genuine attempt to reach a form of truth about a subject. But the area is still controversial. Documentary programme makers aim to achieve a version of reality that is truthful, can illuminate a subject and appeal to a television audience. Sometimes they have to direct contributors to go through movements and activities several times in order to get the required selection of shots. This is normal procedure, although many modern documentaries rely on the use of multiple hidden cameras, or unobtrusive, lightweight cameras with long recording times. The central truthful content of the documentary film need not be obscured by some elements of disguised fabrication.

Interestingly, documentary filmmakers especially in the US are turning to the big screen to show their films in cinemas as well as on television. In 2004, the American documentary filmmaker Michael Moore won cinema's greatest honour, the Palme d'Or, at the Cannes Film Festival for his film *Fahrenheit 9/11*. This was the first time the Cannes jury had awarded its prize to a documentary since Jacques Cousteau's *The Silent World* in 1956. Michael Moore in 2003 won Best Documentary Oscar, for his film *Bowling for Columbine*. Many people feel that Moore is making interesting films, but that they are not fully realised documentaries. He uses the tools and forms of documentary, but manipulates his material to make convincing points. This means, argue his critics, that he is economical with the truth. This notion is compounded because he makes cinema documentaries and so sidesteps some of the safeguards and controls provided by television broadcasters in the way they label and promote programmes. Authored political documentaries have their place on television, but in the UK have to be part of a balanced output.

Some documentary conventions connote unmediated reality, like hand-held camera, 'natural' rather than expressive lighting, and imperfect sound, while other conventions connote drama, argument and interpretation, like voice-over, narrative structure and contrastive editing. The grainy images from closed circuit television in some factual programmes carry powerful political and social connotations. They police the boundaries between normal and deviant or criminal behaviour, and provide evidence of it.

Whereas documentary has a history of representing and arguing for those in society who are the least privileged, the most vulnerable to exploitation, and the most marginalized, the use of footage from closed-circuit television in factual television can reinforce marginalisation, deprive deviant behaviour and deviant people of the opportunity to explain and provide contexts for their actions, and remove their actions from larger social and political contexts. The pleasure for the audience is in seeing something hidden, seeing the very moment when something shocking and disturbing is happening, and the provision of this pleasure or the generation of anxiety take greater precedence than the investigation and exploration of the behaviour portrayed.

Key point

There is a tension between producing a documentary which is representative and 'accurate', and providing the audience with a programme which conforms to the conventions of argument or storytelling.

REALISM AND SOCIAL RESPONSIBILITY

Television audiences are invited to experience the lives of other people through factual TV forms, so factual television carries assumptions of both realism and social responsibility. Factual programmes play a key role in the public service commitment to disseminate information about contemporary events, and the range of attitudes and ways of life among the population. Television documentary and other factual genres aim both to mirror society to itself and to show the diversity that exists within that society. Documentary was initiated in the film medium and was designed to be socially responsible, and to be an art of record in contrast to cinematic fantasy. In television, documentary especially is able to take up the requirement for public service by focusing objectively and with authority on public events. Its realism is a particular form which not only denotes a real world but also makes it public and explains it. Documentary makes an argument and centres on evidence, and this usually includes some reliance on narration and interpretation. In other words, documentary always has a point of view; even it claims to be a neutral one.

Television has always placed great emphasis on the moment of the present, especially in its factual output, partly because live broadcasting has been so significant throughout the development of the medium.

Key point

Documentary's realism is a particular form which not only denotes a real world but also makes it public and explains it.

REFLECTING THE NATION

Programmes about historical figures suggest parallels and contrasts between ancient kings and modern-day rulers, or between ordinary people's ways of life in the past and the way most people live in Britain today. Television has always been used to relay events (like sporting events, royal weddings and general elections) live across the country, thus keeping people in touch with what is thought to be significant. Contemporary television still devotes much of the available broadcast time to factual programmes. All of this derives from the assumption that television informs a national audience about the actual state of society, and that knowledge about what is happening now is essential to a democratic and humane culture. This kind of assumption about what television is for can be seen in the BBC Producers Guidelines (2003), for example, which include this general principle: 'The BBC has a responsibility to serve all sections of society in the United Kingdom. Its domestic services should aim to reflect and represent the composition of the nation.'

Reflecting the nation means representing both what is considered normal and ordinary as well as what is deviant and exceptional. Since the late nineteenth century, photographic media have been used for collecting criminal evidence, and to record scenes of crime. Factual television continues this tradition, by both representing people who might be 'just like me' in *Wife Swap* (Channel 4/E4 2010) for example,

FIGURE 8.1
Archive film: a Supermarine S6B in The Schneider Trophy, 1931, and early outside broadcast (radio) for the BBC

and also people who seem very different from the norm *Supersize vs Superskinny* (Channel 4 2010), for instance. There is still interest in representing the special kind of deviance that constitutes crime, perhaps by using surveillance footage as the raw material for programmes. But because documentary and factual programmes have this role of reflecting reality and representing society, there are continual debates over whether individuals, groups or issues are fairly represented. The medium of TV introduces the notion of a restriction of vision as well as a privileged vision, since the camera can select and emphasise particular shots, and editing and post-production in general will inevitably construct meaning and point of view through selection and combination of images and sound.

Key point

Reflecting the nation means representing both what is considered normal and ordinary as well as what is deviant and exceptional.

THE IMPRESSION OF REALISM

In order to produce the impression of realism in television documentary, several very unnatural procedures have to be carried out. The documentary subject will almost always be aware that he or she is being recorded, witnessed or even pursued by the camera operator and often also by a sound recordist. Once the footage has been gathered, the documentary maker will edit the footage together in order to produce a coherent argument or a narrative. While the finished programme may acknowledge the presence of the documentary maker, it is often the case that documentaries imply that the subject is behaving 'naturally' or at least represen-tatively. There is a tension between producing a documentary which is representative and 'accurate' and providing the audience with a programme that conforms to the conventions of argument or storytelling.

Paradoxically, the impression of reality in documentary television can often depend on supporting narration, testimony or expert commentary that provides an interpretive context for the observational denotation of the camera and diegetic sound. These devices link documentary with other factual genres, where the authority of a narrator provides coherence and continuity, such as in motoring programmes where an on-screen or off-screen narrator explains the features of a new model. Factual programmes always seek new kinds of realism to engage the audience in up-to-the-minute ways.

Key point

Realism is no longer within the TV frame, but is seen to be a construct between the programme maker, the subject and the audience.

AUTHENTICITY

In documentary, testimony of members of the public supports the authenticity of the programme, as it also does in some television commercials, where members of the public declare their preference for a certain brand of headache pill, for example. Expert commentary provides backing for the assertions and arguments of the programme maker or the figures appearing in the programme, and this can also be seen in sports programmes, science programmes, nature programmes and current affairs. So although documentary always makes claims to represent a real world, it borrows some of the codes and conventions from various other kinds of factual and fiction programmes.

Key point

Television documentary's claim to represent the real rests on negotiating with the ideologies that already shape reality for the audience.

METONYMY AND ACCOMMODATION IN DOCUMENTARY

The device of metonymy in documentary enables part of reality to stand for the larger real world.

Definition: metonymy is a term deriving from linguistics that means using one thing to stand in for something else it is part of, or that is related to it.

One day in the life of an airline worker in *Airport* (BBC) metonymically stands for any other day. The work of a rural vicar in *A Country Parish* (BBC) stands metonymically for the everyday experiences of all rural vicars. Specific images or sequences, or specific documentary subjects, have metonymic relationships with the reality of which they are a part. This device is one of the unstated assumptions that enable television programmes to claim implicitly that they represent society to itself, and connect the specific subjects of programmes to larger social contexts. But creating this kind of realism in documentary depends on the relationship between the codes of the programme and the codes available to the audience for interpreting it. Kilborn and Izod (1997: 39) refer to the shaping of documentary programmes to accord with the assumed knowledge of the audience, and they call this 'accommodation'. Documentaries about airlines or vicars accommodate themselves to some extent with ideological assumptions about airlines and vicars that circulate in society, and in other television programmes. Television documentary's claim to represent the real rests on negotiating with the ideologies that already shape reality for the audience.

Accommodation is a key feature of factual forms that not only rely on found footage, but also use covert surveillance systems in order to generate actuality. Programmes such as *Rattrap* (ITV), *Nannies from Hell* and others in the 'from Hell' series, such as *Neighbours from Hell* or *Plumbers from Hell*, have adopted this technique. Programme narrators provide tips and information on how to spot inferior and overpriced work, and give guide prices for what particular common jobs should cost. There is an assumption that they are engaged in a public service, so that, for example, the names of plumbing companies are shown on screen to inform viewers which businesses have been exposed. These programmes feature only the most disturbing and shocking incidents, and are necessarily unrepresentative. But they are successful as formats that can gain large audiences in comparison to traditional forms of documentary. Conventional documentary strands such as *Storyville* (BBC) have lower audiences and later and later positions in the schedule.

DOCUMENTARY TYPES: OBSERVATIONAL DOCUMENTARY

Most theorists do not consider different styles of documentary as genres but as types based on content and programme-making style.

Modern digital recording, with long recording times and small low-light cameras, has revived the type of film making that Grierson first called a documentary – *the observational documentary*. This is the type of programme that looks at how people live their everyday lives as if from an objective viewpoint. It can be based around life in an institution such as a hospital, ship, or prison, or focused around people who live in a certain place.

This approach is also known as 'fly on the wall' as the participants become so used to the cameras and sound equipment they live as if the equipment was not there at all, as invisible as a fly on the wall. This type of documentary can still be original, interesting and provocative.

Key programme makers such as Roger Graef used this technique to observe the intimate lives of people in their own homes. This genre started with Paul Watson's intimate look at the lives of the Walton family in *The Family* (1973). Watson showed that to make strong programmes that were both illuminating and interesting the documentary director had to spend large amounts of time with the people involved. This type of documentary can still be provoking. The genre has mutated into the Reality TV of *Big Brother* formats, which deliver higher ratings, but is not documentary at all in the Grierson sense.

Modern variants of this technique are set up and cleverly managed, and carefully edited to highlight content that is sensational or startling. Often the participants have to do something that they are not used to doing in order to create conflict. This technique is borrowed from Reality TV. The set up becomes the format for the programme, as for example: *Wife Swap* and *Brat camp*.

The documentary continues to evolve. Vibrant filmmakers around the world are turning their cameras on a wide range of subjects. There is an unprecedented complicity between characters, the filmmaker and audience that is evolving in the history of documentary. The characters are encouraged to talk to camera, laugh at their mistakes and involve the viewer in the illusion of reality.

DOCUMENTARY TYPES: AUTHORED DOCUMENTARY

In contrast to the observational documentary which aims to be non-judgemental and unbiased, the authored documentary is presented by the filmmaker and aims to take a very definite point of view. US documentary makers Michael Moore and Morgan Spurlock have made feature film documentaries about socio/political issues. Although not initially made for television they do end up on television albeit as feature films, and thereby evading any constraints about bias and balance. Morgan Spurlock's film *Super Size Me* made in 2004 takes place over one month during which he eats only McDonald's food and tackles issues to do with consumerism and obesity.

One of the best-known examples of an authored documentary is *An Inconvenient Truth* (2006) directed by Davis Guggenheim. It is about former United States Vice President Al Gore's campaign to educate the public about global warming. In this case the 'author' is Al Gore because it presents his case for global warming in a one-sided way. Since the film's release, *An Inconvenient Truth* has been credited for raising international public awareness of climate change. The documentary has also been included in science lessons in schools around the world, which has sparked controversy including a British High Court case, and has not pleased everyone.

Authored documentaries are popular with audiences, as they create a head of steam about a subject. American filmmaker Michael Moore directs and produces documentary films including *Bowling for Columbine*, *Fahrenheit 9/11*, *Sicko* and *Capitalism: A Love Story*. His *Fahrenheit 9/11* is one of the most controversial. It examines America in the aftermath of the attack on the twin towers in New York and suggests there might be links between the families of ex-President George W. Bush and Osama bin Laden.

Key point

The authored documentary is presented by the filmmaker and aims to take a very definite point of view.

DOCUMENTARY TYPES: DRAMA-DOCUMENTARY

The drama-documentary is a hybrid type, and combines the codes of observation, witness and analysis from documentary with the narrative structure, focus on key 'characters' and movement towards resolution that derive from dramatic codes. Television drama-documentary re-tells events, often recent events, in order to review, understand or celebrate them. The key figures and turning-points of the story are often familiar to the audience, and opening statements and captions make clear that they are based on fact. On the other hand, disclaimers may state that some events and characters have been changed, amalgamated or invented and events 'reconstructed'.

Definition: Derek Paget's (1998: 82) definition of drama-documentary is that it:

> uses the sequence of events from a real historical occurrence or situation and the identities of the protagonists to underpin a film script intended to provoke debate . . . The resultant film usually follows a cinematic narrative structure and employs the standard naturalist/realist performance techniques of screen drama.

Drama-documentary offers a single and personalised view of a dramatic situation, in which identification with central figures allows access for the audience, but where the documentation of a historical and situation 'objectively' sets these identifications into a social and political context. Narrative provides the linkage between the forms of documentary and of drama, as John Caughie (1980: 30) describes: 'If the rhetoric of the drama inscribes the document within narrative and experience, the rhetoric of the documentary establishes the experience as an experience of the real, and places it within a system of guarantees and confirmations.'

Key point

British drama-documentary is based in carefully researched journalistic investigation, and follows the conventions of journalistic discourse, such as the sequential unfolding of events and the use of captions to identify key figures.

DOCUMENTARY TYPES: DOCUSOAP

The idea of a series of observational television programmes based around normal people but with continuing story lines has become known as the docusoap. It borrows techniques from television drama, and particularly the structure of a television soap opera. Docusoap combines the observation and interpretation of reality found in documentary with the continuing narrative centring on a group of characters in soap opera. This has several advantages in that the multi-strand format of a drama-soap is a way of generating narrative interest and excitement. The characters and events are from everyday life but the way the stories are told – the narrative drive – is in the format of a soap.

A docusoap has an episodic structure with several interweaving plot lines each involving different characters. This type of documentary has thrown up an unlikely collection of television characters. Maureen the terrible driver from *Driving School*, and Jeremy, the over-friendly fellow from *Airport*. Docusoaps have been part of the democratisation of television, where ordinary people can be both subject and performer. These programmes are very popular and deliver large audiences, and broadcasting institutions like them as they are relatively cheap to make.

Docusoaps have been criticised for lacking the depth of insight into character or situation that television documentary has conventionally aimed for. Formally, docusoaps use rapid cutting between scenes and characters to maintain audience interest, and do not adopt the sustained focus on the subject which has signified television documentary's quest for understanding. A controversial but well-known docusoap was the BBC's *Driving School*, which was scheduled against the popular ITV police drama *The Bill* yet attracted twice as many viewers, peaking at twelve million. The narrative codes of television fiction structured *Driving School*, and it featured quirky 'characters' experiencing dramatic moments and changes of fortune. The dramatic turning points, conflicts and moments of comedy were embedded in a narrative provided by voice-over narration. The emphasis on 'real-life drama' in *Driving School* was the subject of controversy when it was alleged that scenes had been 'faked', effectively scripted like drama rather than observed as in documentary. The 'objectivity' of documentary seemed to have been exchanged for 'entertainment', perverting the expectations of realism in factual television genres. For Graeme Burton (2000: 159), docusoap 'stands for a growing use of viewers to entertain the viewers – an approach familiar from the game-show genre and the use of studio audiences. It creates the illusion that television recognises its audience and works for its audience.' This inclusion of the audience and its perceived demands is even more striking in relation to the factual genre of Reality TV.

The docusoap lost some of its appeal to channel schedulers by 2010 as it was perceived to have been overexploited, and had ran out of 'characters' willing to be exploited. Mini docusoaps, however, where manipulation and control of the format, the situation and characters is transparent, seem to attract channel controllers and obtain reasonable viewing figures.

The rash of relocation programmes from the BBC and Channel 4 has switched the focus away from quirky individuals to the role of the presenter. The programmes still feature the lives of ordinary people, and draw their content and narrative structure from the events that shape their lives, but the presenter takes on a more interactive role.

Key point

A docusoap has an episodic structure with several interweaving plot lines each involving different characters.

DOCUMENTARY TYPES: PRESENTER-LED DOCUMENTARY

The presenter in a factual programme is now a guide and a friend, who helps to realise the dreams of ordinary people or guide the viewer through potentially yawn-inducing terrain such as ancient history. The factual genre has modified to take in more serious subjects. Travelogues are not only easier to make with modern digital cameras, but if the institution ups the profile with a celebrity presenter they can pull in big audiences.

Actress Joanna Lumley had a huge hit with her ostensibly observational documentary travelling from the Mediterranean upstream to the source of the Nile. The clue to the broadcasting institution's intentions is in the title, *Joanna Lumley's Nile* (ITV 2010). National treasure that she is, Joanna Lumley does not own the Nile. She made a conventional documentary into a prime-time emotional and educational crowd pleaser telling a fascinating story, and it held its own over four one-hour episodes (against drama and snooker on the BBC), with an average audience of 4.5 million viewers (about an 18.6 per cent share of the total TV audience). Many documentaries are happy with an audience of a million. The programme's success was entirely due to Lumley's intimate style, her modesty, and her enjoyment and excitement at what she was seeing on the journey.

ITV was less successful with Griff Rhys Jones's mundane *Greatest Cities of the World* (2010) series. Here the celebrity presenter had to work too hard to make anything other than a sight-seeing show. Production teams on this type of programme seem to think the viewer wants to see the presenter humiliating himself by, for example, swimming in a freezing ice-cooled pool in Sydney, Australia. The worst example of this type of show was *Paul Merton in China* (Channel 5 2009) where the viewer found out nothing about China but too much about Merton's ego.

Producers will go to inordinate lengths to link a celebrity with a documentary format. Some of these tenuous links arise from tenuous ideas, and rarely produce ground-breaking television. Comedian Victoria Wood was the presenter and reason for the series *Victoria's Empire* (BBC 2007), where she went round the world looking for other places named after Queen Victoria. The *Guardian* reviewer described it as: 'too "educational" to be an enjoyable travelogue, but it stopped short of transmitting any actual information' (*Guardian*, May 2007).

The celebrity-led travel documentary format was first made sexy and worthy of prime-time viewing by Michael Palin's witty, amusing and engaging travel documentaries. It is extraordinary to think that his first journey began in 1988 and was broadcast a year later: *Around the world in 80 days* (BBC 1989). Palin on his website admits he was a complete novice at factual programme making:

> 'I had volunteered to deliver six fifty-minute documentaries (having only done one in my life before), against the clock, with absolutely no script at all, on a

route that might change without warning. Nothing like it had been attempted before. Perhaps the greatest satisfaction of all was that we brought home so much usable material that the BBC gave us seven shows instead of six, and the seventh pulled in an audience of over 12 million.

Palin was to make many more journeys over the next twenty years that could have put the format in jeopardy, but instead established the travelogue as a very successful format. The obvious veracity of his journey with the setbacks and pitfalls of visiting exotic and far-flung destinations drew wide-ranging and appreciative audiences.

A topic to have refound its televisual form in the first decade of the twenty-first century is the authored history documentary. This type of programming is reliant on an enthusiastic, genuinely knowledgeable and charismatic presenter. He or she can interview experts from a background of understanding and can tell a story to make it alive today using only the evidence of old buildings, historical landscapes or ancient artifacts. Historian Bethany Hughes did this superbly well for Channel 4/E4 in her *Ancient World* (Channel 4 2009) strand looking at the Islamic Moors invasion in the Middle Ages and its subsequent 700-year rule over Spain.

The popularity in broadcaster's minds of the presenter-led format is evident in the excellent historical series *Story of England* (BBC 2010). Experienced presenter Michael Wood led the viewer gently and masterfully into the story of the ordinary people of England through the history of the small town of Kibworth in Leicestershire. Fortunately this likeable, unostentatious and very well-informed presenter leaves the story to the programme contributors and the material they uncover.

Broadcasters like factual programming because it can be popular and it is much cheaper to make than drama – even if you take a top-rank celebrity all the way to the source of the Nile. Adding a well-known presenter can make factual programmes attractive to other international broadcasters, like the Discovery channel, for a complete package price including numerous airings without the cost of residual payments to artists and writers for each broadcast.

Cooking on television did not start with Delia Smith. There were already shows like the *Galloping Gourmet* who magicked up delicious food almost by sleight of hand, and then there was Fanny Cradock showing us how to cook French dinners. However, it was in the 1970s that the BBC's Continuing Education department introduced Delia Smith's first television cooking course. It had an accompanying instructional book with recipes, including how to perfectly boil an egg, and covered everything a novice cook would need to know to successfully cook for family and friends. A whole generation who had not been taught to cook by their parents grew up cooking their Sunday roasts with Delia.

It took some decades before TV cooking became the celebrity cooking circus it is in the second decade of the twenty-first century. Whether it is the easy to watch Jamie Oliver creating a meal in Venice, or the irascible Gordon Ramsay opening a

FIGURE 8.2
Gordon Ramsay: piece to camera (PTC)

new restaurant, audiences seem to find the mixture of food, celebrity, dramatic incidents and on-screen testosterone a heady attraction. These programmes are very successful with large audiences, and there are successful publishing spin offs for the broadcasters.

DOCUMENTARY TYPES: THE MAKE OVER

Some critics see the type of documentary known as the make over as a form of voyeurism; the audience are gaining a form of sexual pleasure by watching people going about their normal lives, while they remain unseen. To a certain extent this is true of all types of documentary but the modern make over seems to often require nudity. The make over idea has spread to all types of programmes – there are make overs for cars, fashion, rooms, kitchens, restaurants, the home, your face and your body. All are popular and some are voyeuristic, because they allow people to expose some of their worst physical characteristics. Channel 4 has made something of a speciality of these type of shows. A typical example is *Embarrassing Bodies: Back to the Clinic* (Channel 4) and *How to Look Good Naked*. At the more demure end of the scale is ITV's *Ladette to Lady*.

Another criticism is that contributors who take part in these 'show all or tell all' documentaries are exhibitionists who have 'no shame'. Well that is what the public in 2010 seem to like both as viewers and as participants. Make over shows of all types throughout the world are always oversubscribed by would-be contributors; it seems that many ordinary people want to participate and be seen on screen as part of embarrassing television programmes. This was not always the case. I remember making documentary programmes in the 1980s when it was very difficult to persuade ordinary people to take part in a documentary on a difficult subject such as mental illness, or obesity – not so in the twenty-first century. All contributors to television documentaries sign a binding agreement that makes clear what they are expected to do, so nobody can say they have been unduly coerced into taking part.

WILDLIFE AND CURRENT AFFAIRS

Some topics fall naturally into the documentary arena. Wildlife programmes are typically observational programmes about nature and animals. They attract large early evening audiences, but are costly due to the length of time taken to film animals in the wild. They are always made by specialist wildlife programme makers such as Simon King and by specialist departments. The BBC Natural History Unit produces globally renowned radio and television programmes including David Attenborough's ground-breaking 1979 series *Life On Earth* and more recently *David Attenborough's First Life* (BBC 2010) where his subject is palaeontology – what we know about ancient life forms through fossils. The output of this department has introduced a world-wide audience to the wonders and mysteries of the Earth's plants, trees and animals, and stimulated a mass audience's interest in conservation of the environment. Currently they are working on *Frozen Planet*, billed as: 'The ultimate portrait of the earth's Polar Regions'.

Current affairs documentaries are about stories to do with people in the news and deal with political and societal issues. They are made by journalists in collaboration with broadcaster's news departments, such as the BBC's *Panorama*. These are serious programmes aiming to do original research on a current topic of political and social interest, such as an issue like ASBOs. They generally do not bring in large audiences as most viewers seem to find them 'worthy' but sometimes too serious after a hard day at work. This prompts the question: can television be a medium that is able to tackle serious topical issues in a popular, unbiased documentary style? It would be a dereliction of duty for PSB television not to take on serious current affairs issues, but commercial broadcasters are increasingly avoiding this genre mainly through cost but also through lack of expertise. It takes talent, time and money to make an interesting and intellectually stimulating *Panorama* programme.

MUSIC DOCUMENTARIES

Music documentaries often mix interviews with current celebrity musicians, and archive material of legendary artists giving insights into a genre or area of music. Factual music programming attracts more than a niche audience. The BBC's award-winning *Story of Song* (BBC updated repeat 2010) and Simon Russell Beale's inspiring and highly praised series *Sacred Music* (BBC 2009) proved how successful this area of programming can be when produced with flair and expertise. Both these series are at the expensive end of documentary making, as live recordings and archive film involving copyright and artists' fees ratchet up the budget. The rarer the footage the more expensive it is. Footage of early Elvis or the Beatles has to be specially budgeted for. Television is a natural home for this style of programming for both classical and rock music as it combines the strengths of documentary – interviews, archive footage, household names, music and a linear timeline for narrative thrust – with the entertainment elements of music video.

Music documentaries about rock stars have come to be known as 'Rockumentaries', pilloried mercilessly in the 1984 mock rockumentary *This is Spinal Tap*, directed by Rob Reiner, about the eponymous fictional heavy metal band. The film satirizes the legendary outlandish personal behaviour of heavy-metal bands, and the hagiographic tendencies of rock documentaries.

POSTMODERN FACTUAL TELEVISION

Participants in a certain form of modern documentary are encouraged to talk to camera, laugh at their mistakes and involve the viewer in the illusion of reality. Realism is no longer within the TV frame, but is seen to be a construct between the filmmaker, the subject and the audience. User-friendly digital cameras allow contributors to record their personal thoughts and intimate moments as video diaries at home, or in a hotel room, without the intrusive presence of a film crew. Some contributors are given cameras and minimum training to shoot their own material. At many points factual television intersects with other television genres such as comedy and drama. The comedian Sacha Baron Cohen took this concept one stage further to create a 'mockumentary', a documentary-comedy. Taking on the persona of Rap star Ali G the actor interviewed real people, such as the former MP Tony Benn, without revealing his true identity. The programmes *Da Ali G Show* (Channel 4, first series 2000) were billed as comedy but built on the codes and conventions of documentary. He went on to exploit this technique in the comedy film *Borat* that caused controversy for blurring traditional lines between documentary and comedy as well as upsetting the government of Kazakhstan.

REFERENCES AND FURTHER READING

Bignell, J. 'Television Realisms', in *Media Semiotics: An Introduction*, 2nd edn, Manchester: Manchester University Press, 2002, pp. 131–54.

Bignell, J. 'Television Realities' in *An Introduction to Television Studies*, London: Routledge, 2004, pp. 183–208.

Bondabjerg, I. 'Public Discourse/Private Fascination: Hybridization in "True-Life-Story" Genres', *Media, Culture & Society* 18:1 (1996), pp. 27–45.

Bruzzi, S. 'Docusoaps', in G. Creeber (ed.), *The Television Genre Book*, London: Routledge, 2001, pp. 132–4.

Burton, G. *Talking Television: An Introduction to the Study of Television*, London: Arnold, 2000.

Caughie, J. 'Progressive Television and Documentary Drama', *Screen* 21: 3 (1980), pp. 4–35.

Ellis, J. *Seeing Things: Television in the Age of Uncertainty*, London: IB Tauris, 2000.

Kilborn, R.W. and Izod, J. *An Introduction to Television Documentary: Confronting Reality*, Manchester: Manchester University Press, 1997.

Paget, D. *No Other Way to Tell It: Dramadoc/Docudrama on Television*, Manchester: Manchester University Press, 1998.

Palin, M.: http://palinstravels.co.uk/static-7.

Sears, J. 'Crimewatch and the Rhetoric of Versimilitude', *Critical Survey* 7:1 (1995), pp. 51–8.

CHAPTER 9

Reality TV

REALITY TV TODAY

Reality TV is a genre of factual programming that is more entertainment than documentary, in spite of the title. The techniques and style employed purport to be of a documentary nature. In fact the 'reality' is tightly controlled by the television company, and ferociously edited for maximum entertainment value.

The way the participants are presented does, in the better shows, allow for the unexpected elements of real life to shape the narrative. There are no script writers as such. Events happen in real time although we see the edited version.

The now demised *Big Brother* (Channel 4) propelled Reality TV programmes into the public's consciousness. There are now many different Reality TV shows in a variety of different formats. The current crop, topped in popularity by ITV's *The X Factor* (in autumn 2010, average audience twelve million), and the BBC's *The Apprentice* (in its sixth series in autumn 2010 with nearly seven million viewers) highlight the competitive aspects of the genre, and have been dubbed Talent TV – a reworking of an earlier generation of TV talent shows. Even the shows that make television out of people's behaviour are not observational in a way that Grierson would consider objective or real. The aim of the many cameras positioned around the locations on a show like *Wife Swap* is to capture entertaining and interesting events in order to create a story line – the more shocking the better. The production team intercede at certain times to control the narrative. The programmes are heavily edited to include spicy content. The contestants are chosen for the maximum potential to make interesting TV. The fact that they are called contestants could put this genre in the game show category. US Reality TV producer Michael Hirschorn considers the emotional truth evident in the best shows as worthy of good drama or documentary:

> *The Apprentice* is Darwinism set loose inside an entrepreneurial Habitrail. Post-9/11, *Survivor* became less a fantasy and more a metaphor for an imagined post apocalyptic future. What happens on these shows might be a Technicolor version of how we behave in real life, but so is most fiction. Creative endeavours – written, scripted, or produced – should be measured not by how literally they replicate actual life but by how effectively they render emotional truths.
>
> *(The Atlantic 2010)*

Nobody is fooled that these programmes are representing anything other than a manipulated reality. This attracts much larger audiences than the conventional documentary programme. Some dedicated documentary makers are turning to the cinema, the internet and DVD distribution to attract attention and enthuse an audience.

A successful reality format outside Talent TV mixes up the staple ingredients – minor celebrities, ordinary people, a competitive element and interesting locations. A prime-time series of programmes called *All At Sea* (ITV 2010) seemed to tick the boxes. Two Z-list 'celebrity landlubbers' were transplanted into two different boats – a sleek vintage motor yacht and a rough fishing trawler and sent for a short journey round the British coast. The trouble was the celebrities were not interesting and there was no real competition in spite of the two colour-coded group teams.

This type of reality show promises to attract good audience figures. The audience started on a high of 3.9 million viewers in the first fifteen minutes, but slipped down to an average of 3.5 million viewers and a 15.6 per cent share during the full hour-long slot. This is not unreasonable for a factual programme, and it did well up against more traditional documentaries on the other channels that evening. In the same slot Channel 4's documentary series *How the Other Half Live* picked up an average of 1.7 million viewers and a 7.5 per cent share of the total audience, compared to BBC 2's *History Cold Case,* a series that is billed as 'exhuming the past by forensically analysing its corpses' which had a slightly lower audience of 1.6 million viewers.

Key point

A typical reality format has to have the right ingredients – minor celebrities, ordinary people, a competitive element and interesting locations.

REALITY TV HISTORY

The first 'people shows' or Reality TV formats in the USA were driven by institutional concerns about audiences. In the US in the 1980s, the competition between four networks, cable channels, and the attractions of home video led to smaller sectors, or 'niches', of the audience being targeted by programme makers and schedulers, defined either by age-group, interest (such as sport), or social class. This was when MTV began, the channel that introduced the Reality TV format in its series *The Real World*. The same problems and opportunities that enabled Reality TV to come to prominence in the USA emerged in Britain during the 1990s as new channels, cable and satellite began to erode and segment traditional audiences. In Britain, the term Reality TV was first applied to the combination of surveillance footage, reconstruction, studio presentation by presenters, and actuality footage in programmes such as *Crimewatch UK* (BBC) and *Police, Camera, Action* (ITV). Both series represent recent crimes in realistic ways, and also, as John Sears (1995: 51) has argued, *Crimewatch* performs 'a social function by helping to solve crime, and drawing on the collective responsibilities, experiences and knowledge of the viewing audience in order to do so'.

The term Reality TV was then extended to include constructed factual programmes such as *Castaway* (Channel 4) where situations were devised for the purpose of filming, and also extended to docusoaps like *Airport* (BBC) which impose on real events the editing techniques of parallel montage, character-focused narrative structure, and basis in a single geographical space and community, that are all found in fictional soap opera. Docusoap launched Reality TV as a more widely used and public term by grabbing large audiences throughout the 1990s. From docusoap, Reality TV has emerged as a term that describes programmes characterised by a controlled environment, free of documentary's heritage of social issues. It is closer to entertainment, and increasingly replaces entertainment in evening schedules. The result is not the authenticity and explanation of documentary, but rather the spectacle of the everyday and an emphasis on the performance of identity. But Mark Andrejevic (2002) argues that the artificiality of these scenarios in reality programmes is countered by their use of non-actor participants, no scripts, and a temporal progression which is close to the linear unfolding of lived daily time.

Key point

Reality TV gives the viewer not the authenticity and explanation of the documentary, but the spectacle of the everyday and an emphasis on the performance of identity.

PROGRAMME PROFILE

Crimewatch UK (BBC)

This monthly BBC1 mid-evening programme has been running since 1984, and often features crimes which have been reported already in television news and newspapers, borrowing intertextual meanings from other media such as news and action drama. Fictionalised reconstruction of crimes aims to achieve change by dramatising events, emphasising particular details, sometimes shocking the audience and drawing them into the dramatic narrative of solving crimes. *Crimewatch* reduces its codes and conventions, and the problems it addresses, to a few highly coded images and devices which engage viewer knowledge derived from other genres of television, particularly crime drama. E-fits (images of suspects derived from witnesses' reports), photographs of stolen property, security camera footage, and physical clues also appear in television police fiction. These coded images are metonyms, parts of the narrative of the crime which are connected with each other and stand in for the crime. Conversely, reconstructions on *Crimewatch* are metaphors that parallel the facts of the crime but are fiction.

Although the programme constructs a sense of community, and works on behalf of society in general, it individualises its address to the viewer, and the crimes it features. The presenters of *Crimewatch* address viewers directly with questions such as 'Were you there that morning? Did you see him? Can you help?' The individual action requested from viewers is represented as a response to crimes perpetrated by individuals against individuals. Abstract and structural problems such as the complex of factors that cause crime, and crimes perpetrated by corporate bodies or government agencies are never represented in *Crimewatch*. The 'reality' of crime for *Crimewatch* is that it is committed by a small group of deviant outsiders, against certain unfortunate individuals. The consequence of this emphasis on individuation in *Crimewatch*, in common with many other programmes concerned with social problems, is blindness to the large-scale factors of social class, economics, and ideologies of gender or race.

PROFILE

PROGRAMME PROFILE

Police, Camera, Action (ITV)

Police, Camera, Action is a factual programme which has connections with both news and police drama. It consists of a collection of extracts from police camera footage that from 1994 to 2002 was linked by the narrating voice of Alastair Stewart, a former newsreader, and the programme gains some of its connotations of public service by his association with the values of objectivity, seriousness and reliability which derive from television news. Since 2010 the programme has been presented by ex-*Blue Peter* presenter Gethin Jones. The footage in the programme mainly comprises shots from the cameras installed in police cars, as they follow or chase drivers either engaged in criminal activities (such as making a getaway from a robbery) or committing dangerous driving errors. The car chase is a conventional element of police drama, and normally occurs as a prelude to the capture of the criminal. Car-chase sequences in *Police, Camera, Action* do not have several camera set-ups available in drama, nor shots of the drivers of the police car or the drivers being pursued. The visual quality of the police camera footage is less polished and there is little alternation between points of view or manipulation of narrative time. But despite these differences, the function of the chase is still as an action sequence as a prelude to the capture of an offender. Since police pursuit drivers give a running commentary on their actions, there is also a diegetic soundtrack that helps to explain the action and provides access to the police understanding of events. Dramatic music is used, and the voice-over narration mediates the pursuing police's commentary and points out the stupidity of errors made by drivers, the recklessness of criminals attempting to escape, and the danger posed to other road users.

Police, Camera, Action draws connotations of public service and authority from news, it draws music, the narrative functions of the car chase and pursuit from the police drama series, and the visual conventions of the surveillance camera and found actuality footage from documentary.

PERFORMANCE AND REALITY TV

Reality TV programmes claim a kind of realism by demonstrating how contestants attempt to keep up the façade of the persona they want to create, and yet reveal a kind of authenticity beneath this. Reality TV therefore borrows, perhaps surprisingly, some of the values attributed in drama to 'realistic' acting, and connects this to documentary's revelation of current social issues by means of telling personal stories. In terms of format, the casting of reality shows demands outgoing people and some possibility of conflict, so producers select people who will annoy each other. They test contestants physically (as in *Lad's Army* (ITV) where contestants endured the hardships of 1950s National Service) and dramatic high-points occur when occasionally contestants break down or are physically injured.

Like drama, Reality TV programmes make use of character types, such as the villain exemplified by 'Nasty Nick' Bateman who plotted to get other contestants to vote against each other in the first series of the British *Big Brother* (Channel 4). The contestants found out and Big Brother ejected him from the house, but Nick became a celebrity and got about £150,000 from the tabloids for his story.

In Reality TV, the key moments in individual programmes are when the performance façade of the contestant falls away. This seems to reveal the real person, since the audience is aware that the rest of the time the contestant is performing the self that they wish to project. The most interesting participants are those who project a big personality and are interesting as characters, but the other side of this is that the audience wants to see those big characters reduced to ordinariness, thus re-connecting them with the audience.

Key point

In drama, actors perform their identities as stars whom the audience think they know, whereas contestants in Reality TV programmes perform both a public persona and also take on the role of ordinary people who are implicitly as fallible as the viewer. Reality TV programmes claim to reveal insights into human behaviour in general, and attitudes among specific groups such as young adults in particular. This claim of representativeness is enhanced by the use of newly developed techniques of live broadcasting, such as webcasting, and viewer interaction.

As Stella Bruzzi (2000: 132–4) and others have noted, reality programmes emphasise character and personality to the extent that individuals become relatively free of social determinants. Bill Nicholls (1991) argues that Reality TV distances the audience from reality, rather than seeking to represent and interpret it. Nicholls demonstrates that the American series *Cops*, beginning in 1989, was one of the first Reality TV programmes and seeks to control the disorder of reality by aligning the camera with the police so that threatening crimes and criminals become banal, and the abnormality and danger that many viewers perceive in the outside world is tamed.

REALITY TV AND THE IDENTITY OF THE MEDIUM

John Ellis (2000) has argued that one of the notable features of contemporary television is its focus on witness. What is at stake in debates about Reality TV is the relationship between television as a technology of record that can bear witness to an authentic truth, and television as a separate arena from actual life. If documentary is legitimate because it witnesses and records what would have been there anyway, Reality TV cannot be documentary because it creates what it records. However, documentary filmmakers and commentators very often confirm that this ideology of transparency was never more than a myth, or perhaps an alibi.

Documentary and Reality TV both select and treat what they film, so the boundary between them suddenly melts away. The general question of boundaries and separation is central to the arguments about Reality TV. The question of why Reality TV matters depends on identifying what it is, and this identification is problematic. The problem occurs partly because of Reality TV's assimilation of elements of various fictional and factual television forms, partly a matter of its audience address, partly a matter of its institutional position in broadcast output, for example. Reality TV poses a question of definition, and encourages viewers, theorists and programme makers to ask what television is and what it is for. Does Reality TV mean TV that records reality? TV that makes a reality so it can be filmed? Is it the Reality of TV? And it asks about the generic boundaries between programmes and genres.

Key point

In Reality TV we see television bearing witness to, and worrying over, fundamental questions of representation.

BOUNDARIES BETWEEN AUTHENTICITY AND PERFORMANCE

The presence in the television schedules of various forms of reality programming, often in combination with generic elements drawn from drama and other light entertainment forms testifies to the continuing demand for new generic combinations and new formats to provide novelty and engagement for the television audience. But it also represents a cultural preoccupation with the increasingly blurred boundaries between authenticity and performance. New consumer video shooting and editing technologies and the ability to exchange images over the internet have led to an increased familiarity among the audience with the production practices, technical codes and structural conventions of video production. Recent years have been marked by debates about video surveillance, and the expectation, particularly among younger people, that they are subject to surveillance in many areas of public space. Blurring the boundaries between events that would have happened anyway and events performed for the purpose of recording is already a characteristic of television factual genres that have been around for a long time, such as the semi-staged interactions on television talk shows.

Reality TV has been blended with genres such as the game show, soap opera, documentary and factual light entertainment programmes (home-improvement, cookery, and gardening, for example). This can be regarded as a perpetuation of a process that is endemic to what television is.

Key point

Television is both an external witness to, and a participant in, reality.

REFERENCES AND FURTHER READING

Andrejevic, M. 'The Kinder, Gentler Gaze of Big Brother: Reality TV in the Era of Digital Capitalism', *New Media and Society* 4:2 (2002), pp. 251–70.

Atlantic, The. 2010: http://theatlantic.com/magazine/archive/2007/05/the-case-for-reality-tv/5791/.

BBC: www.bbc.co.uk/videonation/articles/c/cornwall_sleepless.shtml.

Bruzzi, S. *The New Documentary: A Critical Introduction*, London: Routledge, 2000.

Ellis, J. *Seeing Things: Television in the Age of Uncertainty*, London: I.B. Tauris, 2000.

Hill, Annette. Reality TV: Audiences and Popular Factual Television, London: Routledge, 2005.

Nicholls, B. Representing Reality: Issues and Concepts in Documentary, Bloomingon, Ind.: Indiana University Press, 1991.

Sears, J. 'Crimewatch and the Rhetoric of Verisimilitude', *Critical Survey* 7:1 (1995) 51–8.

CHAPTER 10

Making factual programmes

DOCUMENTARY PRODUCTION

The traditional observational television documentary is not a cheap programme type to make. It involves a long lead time to research the stories, then the director has to interview/recce and select contributors maybe from hundreds of applicants, and then there are long days or weeks of filming, sometimes with more than one film crew and usually a long way from home. There is the cost of travel and hotels, and often a presenter. Six documentaries on say the work of the RNLI will cost tens of thousands of pounds. Postproduction takes time too as there is so much footage with digital cameras – even if the director can see the footage on his laptop in the evenings during the shoot.

Modern cash-strapped broadcasting companies have looked to programme makers to cut costs and produce innovative ideas. This has been a bonus for the independent television producer who has a good idea, and can multi-skill. It might be a film about an almost unknown sect in Siberia who believe that they have the reincarnation of Jesus as their leader or an idea about cowboy builders. Instead of taking a film crew of at least two people – cameraman and sound recordist – the producer/director now has to multi-skill, shooting digital pictures and making the sound recordings on his or her own. A translator may be needed for foreign filming, and a local fixer to book hotels, find transport and see to the everyday needs of the programme makers. Look at the final credits of an interesting documentary and you will inevitably see a line like: Produced, directed and filmed by John Spencer.

Technology has really helped the independent filmmaker and has led to a crop of innovative, fascinating and often very unusual documentaries. There is no loss of quality either. A small HD camera can shoot pictures of amazing quality. It is a great pity that sometimes the quality of the sound is not as good as the pictures, and an embarrassed producer can seek to overcome the problem by engulfing the programme in needless music. The fact is that really high-quality location sound is very difficult to achieve even with modern digital kit, especially if you have to think about shot size, camera angles, cutaways as well as the questions to ask the contributor, and whether the overnight hotel has been booked. Good 'indies' have their own ways of getting round these challenges and producing quality documentaries.

GETTING A PROGRAMME ON THE AIR: TREATMENT

A production starts with a treatment. This is a succinct description of what the programme is trying to show, how it will be shown, and the audience it is aimed at. A TV treatment should be no longer than one page and include the vital statistics of the show. The audience need to be defined – prime time, children, daytime, early evening, late night. The presenter and/or any well-known contributors must be included, and the style of the show – studio, all location, video diary, or a genre, and a suggested budget as well as a description of the content.

COMMISSIONING

The treatment is collated with other material into a full **proposal**. This will contain more detail on each programme, CVs of the presenter and main contributors, and a comprehensive media CV for the producer with DVDs of previous work, as well as a list of media awards (e.g. Bafta) and previously broadcast programmes by the production company. Typically it will be submitted via e-commissioning on the web directly to the Channel's commissioning team. It is vital that the team researches what programmes are being commissioned currently, as priorities change. For example, BBC science commissioning suggest what is currently working for them:

> We need to keep refreshing our science to offer to serve audiences unparalleled content that builds ideas and knowledge, innovates and is engaging and exciting to watch. Science at the BBC ranges from the broad and instantly accessible such as *Bang Goes the Theory* to more challenging pieces like *Chemistry: A Volatile History* on BBC 4.

The proposal will be assessed by the TV channel's commissioning editor for its particular genre. If it is liked and thought suitable for the channel and the time slot, the producer will be asked to attend a number of meetings and the idea will go

EXAMPLE OF A TREATMENT

Programme: BEING THE BEST

Genre: Factual science features

Duration: 5 × 25 minutes

Institution: Independent production (Boffin Productions) suitable for mid-evening on BBC2, BBC4 or Channel 4

Format: (This is the way the content of the programme is presented to an audience. Broadcasters are looking for a returnable format that can become a brand and is exploitable across channels, platforms and territories. Think of *Location, Location Location* as a copyrighted format that can be exploited around the world. Yet it is a straightforward idea – find a couple looking to relocate to a new home and make a programme about how they get on, with the professional help of two charismatic experts – hey presto, Channel 4 have a brandable multi-platform, very successful global format.) The format for this example could be summed up as 'presenter-led popular science meets sport'.

Style: Single HD camera shot on location. Extensive postproduction with graphics.

Audience: Everyone is interested in how the best sports performers become the best and maintain their edge in sport. This series investigates how the mind in top sports performers works – from captains in cricket and rugby, via top coaches and sports psychologists to star performers from golf to amateur tennis players – this series will interest a wide general adult audience.

Talent/Presenter: A charismatic Olympic gold medallist for Great Britain has agreed to front the series.

Aim: The very best in any field condition their mind and body to fully exploit their remarkable skills. This series unlocks the mind games and in-depth mental and psychological calisthenics used in psychological training systems favoured by people at the top of their profession. The advice, help and training methods used are analysed and interpreted for armchair viewers.

Resumé: Top performers in industry, and in sport use psychological training regimes and sports psychologists. They employ a variety of mental techniques including meditation, visualisation and cognitive behavioural techniques to maximise performance. How do these techniques work, and what is going on in the mind? The series explains and explores with a light touch using new modern in-depth research from a leading UK university.

Suggested Elements: The programme will interview a wide range of sports psychologists and leading 'life training' practitioners, and will test their theories. Top athletes, footballers, rugby players and cricketers have agreed to take part. A televisual young professor, who has tested many of these techniques, leads the university research team. She will present their research and explain their results. Using some animation the programme will show how the mind works in relation to specific techniques.

Marketing: Dynamic presenter, charismatic contributors and a firm public service within the field of psychological science inform this series. The series will interest everyone who is likely to watch the 2012 Olympics in the UK, as well as those currently watching *The Apprentice.* Cost: average filming days for a 25 minute programme. Some animation. Average budget for a mid-evening programme.

into development. It is relatively unusual for a one-off programme to be commissioned. In the above scenario the producer has prepared his treatment with an independent company which has a track record in investigative science programming. The company might also submit a bundle of similar programme ideas to a commissioning editor and offer several series of science-based programmes to one or two channels. The commissioning editor will work with the company to refine their ideas during development, and then perhaps offer funding to make a pilot to try out the format and the presenter. If the series fits the criteria that the broadcaster has set out on their website and the independent company is known to be able to deliver broadcast-standard programmes then the series may get a green light. This process can take up to twenty weeks.

PREPRODUCTION

Getting the green light of course is just the start. For an independent factual series a team will be assembled by the producer. There is typically a researcher/PA, and a production manager, and an assistant producer who will also direct some of the programmes. There will be additional staff hired such as a video editor, and camera crews depending on the complexity of the series and the budget. This small production team now does all the research and preparation for filming and then editing. Preproduction is everything that takes place before the actual filming starts. When the research stage reaches a point where each programme has good solid content, contributors are lined up and locations finalised; then the next stage is to write an expanded **running order**. This will give shape to each programme and form the basis for the script. Scripts for factual programmes evolve throughout the production. What might start as a list of interviewees and locations will probably end up as a précis of the content of the interviews, linked by pieces to camera, including text for graphics, and lines of commentary to be recorded later.

THE RESEARCHER

Independent factual programmes are not known for having large resources. A researcher is likely to have to go and interview a contributor, and use a small video camera to bring back pictures of the potential interviewee.

The interview will be set up on the telephone, after prior research. The researcher needs to know what the director wants to get out of the interview. The interviewee may be a world expert in a particular field. It is important to explain to the interviewee that the viewer may have no background knowledge of this area so 'industry jargon' should not be used unless explained.

The researcher can ask on the phone about possible suitable locations for the interview, emphasising a relaxing, quiet place. The director will be looking for an interior location, without busy wallpaper backgrounds, or pure white walls. Book-shelves make a good background or an armchair with the background in subdued light. It is always best not to film people against a bright window unless you can light your subject (see lighting in Part 6).

The researcher should prepare the interviewee about what is going to happen, and how long it will take, and sometimes even what sort of clothes should be worn.

RECCE

Recce comes from the French word reconnaissance and means a location survey. This is the stage where you know what you want to film, and now need to finalise the locations or discover new relevant ones. The recce is linked to the research, and often done at the same time. Researchers carry their own portable digital cameras so that still pictures can be taken on location and discussed later in the production office. It depends on the type of production and the nature of the programme as to how much time and budget is spent on the recce. Filming a re-enactment of a battle in the Middle Ages for a historical programme at a castle clearly needs a precise and accurate recce. An interview in London may be able to be set up with just a phone call. Experienced producers never underestimate the value of a well-planned recce.

FILMING AN INTERVIEW

The sort of person you want for your programme is very likely to be busy. Make sure you do not waste their time. Be organised and efficient. Be positive and not vague or unsure of how the equipment works. Check the camera and sound are working before the interview begins. As soon as you have finished pack up and leave quickly.

- **Release form**. It is most important to ask the interviewee to sign a release form – without this you cannot broadcast the interview.
- **Open questions**. Always ask open questions. These are questions beginning with Who What When Where Why or How, and require more than just a yes or no reply. Ask only one question at a time.
- **Listen carefully** to the answers. Keep eye contact with the interviewee and do not look down or away. Nod occasionally to show that you are listening and encourage the interviewee to keep going. Ask questions leading on from the answers as well as ones that you have prepared. You will usually want to cut out your questions, and just use the answers, so make sure your questions do not overlap the answers.

FIGURE 10.1
F1 racing driver Jarno Trulli being interviewed at Goodwood Festival of Speed

- **Cutaways**. Make sure you shoot enough extra material relevant to the interview (cutaways) to cover all elements of the story and make the video editor happy.

- **Narrative**. Make sure you have a very good idea of the linear narrative, or how the story will be told in your programme, before you shoot your first interview.

SETTING UP THE CAMERA FOR AN INTERVIEW

- Set up the camera on the tripod with the lens at the eye level of the contributor.

- Put a chair next to the camera. The person asking the questions will sit in that chair very close to the camera and with his or her head at the same level as the camera lens. The contributor will look at the interviewer and not into the camera lens.

- Attach the tie mic to the contributor.

- Tell the contributor to look just at you, and not at the camera.

- Check that camera and mic are working by recording a few minutes of the contributor talking. The classic way to do this is to ask the contributor

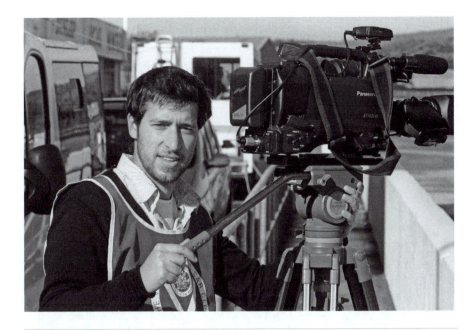

FIGURE 10.2
Brazilian documentary filmmaker with hard disc camera

what he or she had for breakfast that morning. This works as a sound test and a way to set the sound level.

- Identify the contributor by name, and for greater accuracy give the date, while recording. This gives the editor a sound ident for the interview.

- Use three shot sizes for a standard interview. The camera operator will usually change shot size as a question is being asked. This will give greater flexibility in editing. Standard interview shot sizes are: mid shot (MS), mid close-up (MCU) and close-up (CU). If you are on your own start with an MCU and change the shot size after every two or three questions.

LOCATION FILMING

The production team need to do a lot of preparation before filming can take place at a chosen location. The recce will have sorted out things like parking and access. Permission is almost certainly needed to film just about anywhere except the street.

- **Schedule**. For each day of location filming there will be a clearly defined schedule with rendezvous times, meal breaks and what is being filmed. The schedule will show what is going to happen, when and where. It will have a detailed map of each location, and some written directions of how to get there. You cannot just rely on the satnav. Everyone must know how to get to the location by the best possible route.

- **Travel together**. Travelling takes time and time is money – your production money, so use a minibus to transport everyone together and save on costs and you can brief the crew on the way.

- **Overnights**. You may have to stay overnight at the location. The hotel has to be booked and put on the schedule with the address, phone number and details of where the hotel/guest house is in relation to the filming location.

- **Contact details**. Remember to put the contact details of all production and crew on the schedule especially the director/producer's mobile phone number and email. This is handed out to all personnel – remember to keep secure, as personal details should not fall into the wrong hands.

- **Release forms**. All contributors who appear in any production that is going to be broadcast or viewed by the public must sign a release form. It is always better to get the form signed by all contributors, even if you are not sure if everyone you film will appear in the final edited sequence. The Contributor's Release Form covers all known rights in the universe. It is vital that you make sure you have all rights covered. Otherwise, when the broadcaster says that the interview is going on its website, you could find that the copyright for this interview is not covered. The form also covers any subsequent uses of your programme for DVD or internet distribution, or any other exploitation as yet to be discovered.

  The only time when you do not require people to sign a release form is when filming in public places. This applies only to non-speaking members of the public who are filmed in public places going about their business. Public places mean streets and roads and shopping areas, and other areas owned by the community. The rule is that people should be aware that you are filming. They have a right to know what you are filming, and what it is to be used for – news, documentary, entertainment programme or corporate video. They have a right to not take part if they so wish.

- **Clothing suitable for the occasion**. There is a lot of standing around when you are filming, and it is important to keep warm. Old hands say keep your head warm at all times, and do not get too hot in the sun; wear a hat, so that you can think clearly. Hence the ubiquitous use of baseball caps on a film set. In the depths of winter wear heavy waterproof clothing that would be suitable for skiing. When filming in England you probably need a pair of wellies in the boot of the car.

- **Mini office**. Productions take a laptop and use a BlackBerry/iPhone to check emails and produce paperwork with a portable printer to print updates to schedules, and scripts for the presenter. With a fully digital set-up rushes can be downloaded straight into a laptop so that the director can see rushes in the evening and do a rough edit. You will still need a mini-printer to print out scripts, running orders, editing instructions and the odd letter.

EXAMPLE OF A CONTRIBUTOR'S RELEASE FORM

Programme title ....

Television company ....

Address ....

....

Description of contribution (e.g. interview) ....

....

Date of contribution ....

Name of contributor ....

Address ....

....

Mobile no./land line ....

In consideration of the above television company agreeing that I contribute to and participate in the above television programme, the nature of which has been fully explained to me, I hereby consent to the use of my contribution in the above programme. I agree that the copyright of this contribution shall be wholly vested in the television company

....

I agree to any future exploitation of this contribution by the company in all media and formats throughout the universe.

Signed by Contributor ....

Date

....

Signed for the Company ....

Copy given to contributor.

THE FILMING DAY

- **Be prepared.** Have a very clear idea of what you are filming and how you are going to film it. Know which shot size to use in all your set-ups. Allow the cameraman leeway to find the best shots.

- **Communication.** Do discuss the day's filming with other members of the team. You are all working towards the same end – an exciting production.

- **Notes/pictures.** Do make notes of things to do at the editing stage. Do take still pictures. They will be useful for publicity and many other reasons.

- **Budget.** Do not overspend your daily budget – what do you mean you do not know what it is? You must know. Television producers and directors are required to deliver within budget at all times, unlike film directors.

- **Permission.** In private locations that admit members of the public, such as swimming pools, it is not necessary to ask everyone in the pool to sign a release form. The owner of the pool or manager will give the permission needed for filming. It is usual for one area to be put aside for filming.

- **Don't discuss editing.** In no circumstances should you tell anybody you can cut them out of the film in postproduction. You will forget who that person is and what he or she looks like. In the context of getting your

FIGURE 10.3
Documentary production

programme made this will not seem important, but it could land you with a law suit.

- **Celebrity.** If you are filming with a celebrity, or any well-known personality, then you have the problem of excluding the public from the filming area. This usually means employing security personnel, or cordoning off an area that can be used undisturbed.

- **Children.** Making a factual programme with children up to the age of sixteen is more difficult than it used to be. Parents have to give written permission to film their children, and sign a release form. Identifiable children cannot be filmed in public places without parental consent. If children have to miss any schooling to take part in the filming then a Local Authority licence is required. This has to be applied for in advance.

- **Schedule.** Keep to the day's schedule including lunch and coffee breaks. Do not over-run as a professional crew will be very displeased. The quality of work is compromised if everyone is tired.

CUTAWAYS

Think about what pictures are likely to be needed in editing to paste over some of the words of the contributor. These are called cutaways, because the video editor cuts away from the frame showing the interviewee, to something else that is relevant to what he or she is talking about. The editor will cut out repetitions and only keep the core answers. If there are no cutaways available the picture will appear to jump at the place where the sound has been edited. This is called a jump cut and it comes as a visual interruption to the flow of the interview. Cutaways allow smooth transitions through the interview, and allow editing of unwanted words and phrases. Cutaways enhance the visual aspects of the interview, and visually explain elements of what the contributor has said. The audience do not want just a talking head. Many more minutes of cutaways are needed from the location shoot than is at first imagined. The director must remember to shoot everything that is remotely relevant, and use a selection of wide shots and close-ups.

It is useful to have a variety of pictures of the contributor that can be used to introduce him or her or as cutaways. These are known as walking shots. This is because the contributor is videoed walking into their house, or outside in the garden, or just along the street. These shots can be very useful as a way of introducing the contributor or as cutaways.

POSTPRODUCTION

Editing a factual programme is where the major decisions about structure, content, pacing and story are decided. Final Cut Pro is the preferred editing software by

FIGURE 10.4
Location video editing on a laptop

most factual video editors, as it allows so much flexibility. In making a factual programme it is usual to start by editing the interviews for sound only, and not worry about jump cuts. Typically the rushes will be uploaded to the system and editing will begin by compiling a rough first cut where interviews are in more or less the right order, but there are no cutaways or 'visual wallpaper'.

Each interview is at first edited separately, putting together the most important and dramatic sections and placing them in the right order to carry the story forward. It is vital that the internal structure of each interview wholly engages the viewer. The interviews can then be edited into a structure that contributes to the overall story telling of the programme. Small excerpts from the interviews may be used at the beginning and end of the programme to 'bookend' the narrative.

A dramatic opening shot to engage the viewer should then lead on to content of equal value and relevance to the drama of the opening. Viewers need to be led along visual and aural pathways that lead to satisfying resolutions, and are not blind alleys.

When all the interviews are in the most logical order and the structure of the programme is evident then the editor will look for pictures to enhance and complement what the contributors are saying. Video editors use techniques such as slowing down pictures to make a sequence last longer, or freeze framing a landscape or other suitable shot to cover a few seconds of voice over from an interview.

The next stage is to complete a rough cut that has all the major content and is more or less the duration of the finished programme. Some sections may require graphics such as name supers or commentary. Finally, commentary, graphics and any other material such as archive footage are added, and the whole is finely edited to the required duration – this is now the Fine Cut.

COMMENTARY

The commentary has two main functions. It fills in information that has been left out, and it adds extra material to complement the visuals. Commentary works best when written to pictures, so that the words add value to the shots and flow of the programme, rather than trying to make the pictures fit words written previously.

- Commentary is spoken text so it works best written in short sentences, avoiding complex clauses.

- The difficulty is in getting the timing right. The rule of thumb is 'three words equal one second of screen time'.

- Don't rush commentary. It sounds unprofessional. Allow time, or breathing space, for the diegetic sound already edited to do its job and for the visuals to be complemented by the commentary.

- Avoid using commentary to describe what can be seen in the pictures – don't tell viewers what they can see for themselves.

- Be careful about statistics as they are always hard to absorb on their own. Make them as easy to grasp as possible. Instead of saying 'one-fifth of the population' say 'one in five of the population'. One-third is better than 33.3 per cent. Round up decimal points and fractions by saying: 'nearly 40 per cent do not take sugar in their tea' not 38.9 per cent.

- Commentary is usually in the present tense. If you find yourself writing in the past tense, make sure the pictures support it – for example, archive film.

A music documentary could open with pictures edited like this:

Opening wide shot of Alex King's Range Rover coming down the tree-lined drive and pulling up outside his castle home, intercut with close-up shots of him driving from inside the car. Ends with wide shot of arriving at the castle. Cuts to a low-angle shot of a round tower. Cut to interior of Alex entering his sound studio and picking up a guitar. Alex's music begins under the commentary. These opening shots set up the interview, showing who the interviewee is and what he does and where he does it. It leads quickly into the many shots of the recording studio and the essence of the interview. This is the opening commentary for this sequence:

Alex King is almost unknown outside the music industry. But he's more successful than many better-known faces on music television. (Pause.) He lives far from the glitz of the pop world in a castle in Herefordshire. Alex writes film music and he records it in his state-of-the-art sound studio here at his home. His new interest is 3D audio for 3D films.

(No need to say the studio is in one of the round towers as we see that from the pictures, but we do need to say that his home is in Herefordshire otherwise the audience will be wondering just where we are. The 3D clue leads us into his first piece of audio from the interview).

Final commentary tip – short sentences lead to crisp commentary.

STUDENT DOCUMENTARY PRODUCTIONS

Making a documentary at college or university is often part of the requirements of a practical module. This is an exciting project which can lead to an award winning documentary. Some students have a story or topic which they are bursting to film. Other students can spend a lot of time looking around for a topic/story/event that they can make into a suitable documentary. Here are some ground rules for coming up with a very low-budget documentary proposal.

- **Access.** Choose a topic that is possible with access to people and locations. It is best to avoid generic topics such as global warming, or animal rights unless they relate to something specific that is accessible locally, such as a local issue perhaps to do with waste incineration, or the possible closure of an animal sanctuary.

- **Local.** Any topic is fine as long as it has local possibilities. Always look for a local link – it is so much easier to film within your neighbourhood, either at home or at university. A documentary about your local football club is possible – a student production about Manchester United is not.

- **Characters.** Documentaries need characters. Do you know somebody who has an interesting story to tell – it could be your granddad or a street cleaner.

- **Format.** Go for a traditional format – a life in a day of . . . a local band, the park, my Saturday job, or be imaginative – my mobile phone.

- **Footage.** Holidays are the ideal times to shoot footage for a documentary even if you are not quite sure how the finished film will end up. If you have access to a family video camera then use it even if it is just background shots. It is hard to make a bad documentary that has footage of surfing, or sailing or looking for blennies in rock pools, or camping or visiting a foreign city.

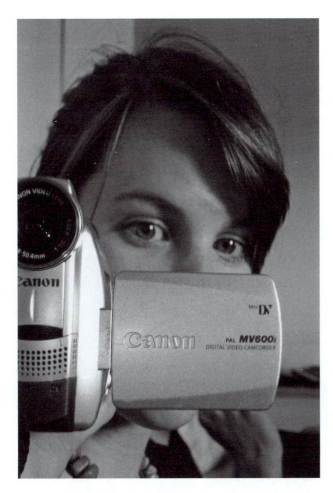

FIGURE 10.5
Student documentary production

- **Sound.** Pay particular attention to the sound and always use an external microphone.

- **Interviews.** A good documentary relies on good interviews with interesting people.

- **Cutaways.** A good documentary must have a lot of footage of relevant pictures of what the interviews are about – in other words you need lots of cutaways, many more than you think you do at the time.

- **Locations.** Choose locations that are visually interesting and add to the story.

- **Story.** Make sure you tell a story with a beginning, middle and end – a life in a day begins in the morning and ends in the evening.

- Good luck and get filming.

For extra advice on video production see Part 6 on Practical Programme Making.

REFERENCES AND FURTHER READING

BBC: www.bbc.co.uk/commissioning/tv/network/genres/features3.shtml
Channel 4: www.channel4.com/4homes/on-tv/location-location-location/
Chapman J. and Kinsey M. *Broadcast Journalism: A Critical Introduction*, London:
    Routledge 2009.

Part 4

News and sport

CHAPTER 11

Television news

THE IDEOLOGY OF NEWS

Television news, because of its liveness or potential liveness, is usually the medium that viewers turn to when major news stories are breaking in order to see pictures of the events and discover the most recent developments. There is a hierarchy of news value in which live actuality pictures are the most attractive to the producers of television news programmes, followed by actuality pictures which have been pre-recorded, and finally those stories which cannot be illustrated by actuality footage or an interview are the stories which are least likely to appear.

Television news claims to denote events objectively and immediately, offering a neutral and transparent channel of communication. The iconic quality of television images, which appear simply to record what is unfolding in front of the camera, are key signifiers of this mythology of transparency. When news events like election results or the Olympics are broadcast live, or when a national event such as a royal wedding or the occurrence and aftermath of disasters are broadcast, it is the accidental detail and unpredictable unfolding of events that are fascinating.

Contemporary networks of electronic mediation allow digital news images to be circulated around the world from television news crews back to their producers at home, and also to the news agencies which sell packages of news pictures to broadcasters.

Key point

Television technologies are not neutral, and the selection of news and the forms in which it is represented have political effects.

One example of the political effects of the selection of news is the perception of the Third World by Western television audiences, where some categories of event are more frequently denoted in news and current affairs. Large-scale political violence and natural disasters are the predominant form of news image broadcast of Third World countries and developing countries such as China. The United States and other Western nations predominantly appear in news as the active agenda-setters, while countries in the developing world are portrayed as passive sufferers of news events. These divisions are parallel to, and derive from, the division between the rich Western nations, which intervene in world affairs and control world institutions such as the World Bank or United Nations, versus the relatively impoverished and politically disempowered nations in the rest of the world. The academic study of news has focused especially on these questions of power, and how the ideologies of news reproduce relationships of dominance in both domestic and overseas news coverage.

THE PUBLIC SPHERE

The cultural theorist Jürgen Habermas argued in favour of rationality and communication as means to improve society. Improved communication and rational debate about politics and society would enable people to liberate themselves from the apparently stifling bureaucracy of contemporary societies. This space of public debate is termed the public sphere (as opposed to the private sphere of home and family). In order to achieve this liberation and debate, access to the media and the free exchange of ideas in the media must be key priorities. The centralisation of ownership and control of the media, and ordinary people's lack of participation in them, are the main problems which he diagnoses: 'Insofar as mass media one-sidedly channel communication flows in a centralized network – from the center to the periphery or from above to below – they considerably strengthen the efficacy of social controls' (1987: 390). In contrast to this, Habermas calls for individuals to take practical action to gain access to media and to use them for reasoned political debate. Now convergence allows audiences to be active users of news content rather than just passive consumers.

For TV news to contribute to the formation of a public sphere, news must be available, accurate, balanced and representative of the events that could be the subjects of debate. There are some aspects of the contemporary (and former) presentation of television news that complicate its contribution to the public sphere. But the organisation of news production and dissemination are also significant. Sources of television news are perceived as unequal by television viewers, with some regarded as more reliable than others, and news tends to flow around the globe from north to south and from west to east. Such a situation provides fuel for arguments that global television news exacerbates the separation between the West and other regions of the world where news seems to happen, and the insulation of television news from the lives of its viewers.

Key point

For TV news to contribute to the formation of a public sphere, news must be available, accurate, balanced and representative of the events that could be the subjects of debate.

The relationship between place and television news is complex, and global TV news channels such as the BBC and CNN and the global newsgathering enabled by satellite transmission make local and regional differences more, not less, important. Local news finds its identity alongside or by resisting the national and global news agenda, so that the dominance of global and national news becomes important to the production of local news. Local, in this connection, can also mean regional, in that television cultures cross national boundaries to include speakers of the same language or audiences which share similar cultural assumptions and ideologies (like the British Asian or British Polish communities, who tune into trans-national news channels for news about their 'home' culture and people who share the same origins).

In the global news landscape the concepts of society and nation are diminishing in usefulness. The concept of society as a unit bounded in time and space loses its force when, for example, live television news or sports coverage confuse time and space by broadcasting across time zones. Because television broadcasts such a range of images of culture, like representations of youth and age, domesticity, work and gender, global television provides the possibility of reflecting on local cultures. Global news provides resources for people to think about themselves and their social environment, in the same ways that local or national television does:

> An Egyptian immigrant in Britain, for example, might think of herself as a Glaswegian when she watches her local Scottish channel, a British resident when she switches over to the BBC, an Islamic Arab expatriate in Europe when she tunes in to the satellite service from the Middle East, and a world citizen when she channel surfs on to CNN.
>
> (Sinclair *et al*. 1999: 187)

Key point

Viewers negotiate their sense of place, time and community in relation to local, regional and global television cultures, by adopting, or resisting, ways of thinking and living that derive from television news and other TV genres.

THE NEWS ECONOMY

Modern viewers have access to numerous news sources and not just from Freeview, cable and satellite television channels, but also internet news, RSS feeds and email news and mobile phone apps such as provided by the *Guardian*. The consumer can enjoy greater diversity and quantity of news, but will be further separated from the experience of news events than people who cannot access so much information. It has often been claimed that the world is not only divided into the rich and the poor, but increasingly into the information-rich and the information-poor. Television news producers gather and exchange news in a kind of news economy, producing a global news market that homogenises news inasmuch as it becomes a commodity for sale. News footage is offered to broadcasters by news agencies, and is accessed by satellite links. As well as using these mechanisms for exchanging news footage, news institutions have exchange agreements with institutions and broadcasters in other countries. The BBC, for example, has an exchange agreement with the ABC network in the USA. Satellite technology and the internet enable the international news machine to operate twenty-four hours a day, sending both raw footage and complete news packages to national and regional clients. Because of the different languages used in different nations, news agencies mainly distribute images without commentary. This reinforces the perception that iconic visual images in news are in themselves objective, though clearly the activities of selection, editing and composition in news footage are as much a meaning-making process as the addition of voice-over commentaries for broadcast.

NEWS AGENDAS

One of the most commonly used words to enter political discourse in the first decade of the twenty-first century has been the term 'spin'. Spin has taken the place of censorship in democratic societies, as the predominant means of manipulating television news agendas, and either concealing possible news stories or bringing them to prominence. It used to be the case (in the Second World War, for example) that governments and official agencies would prohibit the reporting of some news events that, in unusual circumstances such as war, could threaten security or damage public morale. But now, rather than prohibiting reporting, modern conflicts more often involve the channelling of information to the media by specially chosen spokes-people. For example, reporting on the war in Afghanistan is limited almost exclusively to 'embedded' journalists. These journalists live with the US or British Army and are only allowed to film or write about what the armies choose for them to report on.

NEWS ACQUISITION

The acquisition of news is now carried out as much by news gathering from sources provided by the people and institutions that are reported on, as by sending journalists to investigate issues. The discourse of news is increasingly based on the editing, reworking and supplementation of acquired footage and press briefings. In short, news often comes to the news studio, rather than news teams going out to find

FIGURE 11.1
News cameraman

it. In this situation, it is especially easy for a news institution to become a victim of spin, or to intentionally or unintentionally editorialise and comment, thus becoming a producer of spin. But organisations that have a vested interest in providing information to publicise or support their cause can be very helpful; for example charities may be willing to supply packs of information, documents and spokespeople, and may be keen to contribute directly to programmes by providing experts and/or video footage. Some charities, such as Greenpeace, take camera operators with them on direct action activities, and are careful to shoot footage that is of appropriate quality and sufficiently dramatic for news programme packages. From their perspective, it is beneficial for Greenpeace footage to be included in news programmes so that material shot from Greenpeace activists' point of view becomes the illustrative material in a news report. Clearly, the ulterior motives of research sources and contributors need to be assessed carefully by news producers, and occasionally television news organisations are subject to public criticism for too easily accepting information and footage provided to them by a participant in a news story.

CITIZEN JOURNALISM

Citizen journalism (CJ) is also a form of news gathering encouraged by broadcasters. On the internet the citizen journalist becomes the producer. This is especially evident during natural disasters such as the Haiti earthquake (2010). Ordinary people present at newsworthy events email photographs or video footage often taken on mobile phone cameras to news organisations, blogs or websites. Independent online news sites such as *The Huffington Post* (www.huffingtonpost.com) rely on user-generated Content (UGC). The reporting on the Haiti disaster carries an exhortation to participate: 'Send us a photo from the destruction with a description of the image and where it was taken.'

Some commentators believed that citizen journalism and user-generated content could take over newsrooms, and provide content that is more interesting, relevant and democratic than news compiled and edited traditionally. By the end of 2010 this had not happened in any significant way. News organisations do ask audiences for visual and textual content, but traditional news gathering processes supply the majority of news broadcasts. If a broadcaster uses a story initially sent in by an individual it nearly always sends a reporter to investigate and report the story traditionally.

FIGURE 11.2
Citizen journalist in action

With a mobile phone anyone can take a reasonable picture and email it directly to a newspaper or broadcaster. The end user is part of the news gathering process. Anyone can make a short video or audio recording on their mobile and upload it to a news desk, or to YouTube, where it can be accessed by television news organisations. If you happen to be on the spot when a news event happens then your pictures will get on the air or in the newspapers. This raw content, available on the internet, can quickly move up the news hierarchy long before newsroom editorial cycles can process and publish news. For example, photos of the July 2005 London Underground terrorist bombings were spread on the internet by ordinary people who happened to be near the scene of the disaster. These pictures were in the public domain faster, and with more unfiltered information than traditional newsrooms were able to publish or broadcast. The dramatic shots from inside the bombed train underground came from the mobile phone cameras of survivors. Traditional news crews and reporters rushed to the scene to analyse and interpret the events that they had been alerted to by citizen journalists.

News has to be understandable and acceptable to viewers. A sent-in video news story still needs a professional journalist to make it a newsworthy event for the viewer; otherwise it is just another YouTube video.

Traditional news values have relevance and importance in the convergence age. The news gathering, research and fact-checking functions journalists provide are vital to a democratic society. As citizens, we develop relationships with a TV news channel and the particular approach of its editors. We depend on them for consistency and credibility. In the digital world information is democratised, and journalists and citizens are less constrained by an older patriarchal model where decisions about what gets reported and what does not are made by a few editors. A compelling and well-researched story will find an outlet.

Key point

News has to be understandable and acceptable to viewers. Traditional news values still have relevance in the convergence age.

NEWS NARRATIVE

Television news consists of narrative reports, and can be analysed as narrative to discover how priorities and assumptions shared by news broadcasters form a code determining which reports have greatest significance within the news bulletin. The reports with the highest news value appear near the beginning of the bulletin (in the same way as the front pages of newspapers present some stories as having the highest news value to readers). The ranking of reports according to their news value shows how the representation of reality offered by television news is not a

FIGURE 11.3
News interview

denotation of events, but a narrative mediated by the signs and codes of news television. Binary oppositions, like those between crime and law, left-wing and right-wing opinions, or home and abroad, are the basis for news narrative.

News narrative contributes to the process of constructing a common-sense climate of opinion through which audiences perceive their reality. Therefore, television news shares the ideological function of naturalising the public arenas of politics, business and international affairs as newsworthy. News programmes seek to connote balance and objectivity by giving approximately equal time to conflicting parties and interested groups. But balance and objectivity are defined in relation to a common-sense norm, a cultural construct, and will therefore shift according to the current balance of power. News narrative, despite its commitment to balance and objectivity, measures this balance and objectivity against the currently dominant ideologies in society, which occupy an apparently neutral position.

Key point

Television news both shapes and reflects the dominant common-sense assumptions about what is significant, since by definition what is deemed significant is what makes the news.

Television news deals with the potentially infinite meanings of events by narrating them in conventional subject-categories, like 'foreign news' or 'business news'. These divisions reflect the institutional divisions in news broadcasting organisations (Harrison 2000). Some news programmes title news stories with captions on the screen next to the news presenter, and these captions connote both the specificity of each news story, but also the connection between a particular story and others in the same category. The effect of using this code is to restrict the narrative frameworks that are available for representing the story. Placing reports in coded categories restricts the viewer's capacity to make connections between one news report and another in a different category, or to bring an alternative narrative structure to bear.

Television news has to deal with events that are by definition new in each day's news, and to do this it has powerful codes for giving shape and meaning to news reports. Reports use four narrative functions (Hartley 1988: 118–19).

Framing

Framing is the activity of establishing the news topic, usually done by the mediating figure of the newsreader. For example, political news is usually coded as adversarial. Although mediators like news presenters speak in a neutral register and establish themselves and the news broadcasting organisation as neutral too, the effect of this is to make the setting-up of the narrative code appear invisible to viewers: it seems to arise from the news itself rather than from how it is being presented.

Focusing

Focusing refers to the opening out of the news report into further detail, conveyed by reporters and correspondents who speak for the news broadcasting institution. These institutional voices develop the narrative by providing background information, explaining what is at stake in the news event, and introducing comment and actuality footage that illustrates this.

Realising

The interviews, film reports and comment by people involved in the news event are part of the function known as realising, since they ground the news story in evidence and personal commentary from interested individuals and groups. The availability of actuality footage gives important added value to news reports because it is crucial to the narrative function of realising the story. But although actuality footage might seem to be the dominant type of sign in television news programmes, its visual signs never appear without accompanying voice-over commentary. Realisation therefore tends to confirm the work of the news reporters' framing and focusing language.

Closing

Closing refers to the way that a news report moves towards a condensed encap-sulation of the report, likely to be repeated in the closing headlines of the news programme, which reinforces the editorial line decided on to structure the story. Closure might involve ignoring some of the points of view on the news event which have been represented in the report, or repeating key points already introduced by the frame or focus.

NEWS VALUES

In 1965, media researchers Johan Galtung and Mari Ruge closely analysed news stories in a number of media to find out what factors they had in common, and what criteria placed them at the top of a news bulletin. They created a list of criteria for news coverage known as the Galtung and Ruge news values. These have been added to and adapted for modern news, but they are still the basis on which television news editors make their daily judgments. News editors also use their experience of a particular audience, and what it expects to see or hear from a news programme as well as what stories have had an impact on that audience in the past.

Each news organisation has its own system of setting news priorities. Broadcast news organisations such as the BBC, ITN and SKY will agree on many of the same news stories for any one day. The emphasis may lead one broadcaster to headline a particular story while another puts it down to item number three, but the mix of stories is broadly similar. These are the news values adapted from Galtung and Ruge and later refined by Harrison (2006: 137).

Impact – information has impact if it affects a lot of people. For example, a change in the interest rate or the Coalition government cuts in government spending has impact, because they affect all people. The rape of a young girl or the death of a family in a house fire has impact, too. Even though only a few people are directly affected, the audience will feel a strong emotional response to the story.

Recency – TV news broadcasters are very competitive about breaking news. Up-to-the-minute recent news can reach the audience very quickly via rolling news stations. The very latest news is an important criterion for news bulletins. For the rolling TV news channels such as Sky News and BBC News recency is their top priority.

Amplitude – Size of the story. The bigger the story the more impact it has. The Haiti earthquake on 12 January 2010 was a massive disaster and huge news story. It killed more than 250,000 people in the poorest country in the western hemisphere. By contrast, sack the manager of the local football club and the story has very little amplitude.

Unambiguity – News editors like a clear story. It may be: two young girls are missing from a small village in Cambridgeshire. More complex stories are usually simplified so that they are clear and unambiguous. In a TV news bulletin the audience can easily grasp a straightforward story, but could be confused by a complex news story.

Proximity – In our backyard. The closer to home the better. Audiences like to hear news about people from their own locality. News about people from their own country matters more to a national audience than foreign news. An airline accident abroad where many people from the home country die or survive will carry more weight as a news item than if there was no one from the home country on the flight.

Correspondence – This is a more subtle news value. The degree to which the news meets our expectations and corresponds to how we think the news should be. We all have cultural values, and often the news from our favoured news source will correspond to these values. Broadcast news in the UK strives to be balanced, accurate and without bias. A public service news organisation like the BBC is set up to be impartial and 'offer the audience an intelligent and informed account which enables them to form a view' (BBC guidelines). Some assumptions can seem to be universal – all terrorists are evil. But it is worth remembering that your terrorist is someone else's freedom fighter.

Surprise or uniqueness – Events have to be unexpected or rare or preferably both to be newsworthy, and often this category is good news. A comet can be seen streaking through the sky or somebody has unearthed a hoard of Roman coins. These items are surprising as they do not happen very often.

Continuity – the running story. Any news that is already news will continue to be news until it is resolved. The fight against terrorism takes many forms, from government Bills going through Parliament to long queues at airports because of increased security. So this is news that will continue to feature in one way or another in many news bulletins. Certain particular stories – for example, the hunt for the missing young girl Madeleine McCann – often seem to come back again and again. News organisations like to have closure of a story, but if, as in this case, there is no agreed final outcome, then the story tends to return.

Composition – The need for balance between hard and soft news, and the need for variety leads the editor to add a foreign story if all the news has been home news, or a celebrity or sports story if the rest of the news has been glum.

Negativity – Negative news tends to get selected over positive stories – why? Murder, a suicide bombing and events where there is death always get priority. Bad news tends to get a higher priority in a news editor's mind than more positive stories such as a royal occasion, or a successful attempt to row across the Atlantic. Although some success stories such as England regaining the Ashes from Australia in cricket override any bad news on the day. Sadly it doesn't happen very often.

Predictability – News stories often arise out of predictable events such as anniversaries. The 200th anniversary of the battle of Trafalgar (1805) was the trigger for many events and news stories over quite a few weeks. Organisations send news providers a Press Release which announces something that they consider to be newsworthy. It may be a new drug, or new research into a controversial health topic such as obesity, or the result of a survey, or the winner of an award such as the Turner art prize. These are predictable stories in the sense that the news room know about them in advance so can send a reporter to cover the event. Some theorists think that too large a proportion of modern news emanates from uncontested sources such as press releases, press conferences, pressure groups and global companies. They feel that investigative journalism is being sidelined for this 'easy' news content as it is cheap and available.

Personalities or *elite people* are news. We are mainly interested in the powerful people who affect us and the powerful or elite nations such as the United States and our own country which affect the way we live – well, people ask, what has a war in Angola got to do with me?

News will always be driven by what powerful people do, such as political leaders, heads of large organisations, and international figures or what they are saying, e.g. Barack Obama. Some television channels such as Five elevate the latest activities of celebrities, soap opera stars and pop singers to the top of their news agendas as they – probably rightly – believe their core young audience desires fresh news about the personalities that interest them. Celebrity news has crept up the news agendas of many channels in the twenty-first century. Some people argue this dumbs down the news as it leaves less room for other more traditional news stories.

These news values have been condensed into a short bullet list of intrinsic news values by Harrison in *News* (2006). Most researchers agree that the presence of these intrinsic news values in an event defines its TV newsworthiness:

- Pictures or film are available.
- There are short dramatic occurrences which can be sensationalised.
- There is novelty value.
- The events are open to simple reporting.
- The events occur on a grand scale.
- The events are negative or contain violence, crime, confrontation or catastrophe.
- They are highly unexpected; or they contain things which one would expect to happen.
- The events have meaning and relevance to the audience.
- Similar events are already in the news.
- They provide a balanced news programme.
- They contain elite people or nations.
- They allow an event to be reported in personal or human interest terms.

News can be said to be only really effective if it affects the individual personally, or is felt to have an affect on the individual personally. 'I was not affected by schoolgirl Millie's abduction and murder but I do have a teenage daughter so I am worried.' This type of human interest story concerns all parents, as it taps into their worst fears. It also fulfils many of the above criteria.

NEWS AS AN EMPTY FORM

There is a paradox in the increasing quantity and speed of international television news. Television, with its focus on liveness, and the showing of actualities from distant places, draws on Western culture's belief in the power of photographic images to bear witness to real events so that seeing something happen on television news claims the immediacy and veracity of fact. But at the same time, the proliferation of representations of realities on television news distances what the viewer sees from his or her own physical everyday experience. Television always aims to contain and explain the real, especially through the form of narrative, and the desire to produce unmediated access to the real goes along with, but is contradicted by, the necessity to domesticate and contain the material. John Ellis ('Television as Working Through', 1999: 56) argued that television news:

> has been driven by the demand that it should provide ever more instantaneous material, to the extent that flexible digital video formats plus satellite technology are moving us towards an era of "real-time" news in which we can see events more or less as they happen.

But these events are not presented in the raw, since they are always subject to a constructing interpretation. This mediation of news by the conventions and codes of news programme formats has led academic commentators to argue that the form of news takes precedence over its content: the medium becomes the message.

Key point

Television always aims to contain and explain the real through the form of narrative.

INTERPRETING NEWS PROGRAMMES

Main evening news bulletins are scheduled at fixed points, and their scheduling already connotes their importance. The dramatic opening music calls the viewer's attention. The opening shot is normally a head-on address to the viewer by the presenter who is placed against a cycloramic visual background linked to the top news story of the day.

News programmes are complex television texts, in which a large number of segments are linked together. There are likely to be sequences in which the news presenter is speaking directly to the viewer, sequences of news reportage, and dialogue between the presenter and experts in the studio or reporters live in a location where a news story is occurring. In addition, presentational techniques such as graphics, maps, statistics and diagrams will be used either alongside or independently of these forms of content. This level of complexity is managed by news production staff using the kinds of consistent structure and division of responsibilities described above, but because news is necessarily always new and yet news programmes are patterned in very consistent ways there are questions to ask about what viewers actually make of it and what impact it has.

REALITY AND 9/11

The French cultural theorist Jean Baudrillard (1997) claimed that the almost non-stop news coverage of the Gulf War in the early 1990s smothered the reality of the event, so that the war itself was in effect replaced by the television pictures which claimed to represent it. On the 11 September 2001 (known as 9/11) another similar example happened when terrorists attacked targets in the United States. Complex issues surrounding resistance to the power of the United States in various regions, the several terrorist attacks taking place on 11 September, and questions about what the terrorists intended to achieve and what the proper response should be, were overwhelmed by a small number of brief and dramatic sequences of television pictures. A few seconds of footage of airliners crashing into the World Trade Center, a few seconds of the huge towers collapsing to the ground, and a few seconds of reaction to the event from shocked pedestrians in New York became the iconic TV images which represented this complex of issues and events, and were repeated innumerable times. Four airliners were hijacked at the same time, one crashing into the Pentagon, another crashing in Pennsylvania *en route* to another target, and two flown into the towers of the World Trade Center. The television coverage focused primarily on the World Trade Center events, partly because of the larger scale of casualties, but also because of the availability of several different points of view on the attack itself filmed by citizen journalists and the comparative ease of access to eyewitnesses, officials, government spokespeople and experts in the New York metropolitan area. News coverage quickly reduced to extracts of a few seconds duration showing the impacts of each airliner into the twin towers, brief sound bites from witnesses close to the scene, and a grainy still photograph of Osama bin Laden. Nevertheless, the days following the attacks were saturated with television coverage. CNN, for example, broadcast live to a worldwide audience of almost one billion, in ten languages including English, to 900 affiliated television stations, and British channels such as BBC News and Sky News ran open-ended coverage.

Key point

Television news provided the images that encapsulated a complex reality in a few seconds of coverage.

The events seemed to be 'more real' because they were shown almost live around the world to millions of viewers, but were also 'less real' because the events were so quickly accommodated into the formats and routines of news broadcasting. Although channels began to cease open-ended coverage in the evening of the first day, news audiences remained high until the end of the week. BBC adopted the strategy of simultaneous broadcast on its terrestrial BBC1 network and its digital channel BBC News. This strategy simplified the management of news broadcasting in a potentially chaotic situation, and also functioned as an advertisement for the recently launched BBC rolling news channel. ITN, by contrast, provided live news across five different networks: ITV, Channel 4, Channel 5, ITN News and Euronews. This enabled each network to maintain the well-known presenters associated with its programmes and provided different programming to viewers on each of the channels. There was some difference in approach between the BBC and ITN coverage. Although both news organisations often repeated video sequences showing the airliners crashing into the twin towers, the BBC quickly introduced analysis and discussion into their coverage as well as live updates from reporters in the United States. ITN, on the other hand, persisted with live footage (usually of presenters in New York and vox pop interviews) rather than analysis. All commercial breaks were dropped from the schedule during ITN news programmes.

BAUDRILLARD AND THE HYPERREAL

While no one would deny that the events of 11 September happened, their reality was superseded by television news representations. Baudrillard argues that in fact we do not experience reality at all except in terms of the codes of television and other media. For example, family relationships are perceived in terms of the melodramatic narrative structures of soap opera and romance, and perceptions of law and order and crime are mediated through the codes of television police series. Baudrillard termed this state of affairs 'the hyperreal', in which the experience of reality has become indistinguishable from the television and media conventions that shape it. The process by which the hyperreal comes into being is referred to as simulation: the staging of events, feelings and relationships by means of the codes and conventions of television and media culture.

Key point

Baudrillard argues that in fact we do not experience reality at all except in terms of the codes of television and other media.

Western television sources based all of their coverage on a Western, and particularly American, point of view. It was very difficult for news broadcasters to provide actuality footage representing the point of view of anti-American individuals or institutions, particularly in Afghanistan (where the supposed organiser of the attacks, Osama bin Laden, was thought to be). Restrictions on Western television personnel there meant that on 11 September 2001 there were very few Western journalists in Afghanistan. There are very few satellite uplink points in Afghanistan and access to these is strictly controlled. But in any case Afghan government restrictions on Western journalists prevented them from filming in the country in the first place, so for a complex of reasons, explanation or justification of the attacks on the United States could not be represented. The result was that poor quality pictures of Osama bin Laden and a few seconds of controversial footage apparently showing Palestinians jubilantly celebrating the attacks on the United States were the primary images representing alternatives to the vengeful discourses emerging from the United States in the aftermath of the attacks. CNN was exceptional in having a reporter in Kabul (the capital of Afghanistan) equipped with a satellite videophone. This technology allowed CNN reporter Nic Robertson to report live from Kabul by unfolding a satellite antenna, connecting the camera to the videophone, and transmitting live pictures. However, the videophone had to be smuggled across the Afghan border and used illegally for short periods in different locations.

The news coverage of 11 September 2001 is clearly an exceptional case, and some of the arguments made about it by academic theorists are deliberately provocative and extreme. But that day and the days that followed draw attention in a very striking way to the questions about structuring news programmes, using technology, and the political issues of access and agenda-setting faced by TV news staff and analysts of news.

TRUSTING NEWS BROADCASTERS

Four years later the tragedy of the London bombings in July 2005, also initiated by terrorism, provoked a massive television news operation. The many different news sources and websites available in the digital age may offer differing versions of events like this. Viewers are not always able to check the accuracy and veracity of reports with so many websites and news outlets, especially if looking for news of loved ones. Many websites, and some news stations such as Fox News, have their own political agendas which may compromise the accuracy and truth of their news.

After a tragic and life-threatening event such as this on home territory people tend to turn to a trusted source for their news. BBC News has a well-deserved reputation for being the respected public service broadcaster, whom people most trust for truthful and accurate reporting. Writing in the *Guardian* soon after the 2005 event, the head of BBC News Roger Mosey said:

In these times of tragedy, broadcasters have the natural human responses – but also the need to keep our audiences informed of what is happening. Journalism is a vital part of our national response to terrorism: reporting honestly and accurately what has happened, and equipping people with the knowledge to understand the world in which we're living. In all, more than 30 million people watched BBC News last Thursday – more than the other news broadcasters in the UK put together.

NEWS AUDIENCES

It is likely that much of the dense content of TV news often passes the viewer by. Many viewers will find it very difficult to remember the news stories presented in a single broadcast, let alone the nuances of the different points of view and fragments of information in it. Instead, viewers will construct a sense of what is important, often based as much on their pre-existing knowledge of news stories, and on other information sources such as newspapers. Some of this cultural knowledge of news must be shared, since it enables news quizzes, for instance, like *Have I Got News for You* (BBC) to be both comprehensible and entertaining. But studies have tended to show that different audiences are diverse and specific in their response to news, and have capacities for active interpretation (see, for example, Bruhn Jensen (1998) for an analysis comparing audiences in different nations).

In Britain, the long-established researchers The Glasgow Media Group studied the representation of the Israeli and Palestinian Arab conflict in the Middle East and what viewers understood about it (Philo 2002). When the state of Israel was established in 1948, Palestinians living in the country were displaced from their land. In May 1948, a war between Israel and its Arab neighbours produced more refugees, many of whom moved to the Gaza Strip (then controlled by Egypt) and to the West Bank of the River Jordan (controlled by Jordan). In 1967, Israel was at war with its Arab neighbours again and occupied Gaza and the West Bank, bringing the Palestinian refugees there under its control. Eastern Jerusalem (formerly controlled by Jordan) was also occupied by Israel. To cement its control, Israel built settlements in the areas it had occupied. The settlements caused anger among the refugees because of the presence of Israeli citizens in former Arab territories, and also because their farming activities deprived Palestinian farmers of water. The subsequent violence in the Middle East consists of attempts by Israel to maintain its control over occupied territory, and attempts by Palestinians to resist the occupation and regain their land.

The Glasgow Media Group researched viewers' understanding of this conflict by undertaking a content analysis of television news stories on the BBC and ITN (counting how many mentions of the conflict there were, of what type, etc.). They also interviewed twelve sample groups of viewers, totalling eighty-five people, from a cross-section of ages and social backgrounds. In addition they interviewed 300 young people aged between seventeen and twenty-two. Each person was asked what they had understood about the conflict from TV news. In the whole sample, 82 per cent named television news as their main source of information, and said that the main point in the coverage was the prevalence of conflict and violence. The news stories analysed related to the uprising by Palestinians beginning in September 2000 until the middle of October 2000. There were eighty-nine bulletins broadcast, comprising 3,536 lines of transcribed text, of which only seventeen lines explained the history of the conflict. The majority of the people surveyed did not understand who was occupying the occupied territories, or why. Among the sample of 300 young people, 71 per cent did not know that the Israelis were occupying the territory, and 11 per cent believed incorrectly that the Palestinians were occupying it and that the settlers there were Palestinian. Although many more Palestinians have been killed in the conflict than Israelis, only 30 per cent of the sample of young people recognised this.

Greg Philo (2002) of The Glasgow Media Group suggested that the reasons for this level of ignorance and misunderstanding were that journalists did not provide any explanation of the history of the conflict, or referred to it only by brief shorthand phrases that the viewers did not understand. TV news focused more on actuality coverage of violence happening than on explanations for violence. The content analysis revealed that Israelis spoke twice as much on television news as Palestinians, thus favouring the Israeli perception of events. The close relationships between British politicians and the United States government led to TV interviewees favouring the pro-Israeli position adopted by the United States, so this official position was reflected in television coverage.

It is too easy to simply blame TV news staff for the lack of real debate about social and political issues on British TV, and the appalling ignorance of British citizens about affairs in their own country and the wider world. News staff are under huge pressure to get news programmes made on time, and to compete with each other and with other media sources to break the news first and draw audiences. What everyone can expect though, is that the commitment to inform and explain that still underpins television in Britain will lead to greater diversity of news formats, channels of delivery and debates about what the function and effects of TV news can be.

DEFINITIONS

Hard news deals with immediate, time sensitive (i.e. today), dramatic and serious events based on facts. A hard news story will always begin with the most important facts, and then back those up with detail, background and some interpretation. What happened, where did it happen, when did it happen, and who was involved, as well as how did it happen, why did it happen and (perhaps) what does it mean.

PROFILE

Senior Broadcast Journalist at BBC News: Rory Barnett

Rory Barnett works at Broadcasting House in London and is part of the team responsible for compiling the London opt-out TV news that follows the national BBC news at 1.00 pm, 6.00 pm and 10.00 pm.

Each day starts with the news conference at 9.15 am when the stories of the day and what has happened over night are discussed. Beforehand he has gone through all the national newspapers to see if there are any relevant London stories that might be followed up. He has also done a 'wire search' for relevant

FIGURE 11.4
Rory Barnett, news producer

stories. The BBC uses the ENPS software system which collates news from agencies such as Reuters and PA and on which he can prepare a running order for the bulletins. After the news conference Rory selects lead stories, organises film crews (one freelance cameraman/sound recordist) and delegates reporters for the chosen stories. Then he begins work on the running order for the first TV bulletin at 1.30 pm.

Asked about the most important aspect of his job Rory says:

> Safe guarding trust – not misleading viewers. Broadcasting in a way that people can trust what you are putting on your programme. For instance simple things that stop people being misled like telling viewers that footage of say the Olympic stadium being built, which is a big ongoing story for us, is from library pictures, or it is live today.

He says finding, editing and producing twelve and a half minutes of relevant local news stories in just over three hours is not straightforward. His nightmare is not having enough news to fill the time. The 'news where you are' bulletin must end on time to the second, as the network vision mixers always cut to the next scheduled programme at the exact time. Rory does not want the embarrassment of his weather report being suddenly cut off in mid sentence. Safe guarding trust is technical too.

PROFILE

Rory's job involves finding and selecting stories using the basic tenets of Galtung and Ruge's news values, and looking to do ongoing stories from a different angle or to offer a new perspective. His most pressing challenge is to do with logistics – can we get a reporter to that story in East London and back and have the story edited by 1.30? He is helped by having fixed points around his area where the reporter can plug in to an existing high-quality line. In London there are fixed points at obvious places like the Old Bailey, outside the famous revolving sign at Scotland Yard and in Leicester Square – very useful for film premieres.

The different media platforms require different elements. Rory has to consider not only the type of story but which platform is most suitable for it – a particular story perhaps fits better on radio or online than TV:

> Television always needs pictures. A recent story that came through an FOI (Freedom Of Information) request about health visitors visiting only 25% of one year old babies worked better on radio and online than TV. Whereas the closure of a well known A and E department can be fully covered on TV with pictures from outside the hospital and interviews.

The BBC has to maintain a position of neutrality on all things but particularly on political stories. Rory uses the interactive aspects of convergence to keep an eye on how the audience is experiencing the bulletin:

> There are so many ways to respond to our news items – email, Twitter, blogs etc. that we can get a good idea about bias. A correspondent might accuse us of bias one way, and then others will claim the other way – this suggests that somewhere in the middle is where we are and want to be.

The news room is changing to accommodate the effects of convergence, especially citizen journalism, although Rory thinks it is a long way from taking over from the traditional reporter:

> It is wonderful for catching a moment such as the first pictures of the *Cutty Sark* fire taken on a mobile. Or the incident at the G20 protests where Ian Tomlinson, who later died, was pushed by police. A few brief seconds of video footage actually showed this incident and was sent to us. We used it on the bulletin and it was later used in court. So we really welcome audience involvement in this way.

Soft news deals with background events, or time-free news.

Breaking news is very new news that is just coming in.

Developing news is how recent news stories are progressing.

Continuing news is ongoing news stories that need to be updated, for example the building of the Olympic site in London.

REFERENCES AND FURTHER READING

Baudrillard, J. 'The reality gulf', *Guardian*, 11 January 1991, reprinted in P. Brooker and W. Brooker (eds), *Postmodern After-Images: A Reader in Film, Television and Video*, London: Arnold, 1997, pp. 165–7.

BBC guidelines: http://www.bbc.co.uk/guidelines/editorialguidelines.

Boyd, Andrew, *Broadcast Journalism – Techniques of Radio & Television News*, FocalPress 2001.

Bignell, J. 'Television News', in *Media Semiotics: An Introduction*, Manchester: Manchester University Press, 2002, pp. 105–30.

Bourdieu, P. *On Television and Journalism*, London: Pluto, 1998.

Boyd-Barrett, O. and Rantanen, T. *The Globalization of News*, London: Sage, 1998.

Brooker, P. and W. Brooker (eds). *Postmodern After-Images: A Reader in Film, Television and Video*, London: Arnold, 1997, pp. 165–7.

Brown, M. 'War of the news walls', *Guardian* media section, 26 January 2004, p. 2.

Chapman, J. and Kinsey, M. (ed.). *Broadcast Journalism – A Critical Introduction*, London: Routledge, 2009.

Ellis, J. 'Television as Working Through', in J. Gripsrud (ed.), *Television and Common Knowledge*, London: Routledge, 1999, pp. 55–70.

Gillespie, M. 'Ambivalent Positionings: The Gulf War', in P. Brooker and W. Brooker (eds), *Postmodern After-Images: A Reader in Film, Television and Video*, London: Arnold, 1997, pp. 172–81.

Habermao, J. *The Theory of Communicative Action, vol. 2: Lifeworld and System: A Critique of Functionalist Reason*, Cambridge: Polity, 1987.

Harrison, J. *Terrestrial Television News in Britain: The Culture of Production*, Manchester: Manchester University Press, 2000.

Harrison, J. *News*, London Routledge 2006.

Hartley, J. *Understanding News*, London: Methuen, 1988.

Mosey, Roger: http://www.guardian.co.uk/media/2005/jul/13/attackonLondon.tvnews?INTCMP=SRCH.

Norris, C. '"Postscript": Baudrillard's second Gulf War Article', in P. Brooker and W. Brooker (eds), *Postmodern After-Images: A Reader in Film, Television and Video*, London: Arnold, 1997, pp. 168–71.

Philo, G. 'Missing in Action', *Guardian*, Higher Education section, 16 April 2002, pp. 10–11.

Sinclair, J., Jacka, E. and Cunningham, S. 'New Patterns in Global Television', in P. Marris and S. Thornham (eds), *The Media Reader*, Edinburgh: Edinburgh University Press, 1999, pp. 170–90.

Walker, I. 'Desert Stories or Faith in Facts?', in M. Lister (ed.), *The Photographic Image in Digital Culture*, London: Routledge 1998, pp. 236–52.

CHAPTER 12

Television sport

TAKING PART

This chapter stresses the ways that audiences for TV sport are encouraged to feel that they are part of the crowd of spectators present at most sports events, that they can take part in the expert evaluation of what the players do, and that they can share the feelings of achievement or disappointment that players experience. Television sports coverage focuses much more on the kinds of sport that viewers might already have experience of, whether as active players (in their youth at school or college, or as leisure activities) or as spectators. There is far more coverage of football and cricket, for example, than of sports that most people have never played or seen live, such as fencing or fives. An interesting exception to this general rule is the TV coverage of the Olympic Games. Here, the competition is between national teams, so television tends to cover events in which the domestic audience can be expected to be supporting British sportspeople. This occurs even when the British sportspeople who have some chance of doing well are taking part in sports that do not normally get much television coverage. So a strong British Olympics team in an equestrian event or a women's hockey competition might get much more attention at the Olympics than they would at other times. In the Beijing Olympics in 2008 the GB cycling team won more medals than any other country and suddenly the sport had a much higher profile in the UK, making television celebrities out of gold medallists Chris Hoy and Victoria Pendleton.

The two main forces that draw television channels to cover sport are relevance to the audience's assumed knowledge and interests, and the possibilities for covering sport in an interesting way that exploits the possibilities of the television medium.

FIGURE 12.1
F1 racing driver Lewis Hamilton being interviewed

Television sports coverage makes use of the potential to set up multi-camera outside broadcasts (OB) for live presentation of football, cricket and other sports where multiple cameras can be positioned around the various sides of a playing area. The opportunities to shift quickly from camera to camera, and from long shot to close up, deploy OB set-ups so that a coherent sense of space and drama can be introduced into the programme. It is a lot more difficult to exploit these possibilities for a variety of shots in linear or small-scale sports like rowing or darts, though each of these sports do receive some coverage.

Football is most obviously covered by TV in the form of live or recorded screenings of matches. But football is also present in the form of programmes featuring discussion of football and interviews with players and other football personalities. The BBC game shows *A Question of Sport* and *They Think It's All Over* have a strong representation of football players, and mix information and discussion about football with light-hearted competition and banter. Representations of football and footballers also occur in commercials, such as the Walkers Crisps ads featuring Gary Lineker, and fictional representations of matches and footballers' home lives are the premise for the ITV1 drama *Footballers' Wives*. As Britain's national game, it is not surprising that this particular sport crops up so widely across television genres and formats.

SPORT IN A MULTI-CHANNEL ENVIRONMENT

In the digital television environment there are more broadcasting channels, and therefore smaller amounts of money per channel and per programme to spend because the audience sizes for particular programmes are correspondingly smaller than those of conventional terrestrial television. The costs of making programmes are therefore more difficult to recoup from advertisers, and need to be generated from the subscriptions paid by the viewers of interactive digital television channels, or from one-off payments made by viewers to see a particular programme.

Figures released by BARB in May 2010 reveal that twenty-four million households in the UK have digital television and access to multi-channel television. The growth in multi-channel has been led by subscription broadcaster BSkyB buying up sports broadcasting rights, especially football and cricket, and promoting them vigorously for home consumers and for pub and club clients. BSkyB has invested heavily in High Definition sports coverage and by the beginning of 2011 this investment was paying off as it was the most profitable broadcaster in the UK. The BBC broadcasts many hours of live sport on its free-to-air channels including, from late 2009, exclusive rights to all Formula 1 grand prix; the London Olympics in 2012; the Wimbledon tennis championships; world snooker and international rugby. However, it has stopped competing with BSkyB for live football and cricket rights as it considers the costs too high for a public service broadcaster.

FIGURE 12.2
Cameraman at a live broadcast sports event

PROFILE: SPORTS BROADCASTER

British Sky Broadcasting (BSkyB)

BSkyB is a vertically integrated company, owning the digital satellite platform on which its channels are broadcast. It also controls the technology used in set-top boxes to receive satellite programmes and sets the prices paid by rival channels to gain access to the digital platform through its subsidiary Sky Subscriber Services Ltd (SSS). The electronic programme guide (EPG) that allows viewers to navigate between the channels broadcast by the Astra satellite system is also controlled by BSkyB, which charges approx £28,000 a year for a listing on the electronic programme guide.

BSkyB is one of numerous television businesses controlled by the media entrepreneur Rupert Murdoch's company News Corporation, whose media interests include film, television, newspapers, book publishing, and magazines, and also financial stakes in major sports teams whose games are covered in the media. News Corporation owns 40 per cent of BSkyB. In 2010 it announced that it intended to buy a full controlling interest in the company. This sent shivers through the rest of the media industry especially newspaper proprietors who worried that one institution could have too much media power. The companies behind the *Daily Telegraph* and the *Daily Mail* united with the owners of the *Guardian*, the *Daily Mirror* and most uncharacteristically the BBC to petition the government to consider blocking News Corporation's proposed £8 billion full takeover of BSkyB. They said the 'proposed takeover could have serious and far-reaching consequences for media plurality'.

In 2011 British Sky Broadcasting (BSkyB) continued to dominate television sports programming. To keep the high profile of sport on television and to drive profits for broadcasters' continuing technical innovation is necessary. Sport in 3D and High Definition (HD) is driving technical change.

Jeremy Darroch, Chief Executive of BSkyB, said in April 2010:

> Our leading HD box is allowing us to bring more innovation to customers faster and at lower cost. The launch of Sky 3D, Europe's first 3D TV channel has got off to a good start, with more than 1,000 venues signed up so far. We're on track to bring 3D to residential customers later this year along with our new video-on-demand service, Sky Anytime+. All of this will be available through our existing HD box.

PROFILE

A sport gaining a much higher profile on British Television is cycling. This arose out of the success of the British cycling team in the Beijing Olympics 2008. BSkyB, Sky Italia, News Corporation and British Cycling are the main sponsors of a new British cycling team called Sky Pro Cycling that took part in the Tour de France in 2010. With the launch of Sky News HD on election night 6 May 2010, all Sky channel brands are now available in HD, with forty HD channels spanning all genres. At the end of 2009, 2.1 million customers had signed up to receive Sky's HD pack of channels.

INTERACTIVE TELEVISION

The attraction of audiences to televised sport, especially football, has been enhanced by the introduction of interactive services accompanying the broadcast of matches. Around 40 per cent of the subscribers to the Sky Sports Active channel watch football games interactively. Digital technology allows them to select text information relevant to the game, and to choose the camera angle from which the game is presented on their television screen. From the perspective of the television broadcaster, interactive television is a 'premium service' that viewers can be charged additional money to use.

Sport, as a familiar programme genre that has obvious opportunities for interactive supporting services, has been a way into interactive television for many viewers. While interactive television is a decisive and important development in the screening of sport, viewers have always interacted with televised sport, and forms of presentation invite the viewer to become involved and to participate.

Television coverage of sport routinely addresses the viewer as a witness watching the sport along with television commentators and spectators at the event. The spoken discourse of sports commentators also routinely invites viewers to make judgments about the performance of the sportspeople and to evaluate their success. The positioning of cameras in television coverage of sport provides a much closer view of the action than is normally available to spectators at the event itself, and cutting between camera shots allows the television viewer to identify with the efforts and emotions of the competitors. The production and editing of television sport is designed to promote viewer involvement and to stimulate viewers' interaction with the event as it is taking place. Strategies like these are intended to stimulate active viewing of television programmes, where viewers give their full attention to what they are seeing and hearing, and where there may be opportunities for action by the viewer.

Key point

A space is 'hollowed out' for the sports viewer to occupy, in which an active response and involvement is required.

ADVERTISING AROUND SPORTS TV

In an interactive sports schedule, there will also be space for advertising that can also exploit the potential for viewer response and activity. It is generally supposed by advertisers that the greater the attention given by television viewers to programmes, the more chance there is that viewers will also give their attention to advertisements. From an advertiser's point of view, of course, it is very important that viewers watch and remember the advertisements they have seen. Advertisements often include opportunities for viewer activity that may simply be invitations for the viewer to get a joke, solve the puzzle, or simply to figure out what product an advertisement is selling. Being intrigued by a visually interesting advertisement, and enjoying its wit, are in themselves kinds of activity that make the advertisement and its product more memorable. But pressing the red button on a remote control in sports programmes makes it more plausible that viewers might also use their remotes to access information about products advertised in the breaks between matches or at half-time.

SPORTS NARRATIVE

The inclusion of viewers in sports programmes takes place by several means. The most apparently straightforward sports coverage on television is the live broadcasting of a game such as a football match. The position laid out for the viewer is both to identify with any or all the players, but especially the audience at the game who are the viewer's representatives. Sports narrative is a series of confrontations between different discourses, each appealing to one of several kinds of authority and legitimacy. Television coverage of sport not only includes the relay of the game, where television is largely an instrument to bring the event to the viewer. It also includes introductory framing of an event by the studio presenter, and discussion among experts and former players at intervals during the coverage. But the person most recognised by viewers of sport is the commentator who puts the action into linguistic form, pointing out the high-points, moments of controversy or giving behind-the-scenes information about the players and teams.

The role of the commentator is to arrange the different roles of spectator, evaluator and narrator into a single coherent discourse. Since the game unfolds linearly over time, the discourse is sequential, and has moments of greater or lesser intensity, breaks and climaxes, and will finally achieve a closing resolution. The commentator acts as a mediating narrator working on behalf of the audience, and claiming to represent its varied and potentially incompatible concerns.

Key point

Sports narrative is a series of confrontations between different discourses, each appealing to one of several kinds of authority and legitimacy.

In the studio discussion that frequently accompanies television coverage of football, athletics or the Olympics, television formats are designed to replicate the conversations that viewers at home might have about the sporting performances they have seen. But this replication is far from neutral or 'realistic', since the television discussion format adapts it into a hierarchical and ordered form. The hierarchy is presided over by the host presenter, and usually includes professional experts such as former players, team managers and sports journalists. Occasionally, especially in late night programmes addressed to young adult sports fans, these experts may be supplemented by guest members of the public and a studio audience. It is obvious that the studio audience or a guest member of the public represents the audience of viewers, and stands in for them. But the more conventional arrangement of host and experts also plays a representative function for the audience at home.

The role of the host is to mediate between the television viewer and the expertise of the invited guests, by representing the viewer's imagined questions and concerns. Television viewers, along with the expert guests, are invited to evaluate the behaviour and opinions of the sportspeople whose play or performance has been broadcast. In a manner similar to the analysis of television narrative, the structure of the programme and its use of hosts and personalities are designed to encourage the viewer at home to feel included in an evaluation of the sporting action. Sport becomes dramatic, in the sense that high-points and processes of action can be identified, and heroes, villains and supporting characters can be praised or blamed for their contribution to the eventual outcome.

THE IDEOLOGY OF TAKING PART

Television calls for viewers to take up membership of an imaginary community of viewers. This call to belong is parallel to the way in which the French philosopher Louis Althusser (1971) explained the concept of ideology. Ideology is a structure in which people are addressed as particular kinds of subject, and take up a position laid out for them by this call, along with the values inherent in the position to which they are called. People become individual subjects, subject to ideological values and constituted as subjects by ideology as the unique destination to which the call is addressed. Television coverage of sporting events has the ideological function of disciplining the range of ways that viewers are invited to interact with the coverage, drawing sport away from the undisciplined irrationality associated with 'hooliganism' and towards the expert evaluation by rational means that is associated with middle-class expertise and the exercise of knowledge. In sports television, for example, singing football songs and throwing cans of beer at the screen is not expected,

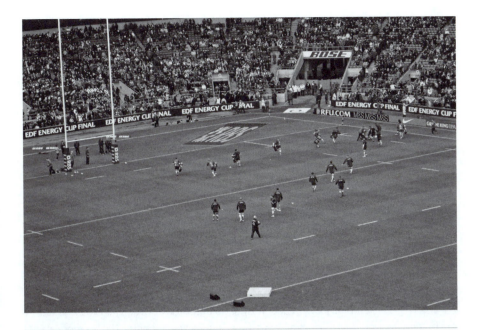

FIGURE 12.3
Sport on TV: international rugby at Twickenham

whereas knowledgeable debate and respect for the rules and conduct of the game are expected. The use of slow-motion replays in sports programmes is a further means of presenting and encouraging this kind of rational and evaluative critique.

The ideology of sports coverage is therefore part of television's more generalised function of shaping the audience and the forms of response to television that it demands. Television sports coverage is constructed in order to invite the viewer's involvement through offering patterns of reaction to the sport directed by the commentator. Studio comment by invited sports experts (former players, managers, sports journalists, etc.) focuses on discourses of evaluation and prediction, and aims to invite the viewer to engage in speculation and judgment in a similar way. This imaginary dialogue between the viewer and the programme therefore lays out codes in which the viewer's response should take place.

Key point

The ideology of sports coverage is part of television's function of shaping the audience and the forms of response to television that it demands.

This process of taking on a specific audience position is enhanced by possibilities for interaction with sports programmes. Some sports coverage, especially football, invites direct forms of viewer interaction. This includes competitions to decide the 'goal of the month' or opportunities to win tickets to important matches.

Sport is not the only television genre to feature opportunities for interaction: comedy programmes invite laughter, television commercials offer puzzles or jokes which the viewer is invited to figure out, and both commercials and programmes provide telephone numbers and websites which offer further information, special offers, or competitions. Television shopping channels are of course entirely predicated on this interaction, since the viewer is explicitly addressed as a potential buyer of the products shown on screen.

Key point

Television institutions provide a sense of activity and involvement for viewers. This can be part of the public service function to show and support initiatives in society, or as part of a commercial imperative to encourage consumption of products and services.

In relation to sport, these initiatives may occasionally have a purpose that seems to contradict the programme or channel's desire for audiences to watch more television. For example, the evaluation of skills in football coverage, or commentary on batting techniques in cricket coverage, implicitly suggests that viewers might wish to go out and play football or cricket themselves. Television is a domestic technology, embedded in the home, and it potentially competes for attention with other domestic activities and possibilities for leaving the home and engaging in sport. However, this can be understood in part as an outcome of the disciplining function discussed above, where the manner of participation in sport can be shaped along the lines of personal achievement and sportspersonship. It also responds to public service intentions to support the playing of sport as a healthy, community-forming and spiritually uplifting activity that contributes to the public sphere and the enhancement of social life.

THE FUTURE OF SPORT ON TELEVISION

Sport used to be available on just a few terrestrial television channels. In the digital world the technology and means of delivering sport to different sections of society is continuing to grow. Sport is now available via many different platforms: High Definition and 3D television, mobile phones, YouTube, web streaming, digital radio, or via playback technologies such as the BBC iPlayer or Skybox +. Sport is also available through games consoles and social networking sites.

High-profile sports events often have their own dedicated websites for just one event with streaming live video, usually with the need for a subscription to watch the action. In 2010, the Indian Premier League streamed its cricket games live on YouTube. There was another challenge to television in October 2009 when England's World Cup game in Ukraine was shown live only on the internet with an audience of about half a million. The rights for live sporting events are usually sold on a

PROFILE

Barbara Slater, BBC Director of Sport

Barbara Slater became Director of BBC Sport in April 2009 and is the first woman in this post. She grew up in Birmingham and has degrees from Birmingham University and Oxford. Barbara is well qualified to be Director of BBC Sport as she is a qualified PE teacher, and was an accomplished international gymnast with twenty International Caps, competing for Great Britain at the Olympic Games in Montreal in 1976.

She has held senior roles for the BBC at many of the biggest sports events in the world, including Wimbledon, the Open and Masters Golf, successive Olympics and Commonwealth Games, the Grand National, Ascot and the Derby. Her job includes working with the governing bodies of sports so that the BBC has a wide range of sports to broadcast. She is leading the controversial sports department move from London to join BBC North in Salford in 2011, and overseeing sports coverage of the biggest planned event ever held in the UK: the London Olympic and Paralympics' Games in 2012.

Barbara joined the BBC in 1983 as a trainee assistant producer in the Natural History Unit in Bristol and the following year joined the sports department as an Assistant Producer. She has spent most of her career as a producer in BBC Television Sport, specialising in outside broadcasts. Barbara is married with three children and lives in west London. She is in charge of a large sports rights portfolio including the rights to the World Cup up to and including 2014, the Olympic Games in 2012, Premier League highlights, the Football League and Carling Cup, Six Nations Rugby, Wimbledon and the Open Golf. When appointed Barbara Slater said:

> I am thrilled to have this opportunity to lead BBC Sport at such an exciting and challenging time, which includes leading the Division to its new home at the heart of BBC North and also ensuring BBC Sport plays its part in making the 2012 Games the success they deserve to be.

(BBC Press Office)

PROFILE

'platform neutral' basis. Mobile, internet and TV rights are all sold together in the same package.

The BBC is the rights-holder to a number of major sporting events, including the Olympics, Wimbledon and Formula 1, and is in a position to maximise this platform neutral development. 'Audiences appreciate our multiplatform approach to covering sport', says Ben Gallop, head of BBC Sport Interactive. 'At the moment (2010) we are looking to maximise our [online] video space, but it is not only about this.' He also points to potential innovations such as the increasing use of games consoles to access the BBC's iPlayer, and showing more sport on 3D television, already available on Sky sports channels (Bill Wilson, BBC 2010). It is important to note that all these new platforms for watching sport are of little interest to audiences without the essential ingredient which is the live event.

'THE CROWN JEWELS'

The most significant debate for television sports audiences is about which live events should be available free-to-air and not encrypted for satellite audiences only. The argument is that some events involve the whole nation and serve to fulfil expectations for a socially cohesive society. The government has agreed with the appropriate sporting bodies that some important televised live sports events have to be shown in some form on available-to-all TV channels. These events are affectionately known as 'The Crown Jewels', and are divided into two lists of sporting events. The idea is to safeguard them for the greater good of the nation. The argument is that if England win the World Cup then we should all be able to see it and share in it. Confusingly there is an A list and a B list. On the A list are those events that can only be broadcast live by terrestrial broadcasters – the BBC, ITV, Channel 4, Channel Five. The A list in 2010 was:

- the Olympics
- football's World Cup and European Championship finals
- the English and Scottish FA Cup finals
- the Grand National, and the Derby
- Wimbledon
- rugby union's World Cup final and rugby league's Challenge Cup final.

An important argument for keeping certain sporting events on available-to-all television is that young people become interested in taking part in sport by seeing it on television. Golfer Paul Casey, for example, gives as his inspiration to become a pro-golfer seeing great British players on television:

> I was watching when I was a kid back in the 80s and early 90s. Faldo, Seve, Woosnam, Langer, Lyle, Monty . . . they got me interested in the game. That

was why I loved to watch and I got to see them live in the Masters. I think if you asked these other Englishmen, Brits and Europeans who have now risen in the world rankings, that's what got them hooked.

(*Independent*, March 2010)

In 1998 a B list was introduced for events that require highlights to be shown on terrestrial TV. Cricket lost out when test matches moved from the A list to the B list much to the anger of many fans. The England and Wales Cricket Board wanted this switch as it would inject more money into the game at grassroots by selling the TV rights to a satellite broadcaster. Other events currently on the B list include the Open Golf Championship, the Ryder Cup, cricket's World Cup, the Commonwealth Games and rugby union's Six Nations.

In December 2008, David Davies, former executive director of the Football Association was asked to review the standing of the 'Crown Jewels' of UK sport in view of the 2012 digital switchover when the analogue TV signal will no longer be available. In 2009, Davies reported back that there should be a list of protected events, but the list of events caused more controversy: 'The decisive factor when considering what events qualify for what list was whether the event unites the nation and provides a moment of resonance' (Robin Scott-Elliot, *Independent*, November 2009*).

Nearly twelve million people watched Andy Murray's epic late-night fourth-round encounter with Stanislas Wawrinka at Wimbledon in 2010 on BBC television. When England won the Ashes at The Oval in 2005 seven million people watched on Channel 4. Four years on, in 2009, when Andrew Strauss's men earned that stunning victory over Australia in August two million tuned in to Sky Sports. Sky simply cannot match the terrestrial broadcasters, particularly the BBC, when it comes to delivering mass audiences. However, the BBC cannot match Sky when it comes to technology, time and money dedicated to a sport such as cricket.

Arguably, these epic sporting encounters because they are available on available-to-all television 'unify' the nation. More realistically, grand television events such as those provided by sport, or international music events such as Live Aid, are no longer the unifying factors that they once purported to be. Television is now only one aspect of the consumer's multimedia experience. Sports events can be experienced through online television, apps on mobile phones, and catch-up players.

In the second decade of the twenty-first century, broadcast television remains the most significant and watched platform for the enjoyment of world class sport both at home and in shared audience groups such as pubs and clubs. One thing is certain, the coverage of live sports on television will continue to be an audience driver and profit accumulator for broadcasters. Viewers have already become used to paying to see live events on television, and this may mean major live sports disappear from PSB schedules. Available-to-all audiences will have to be content with highlights as they did in autumn 2010 for the very exciting Ryder Cup that Europe won at the eighteenth hole.

REFERENCES AND FURTHER READING

Althusser, L. 'Ideology and Ideological State Apparatuses: Notes towards an Investigation', in *Lenin and Philosophy*, London: New Left Books, 1971, pp. 121–73.

Boyle, R. and Haynes, R. *Power Play: Sport, the Media and Popular Culture*, Harlow, UK: Pearson, 2000.

Brookes, R. 'The FIFA World Cup', in G. Creeber (ed.), *Fifty Key Television Programmes*, London: Arnold, 2004, pp. 85–9.

Kelso, P. 'A question of sport', *Guardian*, media section, 8 March 2004, pp. 2–3.

Miller, T., Lawrence, G.McKay, J. and Rowe, D. (eds). *Globalization and Sport: Playing the World*, London: Sage, 2001.

Sharman, M. 'A nation tunes in', *Guardian*, media section, 18 February 2002, pp. 8–9.

Part 5

Television drama

CHAPTER 13

Drama and quality

In television, quality is influenced by production values and the monetary investment made in a programme. It is also a function of the apparent seriousness, creativity or originality of the production. Within the television industry, quality refers to production values, budgets, the skill of programme makers and performers, and the prestige accruing to programmes because of their audience profile and seriousness of purpose.

Within the academic discipline of Television Studies, quality has a broader meaning that also focuses attention on popular television that might be regarded by insiders as merely commercial and generic work that has little aspiration to cultural or artistic value. While the question of quality applies to all television forms and genres, this chapter explores it in relation to drama. One of the reasons for this is that drama is the most expensive and usually the most prestigious kind of television, so it has a special relationship with understandings of quality.

THE WRITER

In television drama, the writer has traditionally had a higher profile than either the director or producer. Writers are considered as uniquely creative originators of programmes, whose work is then realised by the production team. This has two consequences. First, that judging the quality of drama often means judging the quality of the writing rather than the other aspects of a production. Second, as a result, it means that the criteria of quality have a lot in common with the criteria often used in literary criticism, where there is an emphasis on structure, a 'personal vision' or style, and the expectation that a drama has something to say about humanity or society.

Academic thinking has moved away from these literary kinds of evaluation in Television Studies, because they seem to consider writers as a kind of privileged elite and neglect the crucial role of the teamwork that makes TV possible, and also the role of the audience in making meaning from what writers and other creative personnel have produced. Within the television industry, particular writers have been elevated to high status, and publicised to attract audiences and claim prestige for channels and television companies. A writer can function as a brand, a familiar name that alerts the audience to styles and themes that the writer has explored in the past, and distinguishes the programme from the competitors scheduled against it and around it. But the establishment of this authorial prestige is difficult, and only occurs when there are cultures within a television production institution that will support it.

In Britain, the marketing of authors began with the celebration of the unique contribution to television drama by the scriptwriter Dennis Potter, particularly in the 1970s with his serial *Pennies from Heaven* (BBC). Serious marketing of scriptwriters as brands occurred in the 1980s and 1990s in relation to dramas by Lynda LaPlante for example (*Prime Suspect*, *Trial and Retribution*), and classic novel adaptations by Andrew Davies (*Pride and Prejudice*, *Emma*, *Middlemarch*). A few producers have occupied this authorial branding role, such as Tony Garnett (*The Cops*, *Attachments*) and the American Steven Bochco (*Murder One*, *NYPD Blue*). In Chapter 14 a Profile of Lynda LaPlante provides an overview of this writer's contribution to quality TV drama. This chapter also considers kinds of drama that are not associated with authorship, such as British soap opera, and US crime drama and discusses how questions of quality might relate to them.

Key point

A writer can function as a brand, a familiar name that alerts the audience to styles and themes that the writer has explored in the past, and distinguishes the programme from the competitors scheduled against it and around it.

POPULAR DRAMA AND 'QUALITY'

The sociologist Pierre Bourdieu (1984) argues that the cultural products regarded as the best are in fact those that are preferred by the most educated and wealthy segment of a population. Because of their social power, the elite are able to claim their tastes as superior, and as a result, the cultural products that the elite prefer also validate the superior taste of the elite. In this context, academic commentators have looked for ways of discriminating between good and bad television. This becomes especially important in relation to arguments about television policy that seek to counter the consumerist view that broadcasters should simply provide what the largest number of viewers seemed to want. Charlotte Brunsdon (1990: 70) asks

'What are we going to do about bad television? Nothing, if we're not prepared to admit that it exists.'

The debates about how to judge quality result in critics attempting to define it in different ways (see Brunsdon *et al.* 1997: 134–6). It may refer to the public service function of a programme or aesthetic criteria of visual or structural kinds, or relation-ships with the avant-garde or experimentalism of the arts. Or quality could be defined by the ways in which a programme exploits the apparent fundamental properties of the television medium. Or quality may refer to the professional expertise of the makers of the programme, and the exercise of highly developed crafts skills. Or a programme could be described as quality television because of its contribution to definitions of national culture or a perceived heritage of excellence. As channels compete by attempting to challenge a competitor's superiority in one programme genre or format, the values associated with each channel's drama brand can gradually shift.

It is notable the extent to which ITV1 is aiming to present itself differently to its current audience, and trying to attract newer audiences by making programmes that are publicised as quality television. ITV1 delivered a number of highly successful new post-watershed dramas. *Whitechapel* was the highest rating new drama on any channel since 2006. *Collision* was stripped across a week and peaked with 8.4 million viewers. In 2009 seven of the UK's top ten new dramas were on ITV1, for example *Whitechapel, Above Suspicion* and the ongoing *Law & Order: UK*. Bucking the trend for gritty realism, and ITV's most successful drama of 2010, was the costume serial set just before the First World War, *Downton Abbey*, with a Sunday evening audience of over ten million.

Key point

A programme could be described as quality television because of its contribution to definitions of national culture or a perceived heritage of excellence.

COSTUME DRAMA

Costume adaptations of nineteenth-century literature, long regarded as the province of the BBC, are an established form of drama that channels have used in order to claim that they are making 'quality' television. As well as producing classic adaptations the BBC in recent years is also in favour of adaptations of modern literature.

By contrast, ITV's drama productions have included *Micawber*, a prequel to Charles Dickens' nineteenth-century novel *David Copperfield*, and an adaptation in modern dress of Shakespeare's *Othello*. Recently drama on ITV included a new series of the popular twentieth-century costume drama *Foyles War* (ITV 2010) and *Midsomer*

Murders (ITV 2010). Both can be considered quality dramas in terms of high production values. Building on the success of the Jane Austen season in 2007, ITV
introduced a number of new literary adaptations to diversify the range of its drama
output. These included a new adaptation of *Wuthering Heights,* and *Compulsion*,
adapted from Jacobean tragedy *The Changeling*, was also shown in 2009 starring
Ray Winstone.

Costume drama is expensive to produce and in the twenty-first century some critics
think it adds a certain stuffiness to TV schedules. Traditional literary adaptations
will always be seen as significant quality programming but not always the ratings
winners they used to be. Although the high production values of *Downton Abbey*
on ITV1, specially written by Julian Fellowes, demonstrated that quality costume
drama does not need to be an adaptation to be a ratings winner. The BBC prefers
to go down the route of more ironic postmodern costume drama series that attract
young people and a family audience, with long-running series such as *Merlin* and
Robin Hood. Some episodes of *Doctor Who*, such as the famous Shakespearian
episode, can be seen as a costume drama.

QUALITY AND MASS CULTURE

The idea of quality is convenient in its suggestion of fixed standards and allows for
a hierarchy of what is of interest and significance, but academic studies of culture
assume that hierarchies of value conceal unacknowledged assumptions (see
Brunsdon *et al*. 1997, Mulgan 1990). Rather than setting up a single hierarchical
list in which, for example, a made for television film is superior to an episode of a
soap opera, academic studies of culture ask about the purpose against which
a programme is judged, and about the aims and position of the person making
the judgment. John Caughie (1986) argued that the field of cultural studies arose
in the context of an argument over the meaning and value of mass culture, one
of whose components is television. The argument that mass civilisation produced
a mass culture in which cultural value had been lost was applied particularly to
American commercial culture and television. This commercial culture had already
been regarded by powerful voices in the intellectual elite as exploitative and was
stigmatised for encouraging the audience to succumb to emotional appeal rather
than reason and discrimination. The inauthenticity of mass culture was argued to
be the result of its nature as a business where creators of culture exercised
instrumental technical skills rather than artistic creativity and originality. Mass culture
seemed to overwhelm society and drive out quality. In contrast to this, theorists of
television (especially in Britain) looked for ways of valuing the quality of popular,
commercial television as well as prestige authored drama.

Academic commentators have argued that real viewers make distinctions about
quality all the time in their viewing, and that these distinctions are different from
the issues of whether viewers are interested in programmes or enjoy them. Simon

Frith (2000: 46) argues that viewers judge quality 'in terms of the technical (good acting, sets, camera work), the believable, the interesting, the spectacular, the satisfying – terms that echo but do not exactly match the professional concern for originality, authenticity and innovation . . .'. The attribution of quality may depend on the response of viewers, either in terms of audience size or composition. The television industry is a self-enclosed world, with powerful internal hierarchies and codes of shared knowledge, status, competition and gossip. So indicators of success deriving from the industry itself are relatively more significant than indicators deriving from more public sources.

The key indicator within the television industry is the size of the audience, but also the audience share, and the distribution of age groups and social classes. The audience for ITV's terrestrial programmes has been getting older for many years, and has a typically lower average income than the BBC's audience. In terms of the standard measures of income and status, the professional, managerial and skilled sectors of society, who tend to have the highest incomes, are the ABC1 group. It is evidently very important for broadcasters that their audience contains a high proportion of the most economically and socially powerful people in the national audience. Channel 4 has addressed this audience by buying American 'quality' programmes such as *The Wire*, *Desperate Housewives* and *Lost*. It has commissioned original British drama addressed to the ABC1 audience such as the serials *Queer as Folk* and *Shameless*.

Channel 4 through its E4 subsidiary is also attracting the lucrative and difficult to amuse non-TV watching 'late teen/student' audience. In 2010, the popular teen musical-comedy-drama *Glee* was aired on E4 followed by the home grown sexually up-front *The Inbetweeners*. This Bafta-award-winning show returned for its third series on E4 in September 2010 with 2.2 million viewers – the digital channel's highest audience for a home produced show.

US QUALITY TELEVISION DRAMA

A few years into the twenty-first century, US television drama came to be known as American Quality TV Drama. Up until this point UK audiences had rather looked down on US-originated drama even though well-produced TV series such as *Dynasty* had been very popular in the 1980s. This new type of television drama runs in long series and breaks traditional rules such as working with an ensemble cast, and not always having a traditional narrative closure even at the end of the series. The quality comes from the fact that this is writer-led drama, with teams of scriptwriters competing and collaborating to produce high-quality plots, intellectually satisfying narrative arcs and naturalistic dialogue.

The series *The Wire* is considered by many commentators to be the finest crime series ever made for television, even in comparison with the more gangster orientated *The Sopranos*. Other US high-quality crime dramas include *24*, *ER* and *CSI*, and in other genres *Lost*, *Desperate Housewives*, *Ugly Betty* and *The West Wing*, which were all broadcast on British television to high acclaim.

Key point

US quality drama scripts aim for authenticity and relevance to a postmodern audience, often referencing political issues and events.

Channel 4 found US quality drama well suited to its upmarket, well-educated, urban audiences. Each series focuses on a group of characters, rather than one protagonist as British crime drama tends to do. They are postmodern in being self-conscious and using intertextual references to themselves and other TV programmes.

Television writer Peter Jukes considers US TV drama to have overtaken UK output in quality, style and value:

> Starting with HBO more than a decade ago, we've had *The Sopranos*, *Sex and the City*, *Six Feet Under* – ground-breaking dramas that explored the depths of character and the dynamics of group or family, against the larger context of a city, profession or social milieu . . . Not only is the quality of the output high, but so is the diversity of style and genre. This has to be connected to the break-up of the old US network cartel . . . The creative people now have more control and the commissioning process is more open.
>
> (Jukes 2009)

American quality drama has gone back to the principle of being writer based, and the scripts are entirely fit for purpose, carefully tailored to the time slot with deftly written realistic dialogue. The scripts aim for authenticity and relevance to a post-modern audience, often referencing political issues and events. They create a world where realism is the dominant characteristic, with high production values and often elaborate *mise-en-scène* with glossy interiors and emphasis on new technologies.

Much of the popularity of these dramas comes from the viral publicity generated by websites, blogs, chat rooms and social networking sites.

The longest running quality US drama transmitted in the UK from 2005 to 2010 was *Lost* where the first two seasons were broadcast on Channel 4 and then Sky1 from November 2006. Emphasising the high production values Sky1 HD also simulcast *Lost*. The final episode was on 24 May 2010 on Sky1 where an audience of 600,000 tuned in at 5.00 am to watch the denouement, entitled 'The End'. It had a five-minute peak audience of 854,000 viewers, with an average of 635,000 between 5.00 am and 7.15 am showing just how popular this series was. The broadcast was transmitted live from the US. Sky1 simulcast the show's conclusion with US network ABC's west coast transmission. The *Lost* final was the climax of the much discussed, often mystifying, 121 episodes.

PROFILE

ITV drama 2010

It is interesting to look at what ITV are commissioning in the second decade of the twenty-first century. They are looking for scripts for contemporary returning series for 9.00 pm. And for ideas that are 'reflective of what's going on in the world but always delivered in an entertaining, clear mainstream format'.

Another identified priority for ITV is more 'event' drama. With examples including *Torn*, a contemporary family drama, and John Fay's highly original three part *Mobile*, which ITV call 'a good example of a high-concept, contemporary subject with a strong authored voice. We no longer want to be the channel of formulaic, psychological thrillers. We need genre pieces – thrillers and crime drama but are always looking for a fresh angle' (ITV Commissioning).

Laura Mackie, Director, Drama Commissioning identifies what she thinks ITV drama should do:

> ITV Drama should always aim to capture the mood of the nation and to provide a really entertaining or challenging or ideally an entertaining and challenging viewing experience, such as *Torn*, a powerful, emotional domestic thriller and *The Fixer*, a really classy, well executed returning series.

A very successful series in 2009 was *Collision* (ITV), a compelling drama created by Anthony Horowitz, which was stripped across one week and looked at the interweaving lives of a group of people involved in a major road accident and the impact on their families, friends and colleagues. Award-winning writer, Lynda LaPlante launched a new female detective in *Above Suspicion* starring Kelly Reilly.

The highest rating new drama on any channel in 2009 was *Whitechapel* – a darkly atmospheric thriller starring Rupert Penry Jones where someone is carrying out copycat Jack the Ripper murders. ITV Director of Drama, Laura Mackie identifies *Whitechapel* as:

> a very modern take on the detective genre which combines the Victorian intrigue of the original case with the atmospheric backdrop of a contemporary East End of London. This is not simply about bloodthirstily recreating the Ripper murders, but rather focusing on the

PROFILE

three main characters at the heart of the story and the black humour that binds the team together.

(www.primetime.unrealitytv.co.uk)

Across its channels, ITV invests around £540 million in original programming. ITV's channels are delivered free of charge to consumers, funded by advertising and sponsorship revenues, which totalled £1,350 million in 2009 down from £1,966 million in 2000.

The large US franchise CSI is very popular in the UK in its various forms, with some wall to wall broadcasting of many episodes in the summer of 2010 by Channel Five.

Key point

The attribution of quality may depend on the response of viewers, either in terms of audience size or composition.

REPRESENTATIONS IN DRAMA

In relation to the already valued television form of the authored drama series, quality depends not only on the production values of a programme but also on its contribution to the politics of representation and the debates over public issues that are the province of public service broadcasting. For example, Peter Billingham (2005) regards the Channel 4 drama series *Queer as Folk* as an authored intervention in the representation of homosexuality. The series drew on Channel 4's institutional remit to address new configurations of audience and hitherto under-represented social groups, and established patterns of relationships between characters that explored gay identity and the tensions and contradictions around sexuality.

In relation to a much more generic and 'popular' programme, Bignell and Lacey (2005) have also argued that the science fiction series *Doctor Who* has drawn on a tradition of science fiction in film, television and other media that distances it from expectations of quality, but also claims to offer both realist representations of scientific subjects and historical facts that give the programme seriousness of purpose. *Doctor Who* also has a heritage of drawing on new television technologies to emphasise the visual revelation and spectacle that are conventional markers of quality. The meanings of quality shift and draw on different criteria, and are defined in relation to aesthetic forms, institutional constraints and the expectations of audiences.

CASE STUDY

Doctor Who

British television is not as adept as US television in creating long-running television franchises. This is partly because British broadcasting companies commission television programmes in thirteen episode blocks (one quarter of the year), whereas anything that becomes popular on US television is typically commissioned for twenty-six episodes, and the next series as well.

Doctor Who is one of the most successful long-running British television franchises. The BBC TV sci-fi series originally ran from 1963 to 1989. *Doctor Who* is listed in the Guinness book of World Records as the longest-running science fiction television show in the world. It gained a new lease of life when successfully brought back in 2005, largely through the enthusiasm and talent of the main writer Russell T. Davies and high production values by BBC Wales in Cardiff. The series has built in longevity as the main character, the time lord Doctor Who, has the ability to regenerate with a new actor when appropriate.

There have been 751 *Doctor Who* episodes since 1963, and it won a BAFTA for Best Drama Series in 2006. *Doctor Who* has spin-offs in multiple media, including video games, magazines, conventions, apps and the television programmes *Torchwood* and *The Sarah Jane Adventures.* Convergence continues to throw up new ways to exploit successful television brands such as the mini-drama. These are new very short episodes involving the main characters that are produced for internet video only. These mini-dramas aim to maintain interest and excitement in the current series and provide an extra injection of the show between broadcast episodes.

The current Doctor Who, from 2010, is Matt Smith, aged twenty-six, who will be the eleventh Doctor. The BBC says:

> He may be the youngest actor to play the Doctor, but Smith has already built up an impressive CV on stage and the small screen. He has acted opposite *Doctor Who* star Billie Piper three times. His career path could have been very different had a back injury not prevented him pursuing a career in football. He played for the Leicester City and Nottingham Forest youth academies, but was steered towards drama when a teacher at Northampton School for Boys encouraged him to take the subject at A Level. He left

C@SE STUDY

Northampton aged 18 to study drama and creative writing at University of East Anglia in Norwich.

(BBC Press Release)

The important role of the Doctor's new assistant Amy Pond is played by Karen Gillan. The lead writer from 2010 is Stephen Moffat and Piers Wenger is the executive producer for BBC Wales who make *Doctor Who*.

The *Doctor Who* brand

Doctor Who is a potent multimedia brand inside and outside the television series. The BBC owns the brand logo and name, and licenses to merchandising companies the images, names and images of the antagonists and other characters. The brand appeals to adults and children. With the new 2010 series it seems to be aiming at a post-children's audience, with stronger plot lines, impressive CGI and more mature themes. In 1996, the BBC applied for a trademark to use the TARDIS blue police box design in merchandising associated with *Doctor Who*. In 1998, the Metropolitan Police filed an objection to the trademark claim, but in 2002 the Patent Office ruled in favour of the BBC.

There have been eleven different doctors so far, and they are all available on DVD. *Doctor Who* material based on the television series is available in all media including books, magazines, audio, websites, blogs, fanzines, conventions and themed weekends. There is a plethora of licensed merchandise including clothing, mugs, posters, toys, cards, board games and video games. A *Doctor Who* tour of major arenas showcases the Doctor's major antagonists, exciting children and parents with special effects, monsters, Daleks and Cybermen.

Doctor Who codes and conventions

The series has built up its audience by using specific and cleverly articulated objects and characters, which become the codes and conventions over the whole series. The TARDIS and the Doctor himself are the two essential codes that anchor every episode, every series and each regenerated Doctor. The TARDIS stands for Time And Relative Dimensions In Space. It looks like an old-fashioned police phone box and is blue with little windows. Step inside and the dimensions are considerably larger than it appears from the outside, as it is a time-travelling machine that can dematerialise. An important code is the special electronic sound FX of the Tardis dematerialising.

The Doctor is a time lord with two hearts who can move between different space and time dimensions. He is one of us but not one of us – he is other, and that is part of his attraction to audiences. His role as protagonist is to save the planet and people against threats from outer space, and other dimensions. He is helped by a variety of space age devices and his human assistant. Doctor Who always has a human assistant, who is usually female. She is, in a sense, an apprentice. The Doctor has to save her on occasions from his deadly foes but she also rescues the Doctor and helps him in his tasks. The assistant is crucial in making a human link between the Doctor and the audience, and for the Doctor to have an ally he can talk to, which makes for good drama.

Another important code is the Doctor's adversaries. These change with each series but some of the antagonists, such as the Daleks, return to challenge him again.

Antagonists

Doctor Who's enemies are a crucial code in the success of the brand, with the Daleks as the most popular, with strong cross-generational appeal, and possibly the most deadly. The Cybermen are also popular and present a serious threat. Other adversaries that the Doctor has had to combat include, in 1972, The Mutts – pincered, exoskeleton creatures – and the giant Maggots in the 1973 series 'The Green Death', reputedly the only monsters to be made from inflated condoms. More recently, the shape-shifting wasp-like creatures, the Vespiforms, in the 2007 series 'The Unicorn and the Wasps' caused Doctor Who's assistant Donna more than a little trouble. With the introduction of CGI the Doctor's antagonists have taken on new powers and have become considerably more realistic and dangerous, although still not rivalling the Daleks. Tritovores, with insect-like heads in 2009's 'Planet of the Dead', were an entirely new alien race intent on destroying the planet.

Theme tune

The *Doctor Who* theme tune composed by Ron Grainer was originally created in 1963 in the BBC radiophonic workshop. It is widely regarded as a significant and innovative piece of electronic music, and has been updated several times. This was the first theme tune for a television series to be created entirely electronically. To listen to the current *Doctor Who* theme music: http://en.wikipedia.org/wiki/Doctor_Who_theme_music.

Sci-fi genre

A recent code uses the sci-fi genre as a tool to create episodes in a known historical period. The *Doctor Who* episode called '3.2: The

C@SE STUDY

Shakespeare Code' used the Globe Theatre on the South Bank of the Thames in London as part of the plot which involved the conceit of William Shakespeare getting into difficulty writing a play and the Doctor providing the inspiration to finish it.

It could be argued that the appeal of the *Doctor Who* television programmes is due to nostalgia for a treasured past that crosses generations and is most successful when the Doctor travels into the known historical past. One Christmas episode was based on Victorian Christmas celebrations, referencing nostalgia for an old-fashioned Christmas with the postmodern idea of *Doctor Who* itself being nostalgic. This argument ignores the futuristic and intellectual aspects of the show where laws of the universe such as notions of quantum physics and relativity are seen to be understood and acted upon by the Doctor.

Although Doctor Who is a time traveller, stories are rarely about time travel in the same way that science fiction books are. Time travel is the device by which the Doctor arrives in a time or place in order to have an adventure. The series occasionally explores concerns about changing history or altering the future. For example, in one episode, Rose tries to prevent her father's death and in another, she and the Doctor travel to a parallel universe in which she hasn't yet been born. The sci-fi issues found in contemporary science fiction literature such as weird quantum mechanics, singularities, and post-human societies may be mentioned but have yet to feature in *Doctor Who*.

Doctor Who fans

It is impossible to consider *Doctor Who* without reference to the phenomenon of the fans who inhabit the Whoniverse. For example, fan fiction is an odd spin-off that attracts many would be sci-fi writers. To read some of these stories look at the large collection of online fan fiction collected under the title of 'A Teaspoon and an Open Mind: A *Doctor Who* Fan Fiction Archive' (www.whofic.com), which contains over ten thousand stories generated by the creative faculties of more than 1500 *Doctor Who* fans. Another online venture which is audio-based, is Sebastian J. Brook's aptly named Timestream Productions, available on the 'Doctor Who Online' website (www.Doctorwho-online.co.uk). This ongoing project shows that fan fiction is versatile and capable of branching out into diverse media. One of the most professional fan fiction undertakings is the Vancouver-based The *Doctor Who* Project (www.thedoctorwhoproject. com), a multi-award winning collection of fan-written adventures.

C@SE STUDY

Audiences for *Doctor Who*

Audiences for the TV series have nearly always been high. The popularity of the Daleks in 1964–65 attracted audiences of nine to fourteen million. In the late 1970s, the very popular Doctor, Tom Baker, had audiences of over twelve million. Figures remained respectable into the 1980s, but fell noticeably after the programme's 23rd season was postponed in 1985 and the show was off the air for eighteen months. Since returning in 2005 the show has consistently had high ratings. The largest audience for an episode of *Doctor Who* since its revival was the 2007 Christmas special 'Voyage of the Damned', with 13.31 million viewers. This made it the second most watched show of the year. The audience for the 2008 Christmas special was, interestingly, exactly the same as the 2007 Christmas special with 13.31 million people (BARB), which was the second highest audience over the Christmas period beaten only by *EastEnders*. Also the current series achieves the highest Audience Appreciation Index of any non-soap drama on television. That is a considerable achievement.

The TV series was originally created as family entertainment for Saturday evening on BBC television. It has maintained this brief, adapting to the times. The programme's high entertainment values attract audiences of children and families, as well as science fiction fans. Many people remember 'hiding behind the sofa' during the well signposted 'scary bits'. It also is popular with gay audiences. The most dynamic interactive audience are the adult *Doctor Who* fans from all economic demographics who contribute actively to blogs, fan sites, fanzines and who buy merchandise and attend *Doctor Who* conventions, and stadium shows. The series has a fan base all around the world and especially in the United States, where it is shown mainly on public service stations, and in New Zealand, Australia and Canada. Since July 2008, the revived series has been broadcast weekly in forty-two countries.

C@SE STUDY

REFERENCES AND FURTHER READING

BARB: http://www/barb.co.uk.
BBC Press Release: http://www.bbc.co.uk/doctorwho/dw.
Bignell, J. and Lacey, S. (eds) *Popular Television Drama: Critical Perspectives*, Manchester: Manchester University Press, 2005.
Billingham, P. 'Can Kinky Sex be Politically Correct?, *Queer as Folk* and the Geo-ideological Inscription of Gay Sexuality, in J. Bignell and S. Lacey (eds), *Popular Television Drama: Critical Perspectives*, Manchester: Manchester University Press, 2005.

Bourdieu, P. *Distinction: A Social Critique of the Judgement of Taste*, Cambridge, MA: Harvard University Press, 1984.

Brunsdon, C. 'Television: Aesthetics and Audiences', in P. Mellencamp (ed.), *Logics of Television: Essays in Cultural Criticism*, London: BFI, 1990, pp. 59–72.

Brunsdon, C. 'Structure of Anxiety: Recent British TV Crime Fiction', *Screen*, 39: 3 (1998), pp. 223–43.

Brunsdon, C., D'Acci, J. and Spigel, L. (eds) *Feminist Television Criticism: A Reader*, Oxford: Oxford University Press, 1997.

Buckingham, D. *Public Secrets: EastEnders and its Audience*, London: BFI, 1987.

Caughie, J. 'Popular Culture: Notes and Revisions', in C. MacCabe (ed.), *High Theory/Low Culture*, Manchester: Manchester University Press, 1986, pp. 156–71.

Dyer, R., Geraghty, C. Jordan, M. Lovell, T. Paterson, R. and Stewart, J. *Coronation Street*, London: BFI, 1981.

Eaton, M. 'A Fair Cop?: Canteen Culture in *Prime Suspect* and *Between the Lines*', in D. Kitt-Hewitt and R. Osborne (eds), *Crime and the Media: The Postmodern Spectacle*, London: Pluto 1995, pp. 164–84.

Frith, S. 'The Black Box: The Value of Television and the Future of Television Research', *Screen* 41: 1 (2000), pp. 33–50.

Geraghty, C. *Women and Soap Opera: A Study of Prime Time Soaps*, Cambridge: Polity Press, 1991.

Hallam, J. *Lynda LaPlante*, Manchester: Manchester University Press, 2005.

ITV Commissioning: http://www.itv.com/aboutitv/dramacommissioning/default.html.

Jermyn, D. 'Women with a Mission: Lynda LaPlante, DCI Tennison and the Reconfiguration of TV Crime Drama', *International Journal of Cultural Studies* 6: 1 (2003), pp. 46–63.

Jukes, P. 'Why Britain Can't do The Wire', *Prospect Magazine* online, 21 October 2009, Issue 164: http://www.prospectmagazine.co.uk.2009/10/why-britain-cant-do-the-wire/.

Lusted, D. 'The Popular Culture Debate and Light Entertainment on Television', in C. Geraghty and D. Lusted (eds), *The Television Studies Book*, London: Arnold, 1998, pp. 175–90.

Mackie, L.: http://www.itv.com/aboutitv/dramacommissioning/lauramackie/default.html.

Mulgan, G. (ed.). *The Question of Quality*, London: BFI, 1990.

Murdoch, G. 'Authorship and Organization', *Screen Education* 35 (1980), pp. 19–34.

Nelson, R. *TV Drama in Transition: Forms, Values and Cultural Change*, Basingstoke: Macmillan, 1997.

Thornham, S. 'Feminist Interventions: *Prime Suspect 1*', *Critical Survey* 6: 2 (1994), pp. 226–33.

CHAPTER 14

Realism and soaps

THE LANGUAGE OF REALISM IN TV DRAMA

Realism is a particularly ambiguous term. One meaning focuses on television's representation of recognisable and often contemporary experience, such as characters the audience can believe in, or apparently likely chains of events. This kind of realism relies on the familiarity of the codes which represent a reality, and allows viewers to say that a programme has quality if it conforms to their expectations. But another meaning of realism would reject the conventions of established realistic forms, and look for new and different ways to give access to the real. Television has a 'language of realism' which programme makers and audiences share. Finding new ways to deform or undercut that 'language of realism' is a marker of quality too, since it pushes the boundaries of audience expectations and encourages viewers to think about television representation in new ways.

Key point

Television has a 'language of realism' which programme makers and audiences share.

CLASSIC REALISM

The dominant form of realism in television drama, labelled by theorists 'classic realism', is usually what people mean when they describe programmes (especially dramas) as realistic and use this as a criterion for judging that they are high in quality. It can be seen in the majority of television fiction programmes, and also affects representation in factual programmes and documentary. Individuals' character determines their choices and actions, and human nature is seen as a pattern of character-differences. These differences permit the viewer to share the hopes and fears of a wide range of characters. Classic realism represents a world of psychologically consistent individuals, and assumes that viewers are similarly rational and psychologically consistent. The drama will offer identification with the characters and storylines it shows. The viewer's varied and ordered pattern of identifications makes narrative crucial to classic realism, for the different kinds of look, point-of-view, sound and speech in narrative are the forms through which this communication between text and audience is produced.

Key point

Classic realism represents a world of psychologically consistent individuals, and assumes that viewers are similarly rational and psychologically consistent.

CRITICAL REALISM

Realist television discourse resolves contradictions by representing a unified and rational world of causes and effects, actions and consequences, moral choices and rewards or punishments. It distances the viewer from the contradictory and ambiguous aspects of reality and suggests that political action to intervene in the ways that reality is produced day to day is unnecessary. Things are the way they are, and human nature doesn't really change. On the other hand, television could draw the attention of the viewer to the non-equivalence of television and reality.

Since television cannot be a 'true' representation, it could draw the viewer's attention to his or her relationship with the medium and make him or her recognise the social relations that this relationship involves. So perhaps the strangeness or unrealistic nature of television versions of reality, when familiar recognitions and identifications break down, might draw the viewer's attention to the fact that he or she is watching a representation and not a reality. This strategy of 'critical realism' involves recognising a relationship between television and reality, yet resisting television's apparently neutral transcription of that reality. Drama like that would reveal the work that television representation does, and show that TV realism is not natural but cultural and constructed.

Television drama does not usually reveal the production of an illusion of reality in fiction. However, television is an unusual medium in sometimes making its own production, and the failures in its production, part of a drama or a subject for non-fiction television programmes. But this revealing of behind-the-scenes information about how drama is constructed, and drawing attention to mistakes in production, is confined to particular kinds of text. In situation comedy, episodes may end with a compilation of out-takes, but it is very unlikely that a costume drama would do this.

Key point

This strategy of 'critical realism' involves recognising a relationship between television and reality, yet resisting television's apparently neutral transcription of that reality.

POSTMODERNISM

The increasing teleliteracy of the audience makes it less easy for television creators to manufacture realism, because of the audience's awareness of the conventions and codes that it involves. The recognition that television programmes play on their own and each other's conventions of realism is one of the components of postmodernism. This theoretical term rose to prominence in Television Studies in the 1980s, as a way of distinguishing how programmes since that time appear to be more self-conscious and sophisticated than before, indicating a rise in the quality of TV. One of the most useful components of postmodernist critiques of television is the concept of reflexivity to describe the textual and narrative characteristics of programmes. The study of reflexivity entails discovering features of television which display self-consciousness, irony, and the pastiche or imitation of familiar conventions, formats and structures. Examples of this in drama include the pastiche of science fiction conventions in *Red Dwarf* or the pastiche of television and film conventions in *The Simpsons* and *Lost*. The term can also be used to signify a more general shift in television culture, and culture in general, away from classic realism and towards the debunking of illusion. The eventual result of this trend, it is argued, is the scepticism and cynicism that audiences display in their attitudes to the media as a whole.

Key point

The recognition that television programmes play on their own and each other's conventions of realism is one of the components of postmodernism.

BRITISH SOAP OPERA AND AUDIENCES

The continuing serial, more commonly referred to as the soap opera, is a crucial means for channels to attract and retain audiences from week to week, and potentially to bring audiences to programmes scheduled before and after a 'must-see' soap episode that viewers have tuned in for. In 2010, the BBC's most popular prime-time soap *EastEnders* had an audience of between eight and a half and ten million each episode, with four programmes per week. All four are the top programmes of the week for BBC1. ITV's *Coronation Street* over four weekdays achieves a very similar audience of between eight and a half and ten million viewers. The ITV network relies on its main soap operas *Coronation Street* and *Emmerdale* to act as 'banker' programmes at the beginning of mid-evening prime time.

A soap can also act as a 'tent-pole' programme that holds up audience levels in the evening and can also attract 'echo' and 'pre-echo' audiences for the programmes scheduled before and after it. Soaps are a mainstay of drama production, and also act as a proving-ground for performers who will subsequently graduate to series and serial drama with bigger budgets and higher profiles. So although soaps are not part of quality television in its usual sense, they are a sort of nursery for performers and writers who may go on to 'better' things.

TV SOAP AS MELODRAMA

Soap opera has conventionally been regarded as a low-quality genre because of its exaggeration of emotion, its departures from realist conventions, and its comparatively low budgets. Its dramatic form is a kind of melodrama, a term originally signifying dramas accompanied by music, and now used to denote precisely those features of emotionalism and lack of realism. The supposed lack of quality in soap opera dramas is a reflection of the low value given to melodrama as a dramatic form. But melodrama can also be understood as a very effective way of dramatising conflicts of morality and the functioning of community. To force characters into conflict and keep them within the dramatic space for an extended period, restrictions of physical space are placed around them.

The significance of space and setting to the soap genre can be seen in the titles of *Coronation Street*, *Brookside*, *Emmerdale* and *EastEnders*. Location functions as a force linking characters with each other, not only as a positive basis for community but also as a boundary which characters find it difficult to transgress. Characters in soap opera are in a sense trapped by their location, and their proximity to each other within the space creates not only alliances but also rivalries and friction.

The categorisations linking characters together in soap opera include family or work relationship, age group, race or gender. They function in a similar way as either a positive ground for connection or a source of rivalry and tension. The overlapping of these categories among each other also produces possible stories in soap opera, since one character is likely to belong to several different categories, perhaps working in the local shop, belonging to a family, and pursuing solidarity with other characters of the same age group. Soap opera narrative manipulates these connections and distinctions, changing them over time, thus producing different permutations of connection and distinction that form the basis of storylines.

The expression of emotion is an important part of soap opera, and, as David Lusted (1998) notes, it is both a marker of femininity and of working-class culture. While masculine values entail the suppression of emotion in favour of efficiency, achievement and stoicism, feminine values encourage the display of emotion as a way of responding to problems. Similarly, elite class sectors value rational talk and writing as means of expression, versus emotional release.

These culturally produced distinctions have been important to work in Television Studies on the relationship between gender and the different genres of television, where news and current affairs are regarded as masculine, and melodrama as feminine. On the basis of these gender, class and genre distinctions, the role of emotional display takes on increased significance in relation to quality. Because soaps are focused on what seems to be feminine and working-class behaviour, and usually feature a high proportion of women and working class characters, it is not surprising that they are not thought of as quality television. Quality has associations with masculine seriousness and middle-class attitudes, so soap opera has little chance of achieving it.

On the other hand soaps also contribute to public service aims to represent society to itself, and deal with issues of current concern. Phil Redmond (quoted in Nelson 1997: 114–15), the creator and producer of the now defunct Channel 4 soap opera *Brookside*, set in Liverpool, explained that when the programme began in the early 1980s: 'I wanted to use the twice-weekly form to explore social issues, and, hopefully, contribute to any social debate . . . From the outset one of my main aims was to try and reflect Britain in the 1980s.' In this respect, the sometimes contrived storylines that would seem to distance soaps from notions of quality can by contrast be regarded as evidence of responsibility and social purpose, an alternative notion of quality. Soap opera realism allows this transfer between fiction and reality, and enables soaps to claim social responsibility and public service functions.

The balance in soap opera storylines can tip from plot to character and back again, but a focus on either of these tends to reinforce the negative evaluation of soap opera as a low-quality drama form. Granada Television's former director of programmes, John Whiston, talking about *Coronation Street* explains:

> There are tensions between storyliners, who want a story that gets them logically and clearly to a particular point, and writers, who want to free up enough time for their characters to be what they want them to be. If the balance swings too far to the storyliners, you get a very plot-driven show that is a bit 'ploppy' and for my money there has been too much emphasis on the storyliners.
>
> (Moss 2002: 2)

Granada TV executives, and the programme's producers, make strategic management decisions about the programme based on their perceptions of audience demands and the balance of power between the staff in their production team. But the more the producers succeed in attracting large audiences, the more the likelihood that the soap will be evaluated as low quality, since the thrills of melodrama and the popularity of programmes are each reasons to categorise it in this way.

Key point

The sometimes contrived storylines that would seem to distance soaps from notions of quality can by contrast be regarded as evidence of responsibility and social purpose, an alternative notion of quality. Soap opera realism allows this transfer between fiction and reality, and enables soaps to claim social responsibility and public service functions.

ANALYSING DRAMA

Mise-en-scène

Literally means put on the stage, or in the scene. It applies to any sort of programme because all television is a construct, but it is mainly useful in analysing fictional television. *Mise-en-scène* is more than just the physical objects in the scene. It includes the camera angle and any camera movement, the framing, the shot size and the mood of the lighting, the careful placing of the actors, and the make up, and costume. When analysing *mise-en-scène* take a sequence from a programme, or a scene from a drama, and look at the following components.

The setting

Is it a set, or is the action filmed on location – how can you tell, and why is it important? Is it a realistic or naturalistic set? The writer has created a period for the action, and dropped in clues that have been deliberately placed to remind the audience of this period. Examine the objects in a scene which authenticate the period, e.g. the saloon bars in a western, or Albert Square in *EastEnders*. Some props carry forward the narrative, e.g. a knife or a gun. Decide what they are doing in the scene, and what narrative device was used to get them there. The setting may be bland, or in soft focus to place the emphasis on the characters. The director may decide that there should be no extra information in this scene other than close-ups of the characters. This is common in soaps and serials. One of the advantages of these genres is that there is a pool of common knowledge shared by the regular audience. Everyone knows the look and feel of the hospitals in *Holby City* or *Casualty* (BBC). The set will be dressed to look different to emphasise a story line. It can be something simple like Christmas or the tragic death of a character.

Characters

Costume and make up are elements in defining a character and to some extent genre. Comedy uses visual clues to emphasise a character. Fictional television uses costume and make up to signal a range of emotions and traits, including a character's mood, time of life, job, ambitions, anxieties, state of mind and social status. The art of make up for television is often to make the face as naturalistic as possible under the set lights. All presenters and many guests require some form of make up to appear to look perfectly natural in a television studio. This is due to the harsh nature of the lighting, and the way many talk shows want a cheery, sunny visual feel to their shows, which involves high levels of overhead lighting.

For a period drama set in a particular epoch the make up artist will have done extensive research studying photographs and paintings of the time to get the make up to look authentic. Costume and make up often play the most important part in the *mise-en-scène* of any period piece, sometimes hiding the lack of an authentic location.

Lighting

In a two-dimensional medium like television, lighting is most important as it helps create a three-dimensional image that is most convincing to the viewer. Conventional analysis of film lighting is to differentiate between hard and soft lighting. Television lighting directors are versed in these techniques, but also invent new ones. Hard light is associated with well-defined shadows, and is particularly obvious in film noir movies, or classics like *The Third Man.* Soft light is diffuse and has few shadows and works very well for video cameras. Most TV studio shows use large soft lights to illuminate the set without casting any shadows. Television is beamed into the audience's sitting room and most of the time works hard as an entertainment medium not to upset the viewer. Soft lighting helps to create a friendly visual environment. For a location drama lighting has much more to do. The source of the key light is important. A scene can appear to be illuminated by just one light source from a window, or perhaps a candle. This may actually be the case but there will also be other hidden sources of light. Faces usually need separate illumination to make them stand out from the background set. Variations on the three-point lighting plot (see Part 6 on 'Practical programme making') are most commonly used to light a fictional scene. A director of photography (DOP) may use many more lights of different sizes and power to create a particular feeling or atmosphere for a scene. Genre can be defined by the way the set is lit. The under lighting of a character's face, swirling mist and a 'moody' set have become key indicators of the horror genre.

Acting

Everyone feels they can comment on acting in a television programme. The popular criterion for 'good' acting is naturalism. Some of the best-loved actors on television are often anything but naturalistic – for example David Jason in *Only Fools and Horses*. Comedy allows the outrageous as we laugh at exaggerated human traits or foibles – think of John Cleese as Basil Fawlty.

Acting is the hardest element to analyse in a programme. Look for facial expression, movement, gesture and use of the voice. Casting directors for television soaps and serials look for the actor who as himself or herself naturally looks and speaks like the scripted character. Television is a realistic medium. Television acting is not at all like acting on the stage where command of the body and voice is essential. The ability to project character, deliver a meaningful performance and have screen presence is crucial for a major television drama.

Run of the mill television fiction can be accused of relying on the same faces delivering the same type of role. Commissioning Editors are reluctant to take risks and prefer a well-known television face that can fit any part, to a new name who might be exciting but not perhaps to everyone's taste.

Some areas to analyse in TV acting go outside the frame. Television tends not to isolate an acting performance as a film does. The viewer brings to each scene visual luggage from the rest of his or her recent television experience. The worry is that this visual luggage can mean that viewers and broadcasting companies see acting talent as set in stone and eschew the new generation of actors that is always coming up. A film director will spend months looking for a new fresh face; this is unusual in standard television fiction.

Postproduction

The way the pictures are edited together, the choice of music, the selection of background sound, and the mix and balance of the sound all contribute to the *mise-en-scène*. Modern postproduction can completely change the original filmed sequence. Digital effects and animation can be added, the picture colourised or the colour drained from it, the motion slowed or speeded up, unsightly buildings from the location shoot can disappear.

Some TV dramas such as *Doctor Who* have many scenes shot against a bluescreen so that extra background pictures can be added in post production. The advent of CGI has made this form of production more cost effective for television producers, although it is still time consuming and therefore expensive in postproduction. Many special effects are designed to be unobtrusive, or invisible. *Mise-en-scène* analysis attempts to see what has been the effect of postproduction on the meaning and interpretation of the scene or sequence.

PROFILE

Script writer Lynda Laplante

Linda LaPlante is the best known and most successful woman writer in the popular genre of the realistic police series. She began with the serial *Widows* for Thames TV/Euston Films in 1982, and her drama *Prime Suspect* for Granada (1991) has the most enduring reputation among her works. Her work is notable since the police genre is associated with masculinity and yet LaPlante has investigated and critiqued masculinity within the genre at the same time as adopting some of its conventions. As a woman writer, her dramas focus on violence and the graphic depiction of bodily harm has been the subject of criticism, and in some of her work she has drawn on the conventions of melodrama, a form associated with the feminine. Like all drama authors, LaPlante has worked in the context of the collaborative culture of television production. Questions about the relationship between reality, truth and fiction, dramatic creation and authenticity, are also raised by LaPlante's insistence that all of her fictional writing is very closely based on extensive research and interviews conducted with people such as police, lawyers and convicted criminals.

Widows (ITV) was the first crime serial drama written and produced by a female team (see Hallam 2005). Its central characters are the wives of a gang of criminals who take over their former husbands' role as criminal masterminds, and the drama is unusual in depicting the successful outcome of their robbery plan, rather than centring on the investigation of crime by detectives on the right side of the law. LaPlante collaborated on *Widows* with Verity Lambert, one of the few women working in television at the time, and despite being scheduled against *Dallas* in the prime time 9.00–10.00 pm evening slot, *Widows* gained eleven million viewers. The seed of the idea began when LaPlante played a small role in the ITV series *The Gentle Touch* (ITV 1980–4), the first television drama centred on a female detective, and LaPlante offered four story outlines that were all turned down. One of these outlines was the storyline that became *Widows* and secured LaPlante's initial reputation as a television dramatist.

Prime Suspect was commissioned by Granada in 1990. Its central character, Detective Chief Inspector Jane Tennison (Helen Mirren), is a senior female detective whose gradual rise to greater success among the male centred London police force is charted in a series of two-hour double episodes transmitted in mini-series form. In the first series of *Prime Suspect* (ITV) the masculine culture of the police is demonstrated in an aggressive contest between two male policemen who box each other as part of a charity benefit, and the violence against the pursued killer's female victims is demonstrated by forensic photographs of their mutilated bodies, and the evidence of iron manacles and blood stains on the walls of the garage where they were killed. The main character's dispassionate examination of mutilated bodies in the mortuary and of the crime scene are mechanisms for demonstrating the apparently masculine traits that allow her to succeed as a police detective, while her feminine attention to the appearance of female victims, including their clothing and fingernails, enables her to discover clues that male policemen have missed. These contrasts between masculine and feminine characteristics, paralleled by her success at work in contrast to the messiness of her personal life, made *Prime Suspect* a subject of attention both for the popular press and for academic critics interested in gender and representation (see Brunsdon 1998, Eaton 1995, Hallam 2005, Jermyn 2003, Thornham 1994).

PROFILE

After the success of the first *Prime Suspect*, LaPlante produced the storyline for its sequel *Prime Suspect 2* (Granada 1992), but did not write the script, while the third sequel, *Prime Suspect 3* (Granada 1993), was written by LaPlante. *Prime Suspect 4, 5* and *6* (1995) were produced subsequently by Granada, without LaPlante's direct involvement. The BBC producer Ruth Caleb commissioned LaPlante for the series *Civvies* (BBC Wales 1992), about former paratroopers. This developed along side an ITV drama series by LaPlante about a female prison governor, *The Governor* (LaPlante Productions/ITV 1995).

LaPlante started her own production company in 1994, one of the results of the Broadcasting Act of 1990 that shifted some production from the broadcasting instiutions to independent companies. The shift in the broadcasting landscape produced not only organisational changes, but also facilitated representations of a wider range of characters in drama and the creation of new forms, as a new cohort of writers and producers gained access to the airwaves. *Trial and Retribution* (1997) detailed the investigations and court procedures following the murder of a young child, and used split screen format to offer a variety of competing images and narratives. While split screen was criticised for being too demanding on viewers, it is the first significant example of the sustained use of split screen in television drama, and set a precedent for this technique in later work by other writers, such as the film *Timecode* (2000) and the American drama series *24* (2001).

The combination of serious issues relating to sex equality, paedophilia and the Internet in some of LaPlante's dramas, established her as a key writer in the British television drama culture of the time. LaPlante adopted the role of writer and producer that is common in the USA, for the series *Supply and Demand* (LaPlante Productions/ITV 1996, 1997), *Killer Net* (LaPlante Productions/Channel 4 1997) and *Mind Games* (LaPlante Productions/ITV 2000). These series were made for UK transmission but also aimed to penetrate the American television market. LaPlante's position at the top of the British drama hierarchy was demonstrated when she won the Dennis Potter Award for television writing in 2001. This recognised the respect she had gained from her peers among television dramatists, and also from the television institutions that were using her name 'above the title' as a brand that connoted both quality and appeal to large audiences.

The latest from La Plante Productions in 2010 include *Above Suspicion: The Red Dahlia* where DC Anna Travis (Kelly Reilly) is reunited with GCI James Langton (Ciaran Hinds). The first *Above Suspicion* was broadcast in 2009 and attracted eight million viewers.

PROFILE

REFERENCES AND FURTHER READING

Allen, R. *Speaking of Soap Operas*, Chapel Hill, NC: University of North Carolina Press, 1985.

Ang, I. 'Melodramatic Identifications: Television Fiction and Women's Fantasy', in C. Brunsdon, J. D'Acci and L. Spigel (eds), *Feminist Television Criticism: A Reader*, Oxford, Oxford University Press, 1997, pp. 155–66.

Bignell, J. 'Space for "Quality": Negotiating with the Daleks', in J. Bignell and S. Lacey (eds), *Popular Television Drama: Critical Perspectives*, Manchester: Manchester University Press, 2005.

Bignell, J. and Lacey, S. (eds). *Popular Television Drama: Critical Perspectives*, Manchester: Manchester University Press, 2005.

Bignell, J., Lacey, S. and Macmurraugh-Kavanagh, M. (eds). *British Television Drama: Past, Present and Future*, Basingstoke, UK: Palgrave Macmillan, 1999.

Billingham, P. 'Can Kinky Sex be Politically Correct? *Queer as Folk* and the Geo-ideological Inscription of Gay Sexuality', in J. Bignell and S. Lacey (eds), *Popular Television Drama: Critical Perspectives*, Manchester: Manchester University Press, 2005.

Bourdieu, P. *Distinction: A Social Critique of the Judgement of Taste*, Cambridge, Mass.: Harvard University Press, 1984.

Brunsdon, C. 'Structure of Anxiety: Recent British Crime Fiction', *Screen*, 39: 3 (1998), pp. 223–43.

Brunsdon, C. *The Feminist, The Housewife, and the Soap Opera*, Oxford: Oxford University Press, 2000.

Eaton, M. 'A Fair Cop?: Canteen Culture in *Prime Suspect* and *Between the Lines*', in D. Kitt-Hewitt and R. Osborne (eds), *Crime and the Media: The Postmodern Spectacle*, London: Pluto, 1995, pp. 164–84.

Hallam, J. *Lynda LaPlante*, Manchester: Manchester University Press, 2005.

ITV: www.itv.com/dramacommissioning.

Jermyn, D. 'Women with a Mission: Lynda LaPlante, DCI Tennison and the Reconfiguration of TV Crime Drama', *International Journal of Cutural Studies* 6: 1 (2003), pp. 46–63.

Lusted, D. 'The Popular Culture Debate and Light Entertainment on Television', in C. Geraghty and D. Lusted (eds), *The Television Studies Book*, London: Arnold, 1998, pp. 175–90.

Moss, S. 'New Kids on the Block', *Guardian*, Monday 28 January 2002: http://www.guardian.co.uk/media/2002/jan/28/mondaymediasection.

Nelson, R. *TV Drama in Transition: Forms, Values and Cultural Change*, Basingstoke, UK: Macmillan, 1997.

Thornham, S. Feminist Interventions: *Prime Suspect 1*, *Critical Survey* 6: 2 (1994), pp. 226–33.

CHAPTER 15

Drama production – script writing

SCRIPTING THE IDEA

Television programmes of all types have their genesis on the page. One of the definitions of a television drama is that it is a fully scripted programme. The snappy dialogue, sudden twist in plot and the egregious antagonist start life within a developing scenario on a writer's screen. A drama writer uses the three crucial pillars of a good script: story (narrative), characters, and setting to support a distinctive idea. A story starts with an idea. The idea may sit within the genre of perhaps horror, science fiction, suspense, crime, thriller, romance, comedy, teenager drama or a hybrid genre. The idea maybe along the lines of a kickboxing teenager who is involved with the supernatural. It may seem derivative of the *Twilight* series, but it could easily develop a particular take of its own. French director Jean-Luc Godard famously said a film needs a beginning, middle and end, but not necessarily in that order. This is the basis of all narrative, and the linear flow of a story acts as a formidable hook for a television drama.

Some ideas develop from the realisation of an interesting character whom the writer has come across, and who could become an effective secret agent, or the protagonist in a complex romance. John Cleese says he got his idea for the comedy series *Fawlty Towers* from observing hotel owners on childhood holidays in Torquay. Ask a scriptwriter what he does all day. He is likely to say watching, and listening to people – in a café, in the pub, on a train, in a waiting room, or in a supermarket queue – collecting snatches of potential dialogue, and observing potential characters. Main characters in a television drama need to be believable within their context. The audience must be able to believe in them as rounded individuals.

SETTING

Narrative themes can often stem from a particular setting. The plot is how the ideas work out between the characters. The writer may have visited a particularly engaging region, such as Cornwall. The dramatic seascapes and craggy coastline may inspire a story of smuggling, or witchcraft. An ancient stone circle may inspire a script about a young girl who stumbles on a Celtic coin, and then digs up a skeleton. A stylish penthouse apartment in Brighton may be the ideal location to set a romantic drama about a dodgy art dealer who leaves his busy life in London to set up home with a young graffiti artist.

Much of television drama aims to recreate a form of reality set in an urban location that the large audience in towns and cities can easily relate to. This is why it is rare to see science fiction on television, but there are a lot of police and hospital dramas. Soaps create their own sense of place, time and history around a tight specific location such as Albert Square. A drama can work well if it is located in an unusual setting that invites the audience to revel in its beauty, or be engrossed by its very strangeness. A writer has to have a clear imaginative picture of where the story is going to be set. Budding writers are encouraged to choose a location that they know. For a short television drama it can be somewhere intimate – a narrow boat on a canal, a dock side or an interior. There are some definite

FIGURE 15.1
The setting – London at night

advantages in setting a story at one flexible location. 'Whodunit' murder stories are often set in a country house. It makes the drama more intense and claustrophobic.

Scripts take time for the characters to become rounded and for the ideas to mature. This process is called development. This is a state of mind much favoured by Hollywood scriptwriters, where very little appears to get done. But ideas are cooking, characters are being fleshed out, locations are being thoroughly visualised. The creative juices are being stirred, and eventually a script unfolds as if by magic – that is the theory anyway. It always involves a lot of very hard writing and rewriting.

THE PROTAGONIST

The central character is usually the protagonist of the story. The protagonist must have clear motivation to achieve his or her aim in the film. Motivation arises from inner character, and experiences in the central character's past, called 'back story'. The protagonist is the driver of the action. Audiences like to feel sympathetic to the protagonist, and like to feel that there is some development in his or her life. Some action movies just show the main character achieving a particular aspiration. All right if you have a big budget for action special effects, but not much good as a scenario for a television short.

The writer needs to create a protagonist who can achieve a goal, and by doing so go through a transformation of personality as well as getting the girl, or the diamonds. Audiences like a protagonist who goes through psychological or super-natural hoops. The type of psychological and actual journey seen in the film *Erin Brokovich* is captivating. There is something universally appealing about the poor, rejected protagonist who overcomes insurmountable odds to achieve her worthwhile goal. Movies where protagonists do not achieve their goals by the end of the film have a habit of leaving the audience feeling depressed, and downhearted. This may not be the best way to end your first television short.

THE ADVERSARY

In a typical dramatic scenario the protagonist will have an adversary. This is a character who has the job of making it as difficult, and often as dangerous, as possible for the protagonist to achieve his or her goal. In an action film, such as a James Bond movie, there will always be a recognisable, often stereotyped, bad guy. Bad guys often represent a variety of distasteful, or downright anti-human, traits but this need not be immediately apparent. In television, a successful adversary is often a wolf in sheep's clothing. Looking cool, acting normally, but all the time coming from the Norman Bates charm school of psychopaths. The writer matches the cunning of the adversary with the skills and talents of the protagonist.

THE TREATMENT

A television company or broadcasting executive will need to see a treatment of an idea, before commissioning it or putting any money into further development. This is a detailed outline of the drama. A drama treatment tells the story, describes the setting, and the characters. It shows clearly the structure of events. It will definitely show the beginning, middle and end of the story. This is the basic three-act structure – what happens when and why. A well-structured TV drama is often a good drama. Check for yourself by looking at the structures of universally acclaimed dramas such as *The Sopranos* or *Lost*. The treatment should not be a long document. Just one or two pages is quite adequate for a TV short. A longer drama will have a more detailed treatment showing all the twists and turns of the plot, with full characterisations.

It is a good idea to include in the treatment a page of dialogue to show how the characters come to life through the dialogue.

SCRIPT LAYOUT

Writing a script for television is an exciting and exacting process with basic rules and conventions. The basic standards for setting out a TV drama come from Hollywood. The good thing about this format is that one page equals one minute of final screen time. This is most helpful in calculating the length of scenes and how long the piece will run on the screen. A ten minute television script is about ten pages of script.

There is a set format for setting out a page of television script. There is a new scene for each change of location, and each scene has three important parts:

- the heading – scene number and setting
- brief description of the scene
- dialogue.

The heading informs the reader of the scene number and details of where the scene is set and the location. Use capitals. EXTERIOR or INTERIOR; DAY or NIGHT. Put the location in capitals on the same line.

> SCENE 10. EXTERIOR. NIGHT. GRAVEYARD. REMOTE CHURCH.

Be consistent with descriptions of locations. It is either a flat or an apartment, but not both. The names of places should be consistent. The setting of the scene is always written in the present tense. The description is written across the whole page under the heading and single-spaced.

Describe in as few words as possible anything that is relevant to the action or the plot. Do not describe details of the set, or what the characters are wearing, unless it is absolutely relevant to the action. If a character is wearing a coat to conceal a gun, then that is relevant. On a character's first appearance describe salient aspects of the character's psychological and physical make-up. This is more about motivation and potential psychological development than what the actor will eventually look like.

WILLIAM WELTHAM is young, dishevelled and likes to think he is cool. He works in a call centre. Sings and plays guitar at night in a local pub, under a pseudonym. Thinks he should be famous, but is not sure he is ready for a fat recording contract. Ambition is not his second name. Sensitive, and caring, he likes children. Hates commitment. Desperately needs someone to take him on and bring out his true self. Lives alone.

SETTING OUT A PAGE OF DIALOGUE

- Name each character in capital letters, in the middle of the page.
- Use a left margin of about 1.5 inches.
- Put instructions for the actor in brackets at the place where they should happen in the script. (Pulls gun out of glove box in car.)
- Put page numbers in the upper-right corner of the page.
- Set up a template for your script.

Television producers and commissioning editors want to see realistic and sharp dialogue, and a vibrant story structure, with character development.

EXAMPLE OF A DRAMA SCRIPT

A television script has a standard format. Professional script writing software is available, but expensive and not really necessary. Do not put in 'stage' directions unless they are crucial to the plot. Do not put in camera angles, or director's notes. That is for the director to do. This is a script, not a shooting document.

PILTDOWN MAN

by

Angelo Rabelro

11 Farlee Avenue

Angmering

Sussex UK

SCENE 1

FADE IN:

EXT. DAY. CAFÉ BY THE SEA.

SEA WASH on a pebble beach. Sunny.

Wind is flapping the flags. Seagulls overhead. Two men are sitting at a café table. On the table is a SKULL loosely wrapped in a Burberry scarf.

BAILEY is in his early twenties. Studying anthropology he is animated, intense and excited. STEPHEN is an osteopath in his mid-twenties. Successful, well dressed, single.

> BAILEY
>
> It's got to be the one. Nothing else
>
> has this scar feature or . . .

> STEPHEN
>
> How on earth do you know? Why would it
>
> be here anyway?

> BAILEY
>
> When they buried it at Piltdown they
>
> didn't think it was good enough. But it's
>
> better. It's the real thing.

SCENE 2

EXT. THE PROMENADE. DAY

CLAIRE is rollerblading along the sea front with her dog on a lead. Tall, athletic, early twenties. Ambitious. Freelance journalist.

CLAIRE arrives at the café table with a rush. She almost falls into STEPHEN's coffee.

                    CLAIRE

          So that's where my scarf is. I've been looking
          for that all day – you stole it

She picks up the scarf. The skull skids across the table and falls off.

BAILEY dives for it. He catches it as it slides off the table. He almost falls over. The dog barks.

                    CLAIRE

          What the hell is that? . . . Yuck! That's gross.
          Are you into devil worship?

                    STEPHEN

          Don't invoke ancient spirits

                    CLAIRE

          What's so cool about this relic? It's grotesque –
          you can't fool me that's Neanderthal man.

                    BAILEY

          That's a million dollars – that's what
          that is. And you nearly lost the lot.

SCENE 3

EXTERIOR. NIGHT. WOODED AREA. AN OLD QUARRY.

BAILEY is working with a futuristic detector device. There is a bleeping. He gets out a large digger tool and prises something out of the rock crevice.

STEPHEN is crouched over scientific instruments.

Bailey uncovers a medallion-like object.

> BAILEY
>
> Check this out Steve. It's got ferrous. It's also got a sort of bronze . . . It's prehistoric all right.

> CLAIRE
>
> We must have evidence or the paper won't print the story. Wow! The instruments are going crazy.

The instruments are seen to be complex, linked to a laptop. The screen shows animated graphs and scientific displays. They jump about in a frenzy.

> STEPHEN
>
> Now Claire do you believe in the power of the ancients . . . this was a burial site. There must have been burial rites.

> BAILEY
>
> She still thinks it's superstitious rubbish. She's hung up on being an investigative journalist. If you can't interview it, it's not real.

> CLAIRE
>
> Yea OK something's got to be here. I'll believe it when I see it . . . Jeez what is that!

Suddenly the instruments flash. The laptop crashes. There is a mysterious cracking noise from the rock face. The rocks roar and split open. A black void appears with something dark moving inside.

> BAILEY
>
> They're back. They want the skull.

FIGURE 15.2
Italian fishing village of Portofino

STRUCTURE AND SEQUENCE – THE OPENING

In any television drama or film a strong opening is really essential. This is part of the first act – the beginning. If the audience is not hooked in the first few minutes, it is much harder to keep them glued to the screen throughout. Television dramas do not require the sort of dramatic action-packed opening sequence that denotes Hollywood movies. Setting up the character is usually more important. This is small-screen drama viewed at home. The audience will be looking for interesting, believable, 'realistic' characters.

In the opening scene the main character is typically set up – age, job, clothes, mannerisms, and a visual setting that gives the viewer an instant understanding of the type of drama that will unfold. A windswept tower block with broken windows, stark grey sky and poorly dressed young people is going to be about poverty, crime and maybe redemption. This can be explained visually in the first minute or so of the drama. Contrast that with a shot of Canary Wharf in the city, smart-suited young businessmen talking on their mobiles while walking purposefully to work. This could be the opening of a drama about two brothers. One is successful and works in derivatives in the city; the other is down on his luck and selling drugs on a Glasgow housing estate. The enigma for the audience is how this scenario will unfold. It need not be stereotypical. The younger brother could be an undercover police officer staking out a potential cover for Al Qaeda terrorists.

TV drama works well when the plot stems from the motivation of the characters. Successful TV dramas have been located in institutions such as hospitals and schools, but also in a village, small town or recognisable city such as Liverpool or Glasgow. American director Robert Altman has one of the best worked out openings of any movie in his film *The Player*. The beautifully composed opening sequence is one very long shot that sets up the story, introduces the main characters and contains the vital clue to the ending.

GETTING THE PLOT RIGHT

The structure of the story is incredibly important. This includes everything that happens to make the plot work. The plot is the way the story unfolds through the important events that make up the story. The plot stems from the main characters, and what motivates them to achieve their aims. What the main character wants should be clear early on but not necessarily how he or she is going to attain it. The main character develops because of the experiences he or she is going to go through in the drama. Do as much as possible visually, suggesting the relevant experiences with one or two scenes – high-school kid – fresher's ball – CIA – betrayal – loss of friend – determination for survival – new acceptance by father. This can give the rudiments of the story, but very little detail of how the plot will develop. Work out what will happen, and in what order it will happen. This is structure, or plot.

This is a simple scenario:

> Twenty something, career-driven single parent runs a successful fashion business. Father of her little girl is an alcoholic. Disillusioned with men she is sent on holiday by her exasperated business partner. Scuba diving near Portofino she nearly drowns and is rescued by a mysterious handsome stranger. She has to reassess her life. Rejects him and goes for someone she knows who offers security. But he is struggling with his sexual identity. After a series of accidents and trials eventually realises the handsome stranger is the one.

The tease is that the audience thinks she would fall in love with the handsome man who rescues her. She perversely decides to go for the sardonic, gentle child minder who looks after her daughter, but who is having a crisis about being gay. The intrigue is in how her rescuer eventually ends up with the right girl. This is where the details of the plot are crucial.

Making this simple scenario work for TV calls for a closer look at the details of the scenario, how it would affect a real person. A real person could not afford the lavish life style that Hollywood characters seem to follow. She has her two children to think of. Many viewers would empathise with this situation. The character is a mother who is resentful that she has to care for two children with only basic maintenance from the father. This has been her first holiday for over five years. This is a not uncommon scenario. The writer has to make the plot fit a believable situation and be exciting enough to hook the viewer. A typical TV drama would go for realism all the way through, and then create a strong ending, effecting closure with possibly an unrealistic event or twist in the plot to give an emotional climax. On the other hand it may be better to have an ending that is more likely to happen in real life.

As a short film this could all take place in the location of any small town or perhaps the more visually interesting location of a holiday resort such as Newquay in Cornwall.

PACE

The pace of the dialogue should vary according to the action. The action can move between the highs of activity and danger, and quieter periods of self-exploration and revelation through intimate dialogue. In the best scripts the climax grows organically out of the elements of the story. Periods of action can alternate with moments of reflection or character-building dialogue. Writers use devices to enhance the believability and entertainment value of the script.

FORESHADOWING

Foreshadowing gives the audience subtle clues as to what might happen later, or how a character might develop. It sets up possibilities that can be developed later. A cleverly developed scene can plant an unconscious awareness in the viewer of what might happen. Foreshadowing can lead to a more satisfying story.

TREATMENT OF TIME

Everything the viewer sees apparently happens in present time. This does not stop the script from jumping backwards and forwards in time. Soaps and serials almost never do this as they want the viewer to be present in a continuing saga of nowness. Time, however, is always compressed. We accept, for example, the convention that time is compressed in *Friends* to give the impression of an almost timeless day-to-day existence.

A good drama can exploit time to great effect interlacing the past with the present and even foretelling the future. In fact, a writer can create any time period – past, present or future – but it all will appear to be happening now.

The writer decides on the time span that works best for the structure of the film. To create a claustrophobic, intense atmosphere where the characters are under pressure, the film can be set in a tight time span. Perhaps just twenty-four hours. Richard Curtis in his films – e.g. *Love Actually* – always includes Christmas Eve. This is a good day of the year for something dramatic and life enhancing to happen.

Think carefully about the time span of the drama. How long will it take for the main character to fulfil his/her goal? Squeezing the action into a short time span can make a big difference to the pace and feel of the piece.

BACK STORY

Hollywood writers are very keen on back story. This is the unseen part of a character's past life, occasionally alluded to in the text. The writer may know a lot about the main character, but the audience know nothing. The back story illuminates the reasons for the protagonist wanting his or her goal, whether it is for ultimate power, or love, or just greed. Back story may mean dropping into the script factual details about the past. This may be details of where a character was born and grew up. It often works better if the back story can suggest a more psychological history, such as an inability to relate to the opposite sex owing to some trauma in childhood. A believable, contemporary TV character will also suggest back story just by the way he or she talks – a Geordie accent means the character grew up in Newcastle – and the way the actor plays the part is very important in building up the character's personality.

Sometimes it is useful to have a character who has no discernible back story. Think of the Clint Eastwood character in the Sergio Leone films. He comes from nowhere and goes back to nowhere. This can make for powerful drama.

A character's actions, appearance and what he or she says should suggest indirectly what has happened in the past, and what the effect has been. It is important to show how a character changes in the face of adversity or conflict. People can reveal their true nature through their conflicts. Drama thrives on conflict. The choices the characters make in the drama help them to evolve, and become believable, rounded, human beings.

Flashback is the classic way of revealing back story. On television it can be done using short black and white scenes that resemble grainy documentary, or home video shots. This can heighten the sense of realism. Dialogue is the usual way to fill in back story. TV drama is more wordy than a movie. The small screen favours the close-up, and its use to reveal intimate details. Sometimes a simple jump cut offering scenes from the past can effectively fill in back story. Sometimes TV drama writers, or producers, are too cautious about using filmic time shift devices. The audience is sophisticated and can easily cope with instant changes of time as the *CSI* series have shown. Intimate naturalistic stories set in an everyday situation can be effective and are realistic on television. Television is referred to as an intimate medium. This can lead to a more fulfilling experience for the audience.

STORYBOARD

The important word is *story* not *board*. A storyboard is a very good way to work out the visual structure of a drama. It is not necessary to be good at drawing to make a useful storyboard. Some script writers like to storyboard just one scene to see what it could look like on screen. Stick men and simple cartoon-like designs can show how the plot develops, and whether the characters interact well with the setting and the story. At the production stage a storyboard is a tool to help all members of the production get to work on what the director wants to see on the screen. The director creates the final storyboard as he or she is very much in charge of turning the script into a visual experience. The storyboard should show:

- Cuts, wipes, dissolves and other visual effects that are required for the plot.

- The period of the action, such as whether the film is set in the past or future.

- The approach to the film language, such as suggested camera angles but only if they are necessary to the plot or characterisation.

- It is not necessary to storyboard every single moment of the film, just the significant action.

A storyboard is always a work in progress. It may be reworked many times before it is actually used on the set.

REFERENCES AND FURTHER READING

Hart, C. *Television Programme Making*, Oxford: Focal Press, 1999.
Lewis, I. *Guerrilla TV- Low Budget Programme Making*, Oxford: Focal Press, 2000.
Orlebar, J. *Digital Television Production – A Handbook*, London: Arnold, 2002.
Orlebar, J. *Practical Media Dictionary*, London: Arnold, 2003.

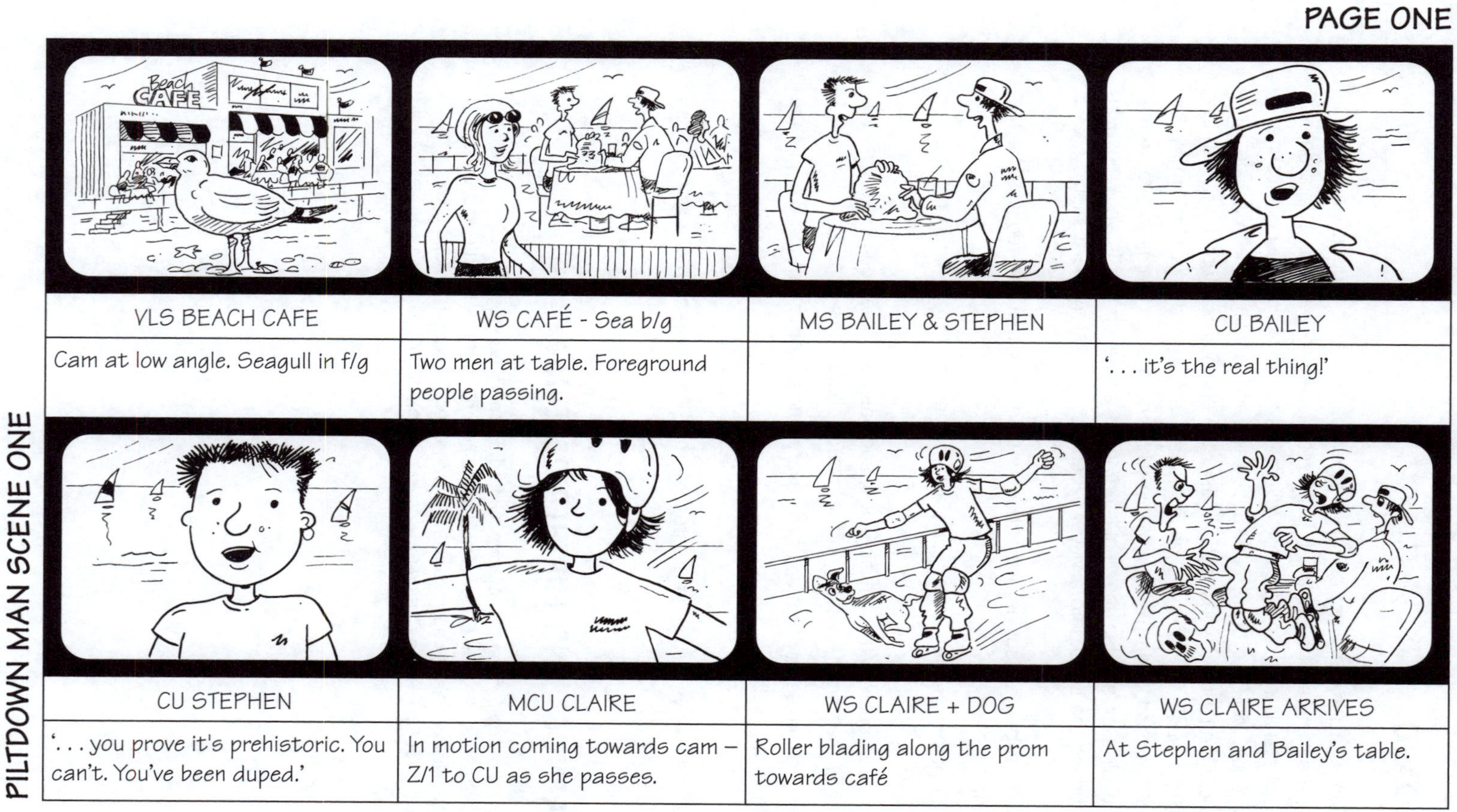

PAGE ONE
PILTDOWN MAN SCENE ONE
Beach CAFE
VLS BEACH CAFE
Cam at low angle. Seagull in f/g
WS CAFÉ - Sea b/g
Two men at table. Foreground people passing.
MS BAILEY & STEPHEN
CU BAILEY
'. . . it's the real thing!'
CU STEPHEN
'. . . you prove it's prehistoric. You can't. You've been duped.'
MCU CLAIRE
In motion coming towards cam – Z/1 to CU as she passes.
WS CLAIRE + DOG
Roller blading along the prom towards café
WS CLAIRE ARRIVES
At Stephen and Bailey's table.

FIGURE 15.3
Example of a storyboard

CHAPTER 16

Crime drama

CRIME DRAMA

Ideologies of good and evil are at the heart of traditional TV crime drama. The police are seen to uphold hegemonic values of society where crime should be seen not to pay. Some episodes of crime dramas, especially US series such as *The Wire*, explore counter-cultural attitudes within the police team. Others deal with tensions concerning policing methods where this ideology can be seen to be strained. The ethics of a utilitarian approach by the police (the outcome of any situation will be for the best possible outcome to society as a whole) can conflict with aspects of human rights issues.

Popular and well-produced recent UK police dramas encode the ideologies of the period in which they are produced. This can be seen in the decade hopping *Ashes to Ashes* and its forerunner *Life on Mars* (BBC). In both series a plot device allows the audience to see the same characters as they are now, and as they were a generation ago. The clothing codes and the changes in language are the keys in anchoring the different periods in *Life on Mars*, which are the twenty-first century and the 1970s. Ideologies of the 1970s include tougher policing with less rules and regulations, allowing non-uniformed police to behave in a 'maverick' manner at times. Policing methods are seen to be different between the two eras. It was not until 1973 that women were integrated directly into the main police force.

Ashes to Ashes (BBC April 2009) is, similarly, a two generation cop crime series set in the 1980s and the twenty-first century. A major appeal of this series is nostalgia. Produced by independent production company Kudos Film and Television, *Ashes to Ashes* uses postmodern self-reflexivity and nostalgia to attract a wide audience. It is a hybrid genre of cop drama with some time travel. The protagonist, Gene Hunt, known to be rather misogynistic in *Life on Mars,* he is paired here with feisty DCI Alex Drake. The series builds on the 'buddy cop' tradition seen in police series such as *Starsky and Hutch*, *Bergerac* and *The Sweeney*.

However, British crime series are not faring well against the high production values and carefully created entertainment culture of US crime dramas such as the CSI franchise. In 2010, ITV's long-running police series *The Bill* finally ended, and *Law and Order: UK* has taken over its role as the ITV flagship regular crime series. The BBC trialled an interesting new high-octane postmodern crime drama *Luther*. It is the first major drama series to have its eponymous hero played by a black actor. DCI John Luther, played by British actor Idris Elba, is familiar from his role as 'Stringer' Bell, the drug lord with business acumen in *The Wire*. In this psychological crime drama the strong-man maverick detective John Luther is brought back into the serious crime unit because he is intuitively capable of solving difficult crimes. Luther has paid a heavy price for his dedication and has recently suffered a mental breakdown. On his return to duty, Luther struggles to balance the psychological demands of his work at the same time as trying to save his marriage to his wife, Zoe.

Neil Cross, the creator of John Luther, looked for inspiration to the most famous detective of all, Sherlock Holmes, to give Luther 'some of that disinterested analytical genius'. This is Luther's ability to engage with horrific crimes such as the murder of three women in episode three and remain detached from the emotional side. This is so that he can concentrate on thinking through how the killer worked and how he can be caught. Cross wanted Luther to have emotional complexity and moral ambiguity: 'combining deductive brilliance and moral passion in one man could make for a powerful and damaged deeply heroic character'.

This type of densely observed lead character with a strong back story is new to British crime drama. The series was relatively successful with an average midweek audience of 3.61 million, but it did attract criticism for going outside the boundaries of conventional TV cop series and for some visceral violence. It was perhaps just too original, although another series has been commissioned. The left-field main female character, the mysterious Alice, enthrallingly played by Ruth Wilson, led the drama into unknown territory that was as dangerous as it was engrossing.

This series provoked serious discussion on BBC websites and in the *Radio Times* about violence in police dramas. One *Radio Times* correspondent wrote: 'I didn't watch *Luther* because my suspicion was it would be yet another helping of misogynist violence.' Another agreed: 'I was so disturbed by the opening of 18 May's *Luther* I actually had to leave the room . . . there are just too many dramas that show women being terrorised, raped, mutilated, and murdered by men' (*Radio Times* 2010).

It is clear that audiences are uneasy about sadistic violent acts against women in television dramas. Writers seem to continually make young women the victims of increasingly depicted sadistic violence by men. BBC drama controller Kate Harwood was asked to comment on the violence in *Luther* and said: 'It is not by a long shot the most violent crime drama on television.' Nevertheless most of the female victims die brutal and violent deaths at the hands of men – why?

It may have all started with the naked female body found in the Thames at the beginning of Dennis Potter's award-winning 1980s TV series *The Singing Detective*.

CRIME DRAMA FORMATS

The format for *Luther* is known as the *inverted detective story*, which is less familiar than the 'whodunit' of the typical TV crime drama. The inverted format works by showing exactly how the detective hero catches the criminal. An inverted detective story, also known as a *'howcatchem'*, starts with the crime actually happening or being described, and usually includes the identity of the criminal. The narrative unfolds following the detective's attempt to solve the mystery and catch the criminal. This format is inverted because it is the opposite of the more typical 'whodunit', where all of the details of the crime and the perpetrator are not revealed until the story's climax. This is the classic Agatha Christie format of the *Poirot* stories and most television detective drama series such as ITV's *Midsomer Murders*.

British detective story writer R. Austin Freeman claimed to have invented the inverted detective story in his 1912 collection of short stories *The Singing Bone*:

> Some years ago I devised, as an experiment, an inverted detective story in two parts. The first part was a minute and detailed description of a crime, setting forth the antecedents, motives, and all attendant circumstances. The reader had seen the crime committed, knew all about the criminal, and was in possession of all the facts ... the second part, which described the investigation of the crime, had to most readers the effect of new matter.
>
> (Freeman 1973)

CRIME DRAMA CODES AND CONVENTIONS

Television crime/cop dramas seek to anchor the representations of police officers as 'believable' characters, with 'realistic' plot lines, and locations in a recognisable urban locale. In US crime series the location can differentiate the series, e.g. *CSI: New York* and *NCIS: Los Angeles*.

In general we can say that crime dramas:

- are constructed realities
- depict constructed versions of reality that appeal to audiences

- encode hegemonic values and ideologies

- represent current, past and future societal responses to crime

- use formulaic structures

- depend on strong characterisation

- employ some stereotypical representations

- make iconic use of gadgets, mobile phones, hand guns, cars, banks, police and explosions

- put the reconstruction of realism at the forefront of their appeal to audiences, particularly in their use of colloquial language

- achieve closure at the end of each episode.

As audiences become more sophisticated so intertextual references and ironic associations with previous crime series increasingly become part of crime drama scenarios. *Life on Mars* showed that audience memories of previous television series last over generations, helped by YouTube clips and DVD box sets.

REPRESENTATIONS

TV crime dramas have ongoing characters who slowly evolve over time, as in a soap opera. Main characters develop slowly and change very little. This is part of the attraction as an audience get to know each main character and see how each character interacts with new and other long-running characters. A typical television crime drama includes four main types of representation:

- Police officers, agents or a special crime solver with fallible human characteristics.

- Ordinary, usually innocent, characters who are victims of crime.

- Damaged or scarred human beings who become caught up in crime, or with police officers.

- Out and out villains seeking unlawful financial gain, revenge, power or sexual domination.

Police officers, victims and villains tend to have stereotypical characteristics. *CSI* revolves around the interaction between the scientifically expert agents and their bosses. These characters are carefully modelled on 'real' three-dimensional people with detailed back stories. Their audience appeal is based on characteristics such as being affable human beings, being highly competent, having an ethical sense of duty, and a touch of legitimate heroism, as well as the 'tough cop–soft cop' representations common in US crime dramas. A victim could be a teenage mother involved in drugs, or an older man who is attacked in his jewellery shop or an older woman terrorised by estate gangs. Victims are there to serve the variety of plot lines. The focus is nearly always on how the police or the agents solve the crime not on how they handle the victim and the victim's situation.

NARRATIVE

An episode narrative typically homes in on the human characteristics of each member of the team to show how a particular character deals with a particular situation. A well-constructed plot line allows a main character to work through a situation to new growth and maturity. Most plots centre on:

- whodunit narrative, or inverted narrative
- how a police officer or agent deals with a horrific crime scene (e.g. badly mutilated body found in a field)
- tension between the uniformed officers and the plain clothes detectives while unravelling a difficult situation
- tension in a police officer's private life.

In crime drama series there is always closure at the end of each episode – the appeal to audiences is how this is achieved or why this outcome is as it is.

Sophisticated series such as *The Wire* and the British crime drama *Luther* are multi-episodic, where the plot is spread over several episodes. Closure is held back to allow the man characters to develop, and increase viewer gratification, which can achieve higher ratings. Some plots include unusual twists or complex multi-stranded plot lines often with a 'relationship' element.

In British TV crime drama, plots depict ordinary 'realistic' events and issues such as are found in newspaper reports from court hearings. In this sense the narrative can have intertextual references (*Ashes to Ashes*) but in regular series such as *Law and Order: UK* the strong focus on realism precludes any ironic or postmodern references to other fictional texts.

The whodunit is for many audiences the most seductive and engaging plot device. Virtually all crime dramas work by posing and resolving a question. The whodunit makes its dramatic question absolutely explicit, and the quest to find the answer is the job of the protagonist. The audience is encouraged to actively participate in the piecing together of the puzzle in a manner that is not possible with many genres. The satisfaction felt by the audience in reaching the solution before the television detective or team of agents is a much appreciated source of entertainment.

CASE STUDY

US crime drama *NCIS* and *CSI*

Both series are ongoing, approximately forty-four minutes running time, and currently aired in the UK on Channel Five, and other digital channels.

The very popular global drama franchises *NCIS* and *CSI* emanate from the US quality television stable. They are both police-style procedural crime series and globally attract large audiences. *CSI, Crime Scene Investigation*, has two spin-offs – *CSI: New York* and *CSI: Miami* and both are also rating successes.

NCIS is an acronym for Naval Criminal Investigative Service, so the US Navy and Marine Corps are involved offering a military rather than police dimension. In 2009, *NCIS* spawned a new integrated spin-off, *NCIS: Los Angeles*, which features the special agents of the NCIS working undercover. The lead characters are played by Chris O'Donnell and, to create a younger audience profile, former rap artist LL Cool J, who says:

> We're maintaining the same wit, the same humour, the same banter as the original, but the undercover aspect gives us a bit of flexibility. The audiences fall in love with characters and that's what we're trying to do – develop characters that people can relate to and have fun with, and want to tune in to every week.
>
> (Bowes 2009)

These well made glossy productions with high production values air in every continent. They epitomise the type of television that the US TV/film industry produces using the expertise, production skills and actual studios of the film industry to create a premier television product with multi-media spin-offs. *CSI* was renewed for an eleventh season in May 2010. *CSI*'s worldwide audience was estimated to be over 73.8 million viewers in 2009. Produced by US network CBS, these crime drama scripts are intelligently conceived involving topical issues such as immigration, or sectarian violence in Iraq, and sharply observed, with realistic crime setups and snappy dialogue. They are deliberately produced to be easily dubbed into other languages. Representations of characters are carefully balanced over the whole series to cover a wide variety of racial and social types. Older silver-haired 'wise' men offer advice to young gung-ho rookie agents. Empowered educated women lead teams and dictate events through knowledge and acumen. Each main character has a forensic speciality.

C@SE STUDY

The structure of these crime dramas is formulaic and ideally suited to commercial television one hour slots. A typical episode of *NCIS* starts with a dramatic crime, such as a modern-style terrorist bomb blast in a city centre. We see the explosion then we see the follow up, with perhaps two agents lost. The team work together looking for forensic evidence which is then analysed in the laboratory. Modern science is used to detect criminals and unpick crimes. This is the classic detective story narrative arc but with agents employing hi-tech forensic science instead of Sherlock Holmes using his magnifying glass. After the initial cinematically filmed crime event the story of why it happened and who is responsible unfolds in forensic labs, the mortuary or other realistic locations.

US TV likes to film in sound studios with realistic sets. There is of course a strong tradition of making realistic movies in studios. *CSI* contains graphic portrayals of body injuries, blood spray patterns, organ damage and big close-ups of forensic evidence, such as fingerprints from unusual places. This attention to visceral corporeal detail gives audiences the sense of being medically involved and enabled.

Realism is created through knowledge of the characters over each series and the apparent credibility of the plot lines. A speciality of the series is the way difficult forensic observations, analysis and conclusions are shown to the audience through scenes where the internal workings of the body are depicted in animated recreations. These animations puncture the realism of the every-day working lives represented by the agents, and give these dramas a postmodern varnish that appeals to educated audiences.

The **media language** is what is now standard postmodern. Big close-ups of the main characters are mixed with steadicam moving sequences and edited with speeded up sections, flashbacks and hi-tech graphics and animation. Slightly soft images give a 'filmic look' to certain scenes. The overall 'washed out' look of the morgue scenes and the heavy use of corporeal details emphasises the tactile pseudo-realism of these dramas. This contrasts with some episodes where fantasy intrudes and characters are seen to come back to life in the morgue and comment on events. These fantasy sequences offer a welcome break from the hard-core realism, and push the shows even more towards a postmodern take on crime drama. This seems to be appreciated by loyal audiences who are used by now to everything from the magical realism of *Desperate Housewives*, where the narrator is apparently speaking from the dead, to the nuanced supposed authenticity of narratives like the *Da Vinci Code*.

The dialogue between agents can resemble a court-room battle which is clearly intended to appeal to TV audiences of court-room dramas. Pace and timing are perfectly managed for the small screen to fit in with ad breaks and hold back the denouement. From the beginning these crime dramas realised the importance of creating fully rounded characters of considerable depth with back stories and contemporary characteristics. The scripts create dramatic conflict out of the interaction of the characters rather than through artificial plot devices.

In *CSI* we are asked to believe in and care about the investigators. We are asked to believe in them as ordinary people fighting difficult and almost impossible situations for the good of society. These, however, are not heroic characters but realistic competent professionals going about their daily tasks.

The underlying ideology of forensic orientated crime drama is to secure the audience's confidence in the judiciary and government system that trains professionals to succeed in combating crime. It is unlikely that a modern active audience are actually affected by this ideology but it may help the audience feel-good factor. *CSI* has been criticised by police and lawyers in the US, who feel the show portrays an inaccurate image of how police solve crimes.

This type of quality US drama is accepted by audiences throughout the world for its entertainment value, and for interesting character relationships and relevant narratives. Some theorists suggest that these long-running crime dramas not only reinforce US social and capitalist values for a home audience, but they also export these US values to many second world audiences. Most audiences will instinctively feel this is a chimera and care only about the entertaining characters, humorous dialogue and intriguing plot lines.

The postmodern ethos of the shows is apparent by the retro title music which for all three *CSI* series is by The Who, and taken from early albums. Roger Daltry made a special appearance in one episode, ironically named 'Living Legend'. Both NCIS and the CSI franchise are globally popular as DVD boxed sets and will no doubt feature on the new TV/internet streamed pay-per-view services offered by Apple and Google. These expensive crime dramas are more than just another cop show. They show up some of the less satisfying, less expensively produced and more homely British cop series such as *The Bill* and must be one reason why it has recently demised. Shows like the BBC's *Luther* are an attempt to create British quality crime drama, which may succeed. Although British broadcasters still seem reluctant to commission long-running series of twenty-six weeks or more as the USA does.

C@SE STUDY

Key point

'US television (crime) dramas have evolved into an art form which explores both the inner psyche and the social world continuously but discretely, so that each fragment contains the fractal beauty of the whole' (Jukes 2009).

REFERENCES AND FURTHER READING

Bowes, Peter. 'NCIS Franchise Reaches Los Angeles', 23 October 2009.
BBC News, Los Angeles: http://news.bbc.co.uk/1/hi/entertainment/8320893.stm.
BBC: http://news.bbc.co.uk/1/hi/entertainment/8320893.stm.
BBC: http://www.bbc.co.uk/blogs/tv/2010/04/introducing-luther-with-love-t.shtml
Freeman, R.A. 'The Art of the Detective Story' in *The Best Dr. Thorndyke Detective Stories*, New York: Dover, 1973.
Jukes, Peter. *Prospect magazine*, 21 October 2009, Issue 164:
    http://www.prospectmagazine.co.uk/2009/10/why-britain-cant-do-the-wire/.
Radio Times, 1–7 May 2010.

Part 6

Practical programme making

CHAPTER 17

Production kit

THE CAMERA

The acquisition of moving pictures and sound for television is now entirely digital. A video camera records in a digital domain, and this digital information is stored in a digital tape format such as DV or DVCAM, or on hard disc, or on a memory card. Virtually all programmes are now made in HD (High Definition) widescreen formats recorded with a resolution of 1080 lines. Professional cameras can record pictures and sound onto a 240GB (or smaller) internal hard disk or external SDXC, SDHC or SD memory card media. A typical video camera for under £900 can record in HD on to a 32GB internal solid state memory or an external memory card giving approximately twelve hours of HD recording. Many news organisations still use the DVCAM or the mini DV tape format because of its robust qualities and easy transfer to editing on Apple's Final Cut Pro, which is the preferred software for most companies. To take steady, well-framed pictures a camera needs a good-quality tripod. Spare batteries are required for the video camera, and a charger to keep them topped up ready for use.

SOUND

A good-quality microphone is essential, and standard camera kits include a rifle mic with hairy wind protector. Professionals do not use the mic built into the video camera except in exceptional circumstances. The pictures are of course important but good sound is equally vital to a well-produced programme, and equally difficult to get just right.

FIGURE 17.1
HD camera

FIGURE 17.2
Sound recordist with rifle microphone with windshield and a hand microphone

A simple interview can be recorded by a cameraman with a lapel radio mic. For anything more complicated a sound recordist should be employed. The sound recordist will have a portable sound mixer, and a variety of microphones that are selected to suit the situation. Television productions are all made in stereo sound which is recorded with the pictures. Factual programmes and news typically employ a rifle mic such as a Sennheiser. This is a directional mic. It is pointed at the sound source, such as a person's mouth, and picks up clear, high-quality sound with little unwanted background noise. Many news and current affairs crews use this as their standard mic.

Personal, or lapel, mics are also used, especially for interviews. The mic is clipped onto an interviewee's shirt collar, and can be plugged straight into the camera. Radio mics are also popular. A radio mic is similar to a personal mic but, instead of a cable, has a small transmitter pack that is hidden in a back pocket, or attached to a belt. The camera can be fitted with a small receiver that picks up the sound from the radio mic. The sound recordist will have receivers for radio mics that are plugged into his or her portable sound mixer, or the camera can have a wireless receiver attached at the back. Any overlapping dialogue required by the script or the director, is achieved by revoicing the dialogue in the sound dubbing suite. This allows complete control in postproduction as each voice can be on a separate track.

THE RIGHT MIC

There are several types of mic that do different jobs in different situations. The following three types most commonly used in television production for location filming:

- rifle mic, hand-held or at the end of a boom/fish pole
- radio personal or lapel mic
- stick mic as used by a presenter.

Rifle mic

A rifle mic is a very useful all purpose mic that can be used in just about any location – for example a Sennheiser MKH416 or similar. These mics are directional, and, as the name suggests, you point the barrel of the mic towards the sound source. Rifle mics are very sensitive to handling and wind noise. The mic can be protected by mounting it in a cradle that allows you to handle and move it without getting 'mic rattle'. The cradle is then put inside a plastic basket windshield to reduce wind noise. The basket can be further protected with a long-haired cover, which makes it ideal for exterior shoots. The rifle mic has many advantages:

- It can be used in a variety of situations.
- It is light and easy to handle.
- It is usually already rigged and therefore immediately available for action.
- It is often preferred for interviews because it is a directional mic and, if used in the correct way, can lose a lot of the extraneous sounds that can spoil a good interview.

Radio personal mic

A personal or lapel mic is a small clip-on mic that can be attached to a shirt, lapel or collar or hidden under a necktie or attached with sticky tape. This type of mic is often fitted with a radio transmitter which is very useful for presenters or contributors moving around within range of the radio mic – usually about fifty metres.

- Personal radio mics are prone to handling noise from body movement or rubbing against clothing. Synthetic fibres may be particularly tricky and can even set up a static charge that affects the mic.
- They are omni-directional and can be rigged pointing up or down.
- A radio mic is entirely dependent on its batteries, and it is essential to use the best alkaline batteries to power radio mics and to change them regularly.

Stick mic

A presenter who wants to talk to contributors or do a piece to camera often uses a stick mic. This is a robust, hand-held mic that does not 'rattle' and is linked to the camera by a strong cable or by a wireless link. It looks the business on camera and the radio mic version can be used by the presenter in all types of moving situations.

FILM LIGHTING KIT

A basic film lighting kit is three or four film lights known as 'red heads' that fit snugly with their stands into a suitcase-type box for portability. A red head is an 800 watt tungsten lamp which is mounted on an adjustable stand. It can be used in a 'flood' position to light a wide area, or in a 'spot' position to focus the light on a smaller area. This is a powerful light and it gets very hot. Operators use heat resistant gloves when adjusting the light. Each light comes with barn doors – four metal flaps that are attached to the front of the light to control the spillage of light into unwanted areas.

There are many types of film lights available from a small 'dink' to a huge several kilowatt 'brute' for large film sets. A standard light that has been used for many years is a 'blonde'. This is an adjustable two kilowatt lamp that makes a very good key light for most occasions. It is, however, a heavy lamp that takes a lot of power. Using a light-weight digital camera the camera operator looks for compact portable lamps. A manufacturer that has won an academy award for technical achievement is Kino Flo. Their equivalent of a blonde is a Diva-lite 400 which is small and very efficient.

A Dedolight kit is an ideal easy-to carry lighting kit to hire. This is a modern light that stays sharp and even across the spread of the beam. It works well with a video camera and is compact, practical, powerful, easy to mount and move, and uses less energy than conventional lights.

CHAPTER 18

Framing and shot size

IMPORTANCE OF FRAMING AND SHOT SIZE

Television programmes of all types utilise framing and shot size as tools to tell the story, illuminate the characters' feelings, refresh the action and develop the tension of the narrative. For a scripted drama the creative use of these tools is essential for a quality production. The way a shot is framed and the selection of shot size should not interfere with, but enhance, how the viewer is experiencing the framed constructed reality of the drama.

The way a shot is framed – where the subject is within the frame, and the size of the shot – the size of the subject within the frame, inform and effect our perception of the person being interviewed or the character in a drama. Shot size and lens selection can make the subject look dominating, powerful, or defeated and downtrodden. It can also make the subject look interesting, involving and the sort of person the viewer would like to talk to, confide in and relate to. This is a basic tenet of the visual grammar of television programme making. It can be adhered to or discarded, but without the visual framework of careful framing and intelligent shot selection television lacks impact and coherence.

Some aspirational TV programmes, particularly for young people, are so concerned about the attention span of their viewers that they define content by style. The interviewing style revels in a postmodern approach of non-traditional shot sizes and camera angles. The out of focus shot, the constantly moving camera, the canted angle, the extreme close-up, the crash zoom, are the over-used visual vocabulary of the ultra-cool programme. Where there is little substance, a lot of style keeps the eye on the screen. For a programme offering real substance the more traditional use of the camera allows the content to reach the viewer.

VISUAL GRAMMAR – SHOT REVERSE SHOT

This is the basic sequence in classical continuity narrative construction. For example, shots of two characters engaged in dialogue will favour first one and then the other. The camera will frame on one person facing camera right and on the other facing camera left. Camera right and left means from the camera's POV.

When these shots are edited together it appears that the two characters are interacting. The audience read the alternation as a link between the two people, even if they were not actually together when the shots were filmed.

There are important things to consider when setting up this structure. First the eye lines of the two characters must match. If one character is standing up then the other character's eye line has to be looking upwards towards the standing character. Their eyes should engage with each other, or appear to do so. Also the shot size should match, so that each character's shot is the same as the other. A change of shot size should be motivated by the dialogue in a drama, or what is said in an interview.

FIGURE 18.1
Shot reverse shot

SHOT SIZE

A selection of shot sizes has developed that fit the TV frame naturally. These standard shot sizes help the viewer deconstruct the image. Used sympathetically they do not come between the viewer and the content. Shot size is more than punctuation. It indicates emotion, content and point of view. There are standard shot sizes that are conventionally used in all forms of television programme making. These sizes fit the 16:9 widescreen TV frame naturally and can be edited together to make visual sense of the content.

Shot sizes are labelled according to how a person is seen in the frame, when looking through the viewfinder of a camera. The camera is placed on a tripod, and the lens is set up at the level of the eye-line of the subject. In television shot sizes are known by their abbreviations.

VBCU (Very Big Close-up) or (ECU Extreme Close-up) Fills the screen with just part of the face of a person. This can be the mouth, or one eye, or both eyes in a typical Sergei Leone shot.

BCU (Big Close-up) The face fills the frame, cutting off some of the forehead or part of the chin, or both. This shot aims to capture depth of feeling and the subject's inner emotional state. Often used when a person is recounting a tragic or important event that has had a profound effect on his or her life.

CU (Close-up) The person's face with the bottom of the frame along the line of the shoulders, just below the knot of a tie.

MCU (Medium Close-up) The most common shot in factual television and news programmes. Shows a person's head and shoulders but not the waist. The bottom of the frame runs along the top of the pocket on a man's shirt.

MS (Medium Shot or Mid Shot) Shows the top half of a person's body. Cuts off at the waist for a person who is standing up or sitting down. Typical shot for a news reader at a desk.

MLS (Medium Long Shot) Typically used for a person standing up. The bottom of the frame is around the knees.

LS (Long Shot) Shows a person in full length, including the feet.

VLS (Very Long Shot) Shows the person or people quite small in the frame, with more dominance given to their relationship with the setting.

ELS (Extreme Long Shot) A very long and wide shot usually of a place but can contain presenters, taken from a long distance away, often from a helicopter or crane. Typically used as an establishing shot, or to note an extreme change a location. Used more in fictional programmes.

WS (Wide Shot) A wide angle of the subject(s) clearly showing the context of a scene and the setting.

Shots are also described by the number of people they contain. Two people in the frame is a TWO SHOT. Three people in the frame is a THREE SHOT, and so on. Movement of the camera alters a shot. The camera can move closer or further way from the subject. The camera may be on tracks or on a wheeled pedestal or a dolly. A camera can move sideways while keeping the subject in shot. This is a **crab shot**. Moving a camera from left to right or vice versa is a **pan**. The pan should be used sparingly and works best for landscape shots where there is a definite beginning point and ending point. Moving the camera lens but keeping the camera in the same position – on a tripod for example – is a ZOOM IN or ZOOM OUT.

FIGURE 18.2
Mid close-up (MCU) and wide shot – guardsmen in Hyde Park

FRAMING

Framing is an important element in the way realism is assessed by the viewer. The director wants the viewer to see a coherent complex of visual signals. These will assist the viewer in interpreting not only the plot and characters but the many other elements that make up a complex narrative. These range from the period that the story is set in to the psychological persona of the characters. This is the *mise-en-scène*.

Framing makes a great difference to the meaning of a shot. Most TV productions use the standard shot sizes when framing a scene. The increasing use of steadicam in drama productions and a natural tendency to break out of the conventions can lead to imaginative framing. There are some basic rules that viewers subconsciously use to deconstruct a scene. The viewer will be able to see who is dominant in a scene by the way the director sets up and frames each shot. Where characters are placed in the frame is crucial to their relationship to each other. A character who is dominant in the frame will typically be camera right, and showing a full face, or more of the face, than the other character who is less dominant. As the relationship changes in the scene so the other character will become larger in the frame, and/or move to the right side of the frame. This can be done by various means:

- Editing – cut to the reverse shot at a different angle.
- The character physically moves round the other character to a dominant position.
- The camera tracks round to put the dominant character in the most dominant position in the frame.
- The camera zooms in to a CU of the dominant character. (Rather too crude for most directors.)

FRAMING AND SHOT SIZE EXAMPLE

A young woman confronts her boss at work over fraud and corruption in the company. The framing will tell the viewer a lot about what is going on which will be reinforced by the dialogue.

Shot 1: long shot. The scene begins with the young woman walking into a long room. The camera is placed in the doorway so she walks past it and towards the boss, who is seated at a large imposing desk at the end of the room. As she walks towards him in a long shot the audience senses her insecurity and lack of power.

Shot 2: two shot low angle. She reaches the desk and she starts to confront the boss. The framing needs to show that she has some power, but is not yet dominating the boss. The low angle two shot from behind and to the side of her shows her back view just dominating the right half of the frame, with the seated boss in the left of the frame. We see his face and not hers so she is still in a subordinate position.

The boss starts to assert some authority and gets up in the shot. He is larger in the frame, and the woman appears to be losing the argument.

Shot 3: close-up photos in folder framed at an angle. She opens a folder and puts onto the desk a sequence of photographs of the boss with a girl in a nightclub.

Shot 4: close-up of woman framed right. The close-up of the woman on the dominant right of the screen shows her looking straight at the boss. She is now fully in control.

Shot 5: two shot. The next shot is a two shot from behind the desk with the man sitting down at the desk, and the woman with her face towards camera. She delivers a line of dialogue, turns round and walks towards the door.

Shot 6: long shot. The last shot is a mirror image of the first. She is walking back down the room towards the camera. The camera sees her face and body getting larger within the frame and the boss looking smaller at the desk. She has made her point.

CAMERA ANGLE

Shots are also described by the position of the camera in relation to normal eye level. This is the camera angle. If the camera is positioned at eye level the person in the frame is looking not quite directly at the audience. Low-angle or high-angle shots each create a specific effect. With the camera placed lower than the eye line the effect is to give the impression of the character being dominant and powerful. This is deployed most successfully by Leni Riefenstahl in her 1935 film *Triumph of the Will*, showing the power of Hitler at the Nuremberg rally.

If the camera is placed high above the eye line and looks down on the character the viewer senses an increased sense of vulnerability in the character. To get the camera really low down a special 'baby legs' tripod is used. A director will use the camera angle to suggest a variety of emotions. The canted or angled camera in Hollywood *film noir* of the 1930s and 1940s suggested to the viewer that the character in this particular scene was not to be trusted, or that something untoward or even evil was happening. In Dennis Potter's TV series *The Singing Detective* the main character Philip Marlowe is an author and he lies in a hospital bed with his consciousness slipping in and out of the thriller he is writing. This mental transition is effected visually by the camera rotating slowly in vision. The close-up of the author/patient becomes a heavily canted angle close-up, leading the viewer to realise that in his mind he is now Philip Marlowe the detective writer. The picture then cuts to the time and period of the thriller.

Other shots labelled by the position of the camera include the top shot. The camera is placed high on a crane to look down on the action in a drama. A top shot can be from a remote camera attached to a blimp in the sky to give a very high angle shot of a cricket match. As cameras have become smaller so they can be fixed almost anywhere. A top shot from a camera fixed overhead in the ceiling adds visual variety to a sequence and may suggest a slightly voyeuristic viewpoint. A top shot can be startling or extremely dramatic. Attached to the top of the mast of a yacht in a storm it can give a view of the boat below that can almost induce nausea. *Top Gear* put very small cameras in all sorts of unlikely places in cars and other locations to get a very wide variety of different shot size and angles.

CAMERA MOVEMENT

Camera movement is a creative tool used in many television programmes. There are two sorts. There is the vertical movement of a static camera known as a tilt up or down, or the horizontal movement of the static camera known as a pan. The whip (very fast) pan has become overused in factual television as a tool to increase the pace of a sequence and apparently hold the viewer's attention. It often ends up annoying the viewer and punctuating the smooth flow of the show.

The second form of camera movement is to move the camera itself. This is done on a track, or with a dolly, and the movement can be from side to side or in or out. A movement sideways is a crab which is common in music programmes. The whole camera moves in or out or around the subject. A tracking shot that moves in to a subject maintains the relationship of the subject to the background. In a zoom-in shot where only the lens is turned, the background changes and goes out of focus making the subject appear to come towards the viewer. A camera track-in allows the viewer to approach the subject and maintain the same relationship with it. A camera track can alter the point of view of the viewer, as the camera movement can reflect the dialogue and change in dominance within a scene.

Camera movements are most effective when suggested by the content or information within a scene, or activity. This is known as a motivated camera move as it follows an action or is prompted by an event within the scene. For example:

- A pan will follow a presenter as she walks across the set to another contributor.
- A track will follow two characters as they walk along a path chatting together.
- A track round two seated characters begins with a two shot to show how the meeting is balanced. The camera moves round to a single shot showing that this character has now become the dominant force in the scene or the instigator of the next action.

To affect a tracking shot the camera needs to be mounted on a dolly, or a crane, or in a TV studio on a pedestal. A dolly is any suitable wheeled mounting for a camera. A crane is a counterweighted, long metal arm with a flexible camera mounting that can be raised and moved either by hand or remotely. Jimmy Jib is the popular name for a camera crane with a multidirectional camera. An operator at ground level using a small monitor and joystick controls the camera remotely.

STEADICAM

The most popular mounting for modern TV productions is now the steadicam. This is a TV camera mounting system where the camera is attached to the operator with a harness. This allows the operator to move or run with the camera and shoot the scene with virtually no camera shake or sideways movement. The operator frames the scene using a small monitor located at waist level. The steadicam offers great flexibility, is able to film on any surface that the operator can walk on and is able to offer superb camera angles from the actor's point of view. Traditionally this shot was accomplished by a hand-held camera giving a hand-held wobbly effect noticeable in documentaries, where it has the caché of suggesting authenticity.

FIGURE 18.3
Steadicam

CROSSING THE LINE

This is a phrase you will hear quite often, especially on a television drama set. It refers to an imaginary line that can be drawn between the eyelines of two interacting characters. That line is crossed by moving the camera to the wrong side of one of the characters. What happens is that, for example, the person facing right suddenly faces left, and so does not appear to be looking at or interacting with the other person. The audience will sense discontinuity. Crossing the line while filming say a rugby match can have the team that was playing from left to right suddenly playing from right to left. If the line is crossed then a cutaway can bridge the gap. Another way is have a shot in which a camera movement allows the audience to observe the participants in the scene changing position in relation to each other.

With so much steadicam filming camera movements are often fluid and undefined. The editor has to choose which sections of the shots will cut together in a way that the audience will understand. Similarly, if several shots show a character travelling, say walking down a street, the character must consistently enter camera right and exit camera left, or there will be the impression of reverse or random movement.

POSTPRODUCTION

Framing and shot size are important for postproduction. If a scene is filmed in such a way that there is little or no variety of shots the video editor has a dilemma as the scene will not cut together. To cut from a long shot to another long shot means a jump cut, and this ruins continuity and can make the viewer lose faith in the 'reality' of the scene. This can happen in factual programmes as well as drama.

The editor will talk to the producer or director about how each sequence should be assembled. They might make a rough edit together. Particular attention will be paid to getting pace, meaning and visual integrity out of the material. For a documentary it greatly helps to have transcripts of the interviews. The editor will work on a full rough cut and then discuss this with the producer/director and then create a fine cut. Music will be added and the sound mix will be balanced in a sound dub. Finally the programme will be transferred onto the transmission format of the broadcasting company.

REFERENCES AND FURTHER READING:

Millerson, G. *Television Production*, 13th edn, Oxford: Focal Press, 1999.
Orlebar, J. *Digital Television Production – A Handbook*, London: Arnold, 2002.

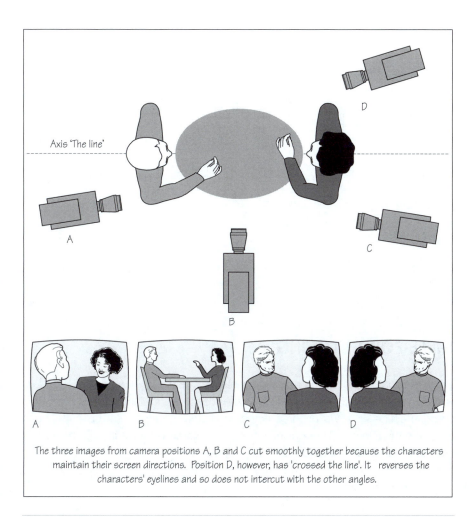

Axis 'The line'

A

B

C

D

A   B   C   D

The three images from camera positions A, B and C cut smoothly together because the characters maintain their screen directions. Position D, however, has 'crossed the line'. It reverses the characters' eyelines and so does not intercut with the other angles.

FIGURE 18.4
Crossing the line

CHAPTER 19

Lighting for television

THREE-POINT LIGHTING

The basic lighting plot for an actor, presenter or contributor in a particular location is the three-point lighting plan. This is the ideal way to light an interview, or a dialogue scene with two or three actors in drama. It can be set up quickly and uses only three lamps. Three-point lighting is so called because it uses three lights from three different points to illuminate a subject:

- the key light
- the fill light
- the back light.

THE KEY LIGHT

The key is the main light to illuminate the face and body of the subject. It is placed in front of the subject, but offset and slightly raised. Looking at people in everyday life we see them lit from above by the sun or in an office by ghastly overhead strip lights, or from the side by light from a window. At home we are more used to seeing our family lit by table lights, sometimes in a pool of light from just one light source in a room.

Three-point lighting is a way of making a subject look three dimensional and as though he or she is lit naturally, in a way that suits the surroundings. Lighting that is seen to be coming principally from the side and is slightly raised typically offers the best and most natural look for an interview.

FIGURE 19.1
Television light – redhead

Imagine that you are going to set up the lights and video an interview with one person who is sitting in an armchair in a domestic room, and looking towards the camera. The key light is set up at an angle to the camera. It should shine into the eyes of the subject, and should be raised above the eye line. The subject will not want to be dazzled. The key light should not be too high, or there will be dark shadows under the eyes. There should not be any highlights or hot spots on the subject. It is possible to use heat proof French tissue type paper, or 'scrim', to tone down the brightness of the light. Pegs or clips hold down the scrim as it is stretched over the film lamp to create a softer light. Hot spots on the face can be toned down with a dab of make-up powder to stop the shine. Over lit subjects do not look as though they are in a naturalistic setting.

The intensity of the light can be altered using the spot/flood adjustment at the back of the lamp. The camera operator will keep looking through the viewfinder to check how the subject looks on camera. The barn doors are used to restrict any spillage from either side of the light. Digital video cameras are very sensitive to light, and work well in low light conditions. It is usually not necessary to flood the set with unnecessary light. It is important, though, to be able to see all the features of the subject's face.

THE FILL LIGHT

The aim of the fill light is to 'fill in' the darker areas that the key light has not reached and to reduce contrast.

The fill light is placed on the other side of the camera to the key, and is as close to the camera as possible The fill light is a soft, diffused light with an intensity that is typically about half that of the key light. By putting scrim (heat proof opaque paper) over a lamp you are effectively increasing the size of the light source and creating a softer light. The camera operator should always check the subject looks 'right' through the viewfinder. If the subject appears to be too bright, the intensity of the light can be reduced by moving it further away from the subject. The aim is to model the face of the subject – this means show the features of nose, eyes and mouth in a flattering way. The fill light should not show up more of the subject's face than the key light. This will not give good modelling of the face.

THE BACK LIGHT

The main purpose of the back light is to create depth and solidity to the appearance of the subject(s) and to give a lighting contrast between foreground and background. This gives a 3D effect, and depth to the picture.

In practice this means illuminating the back of the subject's head and shoulders. This gives a 'glow' or highlight to the hair of the subject, and creates a pleasing effect. The intensity of the back light varies according to the subject. A woman with long black hair needs more light, and a bald man needs less.

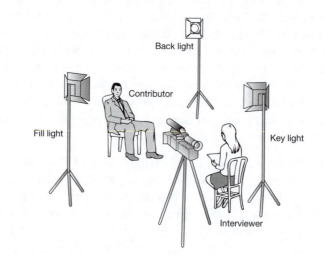

FIGURE 19.2
Three-point lighting

The back light is most effective if placed exactly behind the subject. This may not be possible on location, so a compromise is necessary and it is positioned to one side. The back light should come from the opposite side to the key light. The light can always be made softer with scrim or a light diffuser. The camera operator should check through the viewfinder that the back light is actually creating the desired effect. A helper can be asked to 'flash' the back light – turn it on and off – to see what effect it has. The position of the light can be moved to create greater depth. It is worth checking the difference between each lamp setting on 'flood' and on 'spot'. The barn doors on each light can be repositioned to restrict spillage from the light source.

REFLECTED LIGHT

A reflector is a most useful piece of equipment. It is used to reflect light from the sun, or an artificial light source, onto the subject.

It can be a large piece of white polystyrene, which has to be held with a clip in a lamp stand. More usually camera crews carry a fold-up type reflector that has a white or silver surface on one side, and a gold surface on the other. On an outdoor location where no electricity is available, the reflector can be used to direct sunlight onto the subject's face giving the face a natural lift. A reflected light source gives a naturalistic look to a scene. Reflected light comes from a bigger light source offering softer light.

Sunlight reflector. For exterior scenes a sunlight reflector is often used. This can be a specialist reflector on a stand. These are coated with a reflective white, silver, or gold surface. The gold surface gives a warmer light to create a romantic effect. A reflector is useful as a fill light where the sunlight is providing the key light. If the sunlight is providing back lighting for a sunset shot, then the reflector can 'lift' the face of the subject.

White reflector. A large sheet of white material is held up by a light stand. In India, where they make a large number of movies using the abundant sunlight, you see film workers carrying white stand-mounted reflectors on their backs from one set up to the next – one worker to one reflector. Incidentally, if you see someone carrying a black umbrella on a film set in India, it is not because it is going to rain, but to keep the sun off the director or a star actor. White reflectors can measure two meters by two meters or more. This large reflective area gives a very good soft light source. The white reflector can have a large film light pointed at it to create enough naturalistic reflected light to illuminate a reasonable working area.

Bounce light. This is where an artificial light is reflected back from a white area such as a wall or ceiling in a room, or a reflector, onto an actor or to light a room. A character's face will look rather ill if the wall or ceiling is not pure white.

QUALITIES OF LIGHT

Hard light is direct light from a concentrated source. Direct sunlight is hard light. Sunlight at midday is hard light that casts well-defined shadows. In television, hard light is used to create a sharply defined image, and as a distant light source, such as outside a window, to indicate daylight.

Soft light is diffused or reflected light, as you would find on a cloudy overcast day. Light from the sky is soft light. In television, soft light is useful as a 'fill' light, as it does not create shadows, or to light a whole set. Modern lighting directors tend to go for soft lighting sources to create a more naturalistic look.

To create the most effective television pictures it is useful to know about the qualities of light:

- Light has intensity or brightness. The automatic exposure system in a video camera will react to this quality by changing the aperture (iris). The brighter the light the smaller the aperture and this affects the depth of field.

- Light can be hard, giving shadows, or soft. Generally television prefers soft or diffuse lighting.

- Light creates contrast. This is the relative brightness of the lightest and darkest areas in the frame.

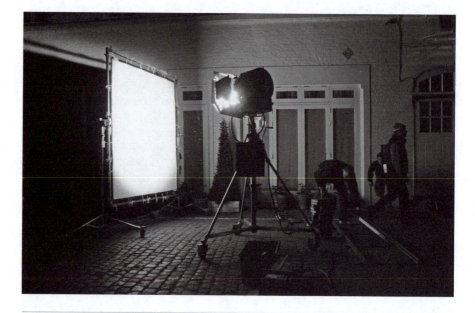

FIGURE 19.3
Night shoot with reflector

- The direction the light is coming from affects how the subject looks.
- The quality of the light is affected by its colour temperature or colour quality.
- An effective way to create good lighting for television is to use soft, diffuse powerful lamps which are carefully positioned for maximum effect.

Lighting cameraman Jonathan Harrison (Broadcast, May 2004) puts it this way: 'Lighting cameramen should try to diminish the depth of field and create layers using light and props, and the considered positioning of your subject. The key is to make your audience focus on the subject of importance in the frame.' For any drama scene he is a great believer in the importance of a recce and in planning ahead. 'Look at the available light sources within the space you'll be filming, and enhance accordingly. Think about your background and perspective and what you'll focus on. Decide in advance on camera positions and what lights you'll use.'

BLUESCREEN

Many factual programmes have a variety of contributors talking about a number of different topics. It can make better television to have control over the visual backgrounds to the interviews. A wildlife expert talking about elephants in India can be videoed against a bluescreen and pictures of elephants added as moving images behind the contributor. Some shows like to have a constantly moving background behind their studio presenters and location contributors. This electronic technique allows one image to be overlaid over part of another image. In TV this technique is known as chromakey, or bluescreen. The bluescreen has to be carefully lit with no shadows to be most effective. The keying that allows two sets of moving pictures to be on screen at the same time is done in the studio by the vision mixer.

An interview can be filmed against a large carefully lit blue sheet, or screen, that can be erected on location, or set up in a studio. Many TV studios have a blue curtain specifically for chromakey work. This blue background is then replaced in postproduction with other moving images relevant to the programme. The very successful BBC factual series *Walking with Dinosaurs* employed CGI extensively. Bluescreen is used in drama productions such as *Doctor Who* (BBC). With this technique actors can walk around futuristic sets, or surf on giant virtual waves without leaving the studio. CGI can be integrated with live action as in the *Lord Of The Rings* films to create startling effects and impressive images.

With bluescreen there is no need to send a reporter to New York to do a story on the Hip-hop clubs – not just for the visuals anyway. She can go into a small studio specially designed for the purpose with all blue floor and walls. Modern sophisticated bluescreen studios allow the director to cut between close-ups and long shots. Carefully selected pictures that have already been shot in New York will replace the blue areas. The reporter will appear actually to be there, in the heart of the city. Hollywood films tend to use green screens, allegedly because so many of the actors wear blue jeans. This technique uses the colour green to act as a key for another set of pictures. Green screen is extensively used in the *Harry Potter* films to facilitate the magic and monsters. An actor wearing blue jeans appearing on television may find his legs dissolve into a scene from somewhere else until the vision mixer sets it up correctly.

LIGHTING FOR DRAMA

The best and most effective lighting for film or television drama is both a science and an art. It takes considerable talent, and many years of experience to understand and know how to 'paint in light'. The possibilities and parameters of High Definition video with its intense detail mean that lighting is a crucial element in the *mise-en-scène* of modern TV drama. Television drama requires a large budget, a dedicated crew and a lot of specialist lights to create the sort of beautiful lighting seen in crime shows like *CSI* (Channel 5), and high-quality period dramas such as *Downton Abbey* (ITV 2010) where each episode cost £1 million.

It is no wonder that the best lighting cameramen, directors of photography (DOP) and cinematographers are in such demand. They can make a television drama look like a million dollars just using light and their camera.

FIGURE 19.4
Location lighting – dedolight

Daylight with the sun shining on a clear day offers full spectrum light that helps create a three-dimensional image on a flat screen. Blue skies mean blue seas, white surf and superb landscape – vistas with depth and clarity. The trouble is if all dramas are set in outstanding landscapes in a sunny climate you would have wall-to-wall westerns.

Not all scenes need a lot of expensive lights to create an effect. A single candle can produce enough light for a modern video camera to record two people at an intimate, romantic candlelit dinner. However, for depth, clarity and 'naturalism' in those pictures, especially those interior scenes, then extra lighting is nearly always needed.

PAINT WITH LIGHT

Lighting can do so much more than just illuminate a scene. It can direct the viewer's attention to a person or object. It can create depth. It can make performers look so much more attractive. Lighting is a wonderful way to create mood and atmosphere. Soft light can be seductive. Harsh light can make an ordinary room into a disturbing and destructive environment with overtones of fear and desolation. Light is the television director's pallet.

The television picture responds well to lighting for depth. Somehow it is more satisfying to watch television pictures that have depth and subtlety. We want to see three-dimensional characters leap out of finely detailed backgrounds straight into our living room. With the advent of 3D this may actually happen. We don't want to see annoying hotspots on faces and foreheads, or nasty shadows on the walls. Above all we want the lighting to help us understand and enjoy the fantasy that has been put on the screen before us. It must not intrude, but it must do its job.

NATURALISM

This is a difficult term that can mean different things to different filmmakers. In lighting it comes from the idea that a scene from a television drama should be lit in a way that recreates a natural situation. One definition might be: naturalism is a look that appears to most people to be something they know and can relate to, because it relates to a scene lit naturally.

Lighting should be subtle for a naturalistic look. Much television drama, such as a soap like *EastEnders* (BBC1), is set in the everyday world of today. The director is attempting to create a recognisable world with characters that would not look out of place in the town where you live. This requires naturalistic lighting.

REFERENCES AND FURTHER READING

Broadcast, May 2004: http://info.broadcastnow.co.uk/?gclid=CJSFtIHQ36cCFUEb4 QodyFxu-g&T=1300709373&JTID=162077356&OGID=67&network=GAW.

Cury, I. *Directing and Producing for Television*, 4th edn, Oxford: Focal Press, 2010.

Millerson, G. and Owens J. *Television Production*, 14th edn, Oxford: Focal Press, 2009.

Orlebar, J. *Digital Television Production – A Handbook*, London: Arnold, 2002.

CHAPTER 20

The television studio

THE TV STUDIO

The television studio is an important part of the TV production process. A TV studio is expensive to run, but it accomplishes a number of objectives in one place and at one time. The essence of a TV studio is that it is a multicamera environment capable of creating whole programmes in one space. Television studios vary in size, availability and complexity of electronic equipment, and what they are capable of doing. Some are able to host a studio audience while others are compact and designed for news bulletins or sports broadcasts.

A TV studio is a sound-proofed area with a flat floor, and a high ceiling where lights can be attached to a grid. There are no exterior windows but interior triple-glazed glass panels that look into the control gallery and sound suite. In a large organisation, like the BBC, some studios have a visitors' area which looks down through glass panels onto the studio floor. In other words this is a vast open space with enormous TV potential.

In the early days of television broadcasting nearly all programmes originated in a TV studio. The studio was television. You could broadcast films as a film or do an outside broadcast. The idea of television was to transmit pictures and sound from a highly controlled live studio to the audience at home. The modern TV studio is now just one element in a vast production process that includes video, hard disc, film, graphics, satellite links, videophone reports, outside broadcasts, online input and the TV studio. At one point in the 1990s, as video camcorders became inexpensive and reliable, some large broadcasting companies thought they could dispense with their studio facilities. This was a false economy as the studio can be the central linking point of a simple or complex production process. Studio production is now back in business although as a leaner and more flexible option for producers.

The sort of programmes that are made successfully and reasonably economically in a multi-camera TV studio vary from chat shows like *The One Show* (BBC1) to glossy light entertainment shows such as *Strictly Come Dancing* (BBC1) and reality/talent shows such as *The X Factor* (ITV1). In the twenty-first century there are virtually no drama productions working in a TV studio. The logistics of drama make it more efficient to film on location and use film studios with sophisticated bluescreen set ups for interiors and other scenes. A film studio is quite different from a TV studio. A film studio, such as the ones at Ealing in west London, is a vast empty sound-proofed space that has to be filled with everything – set, lights, camera and sound kit as well as actors and crew.

A TV studio is also a sound-proofed space but it comes equipped with a minimum of four or five cameras, a sound boom, a sound mixing desk, permanent lighting rig and a vision control gallery for mixing all the video inputs. Even the smallest studios have a vision mixing desk and a sound mixing desk. The studio is cabled up with a computerised lighting rig, sound and vision outlets in the walls cabled to the control gallery, and large doors for easy access for scenery and sets. There is nearby storage for scenery. There are nearby rooms for make up, and a green room for contributors to sit in while waiting to take part in a show. Some studios

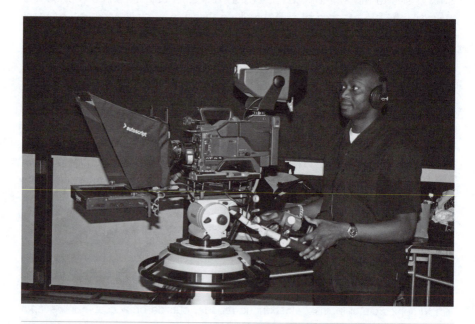

FIGURE 20.1
TV studio camera operator with autocue

are capable of going directly on air; all have facilities for recording the output of the studio onto high-end digital recorders or hard disc.

A TV studio has links to videotape input machines (VT), telecine (TK) which transfers film to video, and sophisticated graphics. In a nutshell a TV studio offers the space and all the technical facilities to make broadcast standard television programmes under one roof. This is its attraction to programme makers.

It is always interesting to look critically at a live TV show coming from a complex studio set up where the highest quality HD pictures and sound are transmitted directly to the viewer. *Later live . . . with Jools Holland* (BBC2) is an excellent example of what can be achieved from one live studio. The studio has four or five bands grouped in a circle around the set with a small audience seated in groups. The presenter moves around the set and introduces each band or talks to audience members. The viewer has the sense of being present in a sophisticated club where there is an intimate relationship with top-class musicians. The fact that they are playing live gives the whole show an edgy excitement which transmits to the viewer. The live studio creates an intense and relaxed space which is ideal for musicians to perform to their best abilities without the distractions often found at outdoor live events.

STUDIO PERSONNEL

On the studio floor

Floor manager (FM) Responsible for everything that happens on the studio floor. He or she is an important member of the studio crew who is responsible for safe and efficient working on the floor. This includes the entire performance area and the audience seating (if appropriate), and camera movement areas. The Floor Manager has two-way communications with the studio gallery, and relays directions from the director to the presenter and other contributors, who are not able to hear talkback from the gallery. He or she is helped by an AFM.

Assistant floor manager (AFM) He or she works to the Floor Manager, and wears headphones to be able to hear talkback from the control gallery. The AFM has a variety of duties including collecting guests and actors from dressing rooms and the green room, and ensuring props are in the right place.

Floor assistant Helps AFM and the Floor Manager. This is a good first job as the Floor Assistant does anything he or she is asked to do, especially greeting guests and contributors in reception and taking them down to the green room. He or she gets artists to the right place at the right time.

Camera supervisor Experienced camera operator in charge of all the camera crew, who typically operates camera 1. He or she advises on difficult shots and camera angles.

Camera operator Part of the camera crew. He or she operates a camera on a pedestal, handheld, or mounted on a crane, and is in constant touch with the director via headphones.

Assistant camera operator Works with a camera operator, helps set up the cameras, holds and carries cables.

Boom operator Operates the sound boom. The boom is part of the sound equipment and is a mobile device for holding a high-quality microphone at the end of a telescopic tube to swing above the cameras, getting the microphone as close as possible to the talent without being in shot. The boom is used less than it used to be, as lapel mics are more flexible.

Autocue/portaprompt operator Operates the prompting equipment that displays the script on a screen in front of the camera. He or she can control the speed, movement and size of the script, slowing down or speeding up according to how the presenter reads.

Set designer Creates and draws up the complex scale architectural plans of the set, and the positioning of all relevant objects on the studio floor known as the Floor Plan. The set is built and then put in place on the studio day under the supervision of the set designer.

Make up Supervises the make up of the presenters and contributors.

Costume The costume designer selects the wardrobe for presenters and supervises the style and design of costume for any actors or contributors.

Stage hands Move scenery and make final adjustments to the set.

The control gallery

The main feature of the control gallery is the very large bank of television monitors arranged across a long wall. In front of this is the vision mixing desk that controls all these vision inputs. The gallery is the bridge of the studio ship. The gallery controls all the activity in the studio. Audio is controlled in an adjacent gallery, or sound suite. The lighting gallery and technical control are nearby.

Director Responsible for the artistic interpretation of the show. He or she calls the shots and generates the energy and drive for the whole studio day. The director writes the studio camera script, and works with the production team to make the best use of the studio. Camera and sound operators, the FM and the AFMs are all able to hear everything the director says in the gallery through the talk-back system – they can if necessary communicate back to the director via their headsets.

Production assistant Sits next to the director in the gallery. She or he has prepared the camera script and running order for the show, and works on the precise timings

FIGURE 20.2
College TV studio

of the show, and keeps continuity notes. This role involves assisting the director in all administrative details leading up to the studio day: booking contributors, checking copyright on music and setting up contracts. It is a busy job – see Profile: TV studio Production assistant.

Vision mixer Operates the vision mixing desk or panel, cuts, mixes, wipes from one visual source to another. The vision mixer works closely with the director, needs a good sense of timing and rhythm, and an ability to work in a sometimes stressful environment. On a large show he or she will work with another vision mixer who sets up and controls the digital video effects (DVE).

Technical manager Oversees all the technical facilities of the studio. This ranges from video source inputs and video recording, to phone lines and OB (outside broadcast) sources. Crucially, he or she is responsible for making sure the show is recorded onto a suitable recording format for transmission or goes out live.

Lighting director Devises the lighting plot for the show in consultation with the director, and set designer. He or she supervises a number of lighting personnel who set up, move and control the many light sources needed on a studio show.

Vision supervisor (racks) Supervises the colour balance and exposure of the cameras, and balances the cameras to give a uniform picture from each camera and other incoming vision sources.

PROFILE

TV studio Production Assistant: Vicky Andrews

Vicky gained work experience as a runner on darts outside broadcasts while she was doing her degree in Media Technology. This sparked an interest in working on live TV programmes, and she honed her skills doing productions in the college's TV studio. On graduation Satanta sports took her on as a trainee PA working on live sports programmes and studio chat shows. After a year's training she moved to Al Jazeera as a studio PA working on four live studios a week. With the World Cup coming up ITV Sport were recruiting studio personnel and Vicky got the job as a fully fledged studio PA working on live World Cup transmissions in South Africa.

FIGURE 20.3
Vicky Andrews: live sports PA

Returning home she found that most studio PAs were freelancers employed on a daily basis. She is currently the youngest freelance studio PA and works for ITV and other broadcasting companies on live sport and chat shows.

Being a studio PA requires good computer skills, concentration, a cool head and stamina – early starts and late finishes – as well as an all round ability to get on with people in the stressful environment of live broadcasting.

A typical day for a live football broadcast with studio discussion starts four hours before transmission. Vicky has to type up the director's notes and put them into a running order format, print our copies, create an autocue document and brief the presenter. One hour before transmission she has to finalise all the durations and in and out words of the VT inserts, check the graphics – name supers etc. – and make sure everything is ready in the studio gallery. Her job is to run in the title sequence, make sure all the timings are accurate and the show is running to time and count down to the advertising breaks. Timings rest entirely on her. She has to back time the whole show so that the director always knows how much time is left as well as the exact duration of each item: 'I run four electronic stop watches throughout the show and keep an eye on all timings. The director, VT and the presenter all depend on me getting the timings spot on – it's a really enjoyable job, the people are really friendly and every day is different. I see lots of different places but I do work six or seven days a week – I just don't like to turn work down.'

Vicky has worked really hard and done extremely well. In her early twenties she earns over £50K a year, and is a charming, calm, dedicated professional who is very popular wherever she works.

Sound supervisor Mixes and monitors the quality and level of sound from the studio. Controls the final sound output which is likely to come from several audio sources.

Sound assistants Assist sound supervisor in the sound suite and on the studio floor. He or she sets up microphones and operates computer sound sources, tape or CD players or telephone and outside broadcast inputs.

PREPRODUCTION

Preproduction for a studio day where a whole programme is recorded or transmitted live involves a large team and a lot of careful planning. The result of all the research and preproduction is the studio script. This has its genesis in the running order. The running order is created by the producer working with the PA, and is the order in which the various items that make up the programme are to appear. This is the start of the studio process, and begins on the first day of preproduction when the producer opens up the computer and writes: 'Hello and welcome to the . . . show.' The rest of the running order may take many days to finalise.

For a magazine programme video items will have been shot and other material gathered. A presenter will almost certainly be on board and the production team will have ideas for studio items and guests for the show. Magazine programmes are particularly suited to studio shows because all the items can come together and be smoothed into one flowing programme on the studio day. The producer and assistant producers will be working on booking guests, selecting music, finalising videoed items and writing the linking script for the presenter. They will try and get a balance of items, with a large important piece that carries some dramatic televisual clout as the last item. Graphics will have to be ordered from the graphic designer. Possibly archive footage will be required to illustrate an interview. This needs researching and dubbing to video, and the copyright cleared. Props have to be selected and sometimes made especially for the programme.

There are the logistics of getting the presenters and the guests to the TV studio and home again – normally another job for the PA. When the running order is finalised it will need to be agreed by an executive producer. There may be budget implications of certain apparently expensive items. The producer has to make sure that the show does not overspend. If the show has a celebrity guest, that could require extra planning. The celebrity may only be available at the studio for a very short time. He or she will want to know in advance what questions are going to be asked. The contract could pose problems. Normally a contract expert will draw up watertight contracts for guests on broadcast programmes with a scale of appropriate fees. Above all, the production team will want to make the show interesting, entertaining and relevant to the target audience. They will make sure they are very well prepared with an excellent studio script.

THE STUDIO SCRIPT

The studio script is the 'bible' of the studio day. This is a meticulously prepared schedule, and script that includes everything that is going to happen on the day. Because so many people work in a TV studio everyone needs to know exactly what is happening when and where.

For example, everybody must know at what time the first rehearsal begins. The AFMs look at the script to see who the guests are and what dressing rooms they are in. The floor manager learns from the studio script who needs to be where on the set and at what time. Anyone working on the studio floor will at some time during the day need to look at the studio floor plan. This shows where all the items of the set, such as the presenters' chairs are positioned, and how the cameras are plotted to be able to show the presenters and guests without blocking each other.

The central section of the 'bible' is the actual camera script itself. This is a shot by shot break down of the whole show. It has all the visual and audio information that make up the particular show, including sound and vision cues, dialogue, camera angles and shot sizes.

Each shot is numbered on the left. A line leads to the place in the dialogue where the shot starts. The number of the camera taking that shot is above the line and next to that is a letter which denotes the camera position on the floor plan. Under the line is the shot size – MS or MCU and the name of the person who is in the shot – presenter or guest. On the right of the page is the dialogue and the line indicates the cut point, which may be at the beginning of a line or at any point that the director thinks is relevant and adds to the visual narrative. There will be other directions on the script for the cameras such as PAN TO 2 SHOT, or for the vision mixer such as WIPE or MIX.

Away from the studio in a video playback area the operator playing in the video inserts will have a copy of the studio script and will note carefully where the VT comes in and ends. Full details of each insert are given including the tape number, the in words or first frames, and the out words or end visual sequence. Most importantly there is the duration of the insert.

The PA will be constantly timing each section of the show, and adding them together to give an overall timing, as well as doing a back timing (how many minutes left before the end of the show). At any point the director knows how much time there is left, or very occasionally if the show is short. The script will indicate where any music that is to be played into the programme starts and stops. If the show has live music like *Later Live . . . with Jools Holland* (BBC2) the lyrics of each song will be printed, the time signature of the music shown, and the number of bars in the instrumental sections. The PA will count each bar of the song so that the vision mixer can cut on the beat.

The script is a lengthy document which has been skilfully put together over the preceding week(s) by the production team. It can still only be an anticipated version of how the studio day will run. Everyone marks up their own copy of the script according to their role in the programme. The director, PA and vision mixer mark up in pencil as they know there are likely to be many small changes as the day goes on. A well-run studio day is an efficient and compelling way to get a programme on the air. It is immediate and can cover many different elements. Performers will rise to the occasion or respond to a live audience. Everyone will strive to perfect their particular contribution and work to a thoroughly professional standard. There is a lot of professional pride at stake in creating a satisfying studio show.

THE STUDIO DAY

A regular live studio programme such as BBC1's *The One Show* needs a crew of about thirty to get it on the air. The day starts early in the morning for the set designer and the stage hands who have to wheel the set into place and secure it in the specified position. This has been marked on a grid floor plan. Just because it is a regular programme does not mean that the set is exactly the same each time. Depending on the items in the programme and the guests, the set will be adapted. If an elephant is going to be part of the show – it has happened on *Blue Peter* – then arrangements are made to create an area that would suit an elephant. The lighting designer then has to rearrange all the overhead lights for that particular set on that particular day. This is all done well before the first rehearsal.

Traditionally a studio day begins on the dot at 10.00 am with a camera rehearsal. This is where the director does a 'stagger through' – so called because it is a stop start procedure – going through each sequence of the script. Each shot may need some explanation for the cameras, and all the other technical elements in the show such as explaining last minute changes, or tricky moves or visual effects. For a regular show the camera operators and other studio personnel will know what to expect and how things will run. After the stagger through there will be a full rehearsal with the presenters but not the guests. This is to check the lines of the presenter and that the autocue can be easily read. The director will go over all the moves each presenter has to make and explain where the guests will sit, and which cameras will get that shot of the elephant.

It will probably be time for lunch after the rehearsal. All these people need feeding. *The One Show* goes out in the early evening. Other shows may not go out until fairly late in the evening, or there might be an evening recording with a studio audience. A studio day is rarely less than ten hours and can be much longer. Because a studio show is multi-camera, the aim is to produce as complete a programme as possible that needs very little editing, or that can transmit live. This leaves no room for mistakes and retakes as on a feature film. The performances, the technical arrangements, and the length of the show have to be absolutely spot on. In practice nearly all shows, other than live shows, are pre-recorded. The programme is edited for time, and to tie together the number of different sections that may be recorded out of sequence. Conventional high-end video editing in a final editing facility is expensive, so as much as possible is compiled and completed in the studio.

STUDENT TV STUDIO

Many universities and colleges have a fully operational TV studio. It may not have the very latest electronic effects, but it will provide an excellent training ground to work with TV studio equipment, and learn how to put together a studio show. A very professional looking show can be produced in a student TV studio session. A student band can play and record live, or mime to a CD. Presenters can interview the band members, and special guests. The whole show can be 'broadcast' live on a monitor in the students' union as part of a student run TV magazine programme with university news, gossip and what's on guide. Extracts can be downloaded to YouTube as a teaser.

FIGURE 20.4
College TV studio

DEFINITIONS

Camera card Each studio camera has a number. The PA will print a card for each camera that lists all that camera's shots and moves.

Chromakey Electronic system that overlays one picture on sections of another picture. Widely used in television for a variety of effects from putting a presenter apparently in another city or landscape to creating sci-fi backgrounds and effects, e.g. *Doctor Who.* The colour (chroma) blue in the picture is used to key (be replaced by) other images. Some TV studios have a large blue curtain that can be pulled across the back of the set so that a presenter can stand against a blue background that can be replaced via chromakey. The vision mixing desk has a button that sets up the chromakey effect.

DVE Digital video effects. These are visual effects, such as spinning the picture or superimposing one picture over another, that are created by the vision mixing desk in the gallery.

Floor plan A diagrammatic map of the TV studio floor superimposed on a grid reference system that shows the exact positioning of the scenery, relevant large props, studio cameras, microphone boom, and other important items as well as entrances and exits.

Foldback Sound played through a speaker situated on the TV studio floor, or in a radio or sound studio, so that artists or audience can hear the studio sound or sound that has been pre-recorded or originated elsewhere. It is particularly useful for a singer miming to a recording as the recording can be heard from studio speakers, but the singer can still sing into a live mic.

Graphics Generic term that describes any lettering or other artwork created for the television show, e.g. the cast list, names of contributors or title sequence to a programme.

Name super Means name superimposition. This is the standard way to name a contributor to a TV studio show. It appears in the lower third of the screen and is superimposed over the image of the person. Created by a caption generator such as ASTON.

Pedestal A wheeled mounting for a studio camera that allows the camera to go up and down as well as move sideways and backwards and forwards. It has a small black and white monitor as a view finder and headphone links to the gallery.

T/K or Telecine Electronic equipment that scans 16mm or 35mm film and allows it to be videotaped or stored digitally.

STUDIO DIRECTING

Some of the terms you will hear a director using in a TV studio gallery:

Cut This asks the vision mixer in a TV studio gallery to make a sudden, clean transition from one picture to another. This is not the same as on a film set, or video location shoot where cut means stop the action. It never means this in a TV studio. To stop all the action on the studio floor the director's command to the floor manager is **hold it**.

Cut to three This asks the vision mixer to cut to camera 3.

Mix This asks the vision mixer to make a gradual transitional from one image to another, known on film or in editing as a dissolve.

Wipe This asks the vision mixer to make an electronic video transition where the incoming picture wipes away the picture already on the screen. There are a large variety of wipes with names that reflect what they look like, e.g. clock wipe that wipes in the next picture on the screen like a fast clock hand.

Super This asks the vision mixer to introduce a new image, usually a graphic such as the name of the studio guest, and overlay it onto the existing picture which is likely to be a shot of the guest.

Fade up This asks the vision mixer to slowly fade in the picture from a blank screen, or as an extra visual source that might be superimposed onto the existing picture.

Fade to black Fades the picture to a black screen to indicate the end of the show or the end of a sequence. Typically this is the last action on completion of the show. Also used is **fade sound and vision**.

Lose This command from the director can be either to the vision mixer or to the floor manager. To the vision mixer it means take out a superimposed picture such as a caption. To the floor manager it means take away some object from the set that is no longer needed, or is in the way.

Take out Asks the vision mixer to take out a caption, electronic effect, or other superimposition.

Run VT Asks the video tape operator to play the insert tape. This has been set up at a starting point agreed during rehearsal.

Go sound The command to run a CD or any other sound source from the sound gallery during the programme is **go sound** or **go** and the name of the source, e.g. CD.

Cue Anna Asks the floor manager to make a sign to the artist Anna to start speaking.

Wind up Asks the floor manager to make the wind up sign to the current speaker, meaning it is time to come to the end of your piece. This instruction is particularly used during studio interviews.

REFERENCES AND FURTHER READING

Cury, I. *Directing and Producing for Television*, 4th edn, Oxford: Focal Press, 2010.
Millerson, G. and Owens J. *Television Production*, 14th edn, Oxford: Focal Press, 2009.
Orlebar, J. *Digital Television Production – A Handbook*, London: Arnold, 2002.

CHAPTER 21

Postproduction and creative editing

Postproduction happens after the production phase where all the moving images have been acquired as well as much of the sound needed to make a programme. The process of postproduction is everything that is needed to finish the programme and make it ready for transmission. The technical aspects of this process are digital and are done on computer or in a video editing facility. It can be a costly and complex process using sophisticated high-end editing facilities to create computer generated images (CGI) and integrate live footage with CGI material, although straightforward bluescreen techniques are available with professional video-editing software for a desktop computer.

Other aspects of postproduction deal with finalising the paperwork, checking copyright and contracts, creating material for the website, making a trailer and marketing the programme. It may have a broadcast slot on a main channel but look at how busy those schedules are. To make your programme stand out and be noticed requires a clever marketing strategy. The broadcaster will help with this if the programme is high profile but may not bother for an excellent, but schedule-wise run-of-the-mill, documentary. Viral marketing, newspaper and magazine interviews with exciting contributors can all contribute to building up a profile for a programme that will attract audiences.

VIDEO EDITING

All programmes, except live broadcasts, are edited. Professional video-editing software packages provide the technology to transform raw video footage into sophisticated television programmes and include AVID and the currently more popular

Apple's Final Cut Pro video-editing systems. What they do not provide is the human expertise in selecting and editing pictures and sound into coherent TV stories – this is a sophisticated skill learned through experience and a sort of sixth sense as to what works best in any given situation.

The director of the programme works with an experienced editor to arrange the pictures and sound in the best way to tell the story. Most television programmes are shot with a ratio of at least 10:1. Ten minutes of video material will yield one minute of edited programme. In a large television production company a thirty-minute factual programme will take a few weeks to edit. Drama could take longer. Then it will be approved by the producer, the executive producer and maybe the channel controller.

A freelance director working with digital video for a small production company, may edit a similar thirty-minute programme on a computer at home, using an effective but relatively inexpensive editing software such as Adobe Premiere, or a less expensive version of Final Cut Pro. The result is the same. The programme can be fully edited for content with effects, mixes, wipes and dissolves all in place. A factual programme could be ready for transmission needing only a minimum of finishing.

Nearly all programmes for broadcasting on terrestrial channels go through a finishing process. This is a digital process to refine the edited programme. It involves colour correction and grading, adding effects, tidying up any images that may not look right or have unwanted content, and making a broadcast format master recording of the programme. Different channels have different format requirements. The sound may be remixed and balanced in a sound dub. This process used to be known as the online edit, where the original pictures and sound were conformed from an offline version of the programme. The increased power of computing systems and improved software means desktop editing is now fully capable of manipulating the actual images and adding real-time effects. Sound too can be mixed in the edit to produce a broadcast-quality programme.

The aim of postproduction is to produce a programme that meets the highest technical standards, is complete with all graphics, title and end credit sequences, and conforms to the format, style and reputation of the broadcaster. Some satellite channels will not require the postproduction resources of a prime-time BBC, ITV or Channel 4 programme with millions of viewers. Lower budget and news channels can transmit programmes directly from the desktop edit.

The advent of digital video means that quality is no longer the preserve of the professional. Small video cameras are used by broadcasters and have their place in factual and entertainment programming. The hugely costly star vehicle entertainment shows, and quality broadcast drama will continue to use high-end technology, such as digital HD formats. Some directors prefer to shoot flagship drama in 35mm film with a more extensive postproduction process, although it is likely to be edited on an AVID or Final Cut Pro system as are most movies.

STUDENT VIDEO EDITING

The DV format has established itself as a popular and cheap digital shooting and editing format for television, although memory card cameras are taking over. Colleges and universities with media courses have digital video cameras and editing systems with versions of Adobe Premiere, or AVID Xpress Pro or Final Cut Pro.

Some students have their own video cameras and editing software and can edit short programmes on a laptop but a lot of memory is needed for longer items. The hard drive needs to have a large amount of storage space.

The DV format uses a standard compression ratio of 5:1. Five minutes of pictures require at least 1GB of hard disc space. Digital video files are large, and need a fast interface to transfer from the video camera to a PC. This is done with a FireWire (developed by Apple) and with the international standard IEEE 1394. Since FireWire remains an Apple trademark, many other companies use the IEEE 1394 label. Sony refers to it as 'i.LINK'. DV is carried by FireWire in its compressed digital state. Copies made in this manner ought, in theory, to be exact clones of the original. However, whilst the copying process has effective error masking, it doesn't employ any error correction technology, and there can occasionally be drop out problems.

This technology in 2010 is ubiquitous and more reliable than it used to be. The PC industry has worked closely with companies such as Sony, to incorporate IEEE 1394 into PCs. This means the communication, control and interchange of digital, audio and video data is available to everyone with a modern large capacity computer.

One aspect of digital editing that can be annoying is audio drift. This has dogged digital video editing systems since they first appeared. Minute variations in data rate and the logistics of synchronising a video card and a sound card cause some audio tracks in AVI files to drift out of sync. Better quality video capture cards circumvent this problem by incorporating their own sound recording hardware and by using their own playback software rather than using a standard component, such as video for Windows. It is possible to edit on basic video-editing software such as Apple's iMovie or Windows Movie Maker to make short videos for educational purposes or that can be uploaded to a website. However, the ability to manipulate sound and images is limited compared to, for example, a £300 version of Final Cut Pro which supports virtually any video format and gives many creative and technical options.

VIDEO-EDITING TECHNIQUES

The art of storytelling for television relies on a good story, and a strong, effective storytelling technique. The story has to be in the right order and it has to be told with an assured delivery, varying the pace and rhythm. There needs to be light and shade with climaxes and quiet periods. These are the skills needed for video editing. Many television programmes are formed and fashioned in the postproduction process. Good editing can make everything in the production look better, but it cannot rescue a bad script or disguise terrible camerawork. There is very little you can do with off-mic badly recorded sound – except record it again. Postproduction cannot be relied on to sort out all the problems that occur on a shoot. It can do a great deal technically such as flip pictures, reconstruct sequences, create slow motion and even change a grey sky to a blue one. However, sequences without those vital close-ups cannot be miraculously saved in postproduction. The editor can't tell a story if there is not one there to tell.

VISUAL CONTINUITY

For a smooth flow that does not jolt the audience out of the illusion of continuity, certain conventions are followed. These are devices by which the actual space that exists between each shot is smoothed out in the finished programme. The illusion of continuity is maintained first of all in production. Visual detail must be consistent. This is of paramount importance in drama, where all the professionals involved share the task of checking continuity. Make up, costume and props are helped by the continuity PA who takes digital pictures of each set up. Each day the set is checked against a video of how it looked in the last shot. Objects should not disappear from a mantelpiece, and turn up on a nearby table. Clothing, make up, hairstyle and the hand that carries the bag or gun have to be consistent, or the viewer will notice that something is wrong. Any suggestion of discontinuity destroys the flow of the narrative, steers the viewer away from the characters and provokes feelings of unease. Visual continuity is also concerned with movement. A hand gesture begun in a wide shot has to be seen as the same movement when the editor cuts to the close-up.

Imagine two characters running after each other in a chase scene. If they leave the shot running, then the next shot should not show them walking along slowly. An entrance through a door should not show the doorknob being turned in both the interior and the exterior shots. The editor cuts the shots to show continuity of action, period, place and space and to compress time. An action that takes place in real time takes much longer than we tolerate in a drama or a factual programme. The editor can use the audience's understanding of visual conventions to move the action along, or it can be subverted. French alternative film director Jean Luc Godard uses jump cuts for political and cultural reasons in his films, for example *Weekend*. He wants the audience to notice the jump cut and be reminded that they are watching a film. He wants them to be aware of the illusion of cinema, and in a sense the political trick that they have consented to, in order to question the form and content of cinema itself. Postmodern television drama shows like *CSI* (Channel 5) are exploiting these techniques as well as the more familiar multi-screen devices to tell a story smoothly and with pace and flair.

SHOT REVERSE SHOT

The basic sequence in classical continuity narrative construction is the shot reverse shot technique. For example, shots of two characters engaged in dialogue will favour first one and then the other. The camera will frame the first character – a man – facing right of frame. This means that from the camera's POV he is looking to the right of the frame. The other character – a woman – will be framed from the camera's POV, looking to the left of the frame. Edited together the audience will think that the two characters are facing each other. In a drama the whole scene will be shot once with the camera framing the man facing to the right, and then again with the camera framing the woman facing to the left. Both characters will repeat their dialogue even when the camera is on the other character. The director has to make sure that the eyelines of the two characters match. If their eyes do not appear to engage with each other the audience will be disorientated. The editor can cut at any point from one shot to the other, depending on what is said and how it affects each character. This sequence is the basis for every film and TV drama, and is especially evident in soaps. A clever use of variety of shot sizes adds to the drama, and the audience's understanding of the relationship between the characters.

In factual programmes the technique is also employed even though the two characters are now an interviewer and a contributor, and may not be in the same room. It is used to carry out a standard interview or juxtapose opposing views. In most filmed interview situations the interviewer is asking the questions out of shot. After the interview the contributor may leave the location. The cameraman then films the interviewer asking the 'reverse questions', making sure that he or she is facing the opposite way to the contributor, and that the eyelines match. The illusion is preserved in that the questions appear to be being asked at the same time as the contributor is answering them. The reverse questions and pictures of the interviewer nodding help greatly with the editing. The editor can cut out parts of the interview, and insert a 'noddy' of the interviewer to cover the cut. This is not considered dishonest, or to undermine the veracity of the interview.

Journalistic ethics and broadcasting compliance do not allow for a change of meaning to be exploited by this technique. It is a technique to help the viewer stay with the programme. Some programme makers try to do away with this illusion, and make the cut in an interview more obvious, either with a little dissolve or a straight jump cut. This can be a useful tool in certain cases where authenticity and credibility are at stake, but it can also look too contrived and get in the way of what the contributor is saying.

POSTMODERN TECHNIQUES

A postmodern audience accepts many of the subversions of the conventional, such as the jump cut, the use of multi-screen effects, the exaggerated compression of time and slow motion. A visual trick observable in many documentaries is the speeding up of part of a sequence or long shot. A group of young clubbers may be hurrying along the street to their club destination. The camera pans them across a road at which point the editor speeds up the movement in vision so that the clubbers reach the entrance to the club very quickly. The movement then slows down to normal speed. This completely undermines the conventional continuity, but is acceptable as a postmodern stylistic embellishment that appeals to viewers brought up on the discontinuous visual world of music videos. It also brings pace and time acceleration to the sequence.

Postmodern audiences are aware of how technical elements are used to create perspective or viewpoint within a sequence. This can affect how the audience is positioned in relation to the representations on the screen, leading to some representations being privileged where others are marginalised. Judicious editing can change the viewer's relationship towards the dominant views of gender in different scenes. Modern audiences are used to the way sequences are edited to show or withhold narrative information from the audience so as to encourage identification or rejection of a particular character.

Digital video editing has opened up to the home editor many of the effects, visual tricks and picture manipulation that was previously only available in the cinema, or by hiring extremely expensive high-end digital technology in a facility house. Whether this leads to more audience involvement with programmes, or more incisive

FIGURE 21.1
Video editing on Final Cut Pro

documentaries, or richer storytelling is up for debate. What is certain is that televisual forms, styles and conventions will evolve as the technology develops, and as producers and editors look for more ways to grab an audience.

THE POSTPRODUCTION PROCESS

This is the sequence of events for a factual programme. It is very similar for a drama.

1 View rushes.

2 Log rushes. For any programme, or even a short insert item, it is worth making a record on paper of everything filmed. Logging means writing down the 'in' timecode and 'out' timecode of all useable material, and briefly commenting on the shot. e.g. WS river. Speedboat comes in left. 22" (22 secs).

3 Send DVD of long interviews to be transcribed. This will turn the audio of the interviews into a written form. Most people find it easier and more accurate to edit long interviews in written form on paper or on the screen. It is also possible to edit the audio on audio editing software (e.g. Audacity) available for any computer. Short interviews are straightforward to edit in video editing without transcriptions.

4 The cutting order for the programme. This is the sequence of shots and the edited extracts from the interviews in the order that the director/producer thinks will make most sense, and give a shape and structure to the programme. This will not be the final order for all the sequences. The cutting order is a structured starting point that can be put together for the first assembly. The duration should be over long. This is normal.

5 Marking up the transcripts. This is where the benefit of a written transcript of all those long interviews that were done months ago becomes clear. Highlight the sections that are to be used in the programme in colour on the computer – yellow is an easy to read background colour for black print. Identify each block of words with the name of the interviewee and a number, e.g. John S. 4. Make sure the full transcript is retained as the editor will need to find each section from the full interview. It is impossible to find short extracts without referring to the full transcript.

6 First assembly. The editor follows the cutting order and uses the selected sections from the transcript of the interviews to assemble all the shots and sound together. At this stage the editor will not worry about jump cuts, poor sound or anything technical. The aim is just to get the story together with a beginning, middle and end.

7 Rough cut. If the assembly shows a clear structure, and contains all the relevant material, it is now time to make a rough cut. This should be within

a few minutes of the final duration, have a definite structure and include the cutaways. Irrelevant material should all go at the rough cut stage. It is essential to be ruthless and only keep what is essential to drive forward the story.

8 Commentary. Most factual programmes need commentary of some sort. There will be sections of the programme where interesting and hopefully relevant shots need an explanation, or an introduction to a new contributor. The rule of thumb is that three words of commentary equal one second of programme time – thirty words need ten seconds of pictures – quite a lot.

9 First fine cut. At this stage the commentary is added on a separate audio track and the pictures adjusted so that they make sense with the commentary. Music is selected and added. The programme is trimmed to within thirty seconds of the final duration and the sound checked for overlaps, cutaways and any tight edits. Archive material is inserted, and a rough version of graphics, such as name supers added.

10 Fine cut. The programme is trimmed to the exact duration for transmission. Final graphics, mixes, effects and opening titles, and credits are added. The sound is track laid for the sound dub. If necessary the fine cut is taken to a facilities house for finishing.

11 Enjoy the BAFTA.

POSTPRODUCTION POSTSCRIPT

Postproduction is a major cost in time and resources for any production. The major resource is the time required to edit the programme and then finish it. The editing process is time-consuming. It takes thinking time, and editing skill, to get the most expressive combination of pictures and sound to tell the story in a way that will satisfy an audience. A senior or executive producer will need to see a rough cut of the programme and changes will be suggested. After the fine cut has been agreed then the programme has to be finished. This will involve a sound dub to smooth out the sound and add music if required. The final process is to create a master tape for transmission. This can include adding graphics, a title sequence and channel logos and copyright as required by the broadcaster. Short sequences of evocative images that will work as a trailer are usually required for publicity.

But here is a health warning – postproduction always takes longer and costs more than expected. Allow twice as much time as you first think will be needed. Allow time for other people to make changes. Broadcasting companies are apt to make last-minute changes in schedule and programme duration. Leave plenty of time before the delivery date. Above all, start postproduction as early as possible. With a laptop it is possible to rough edit the rushes as soon as the pictures are available – what a good idea!

REFERENCES AND FURTHER READING

Amyes, T. *Audio Postproduction in Video and Film*, Oxford: Focal Press, 1999.
McGrath, D. *Editing & Post Production (Screencraft Series)*, Oxford: Focal Press 2001.

CHAPTER 22

Working in television

WORKING IN TELEVISION

The television and video businesses have a large variety of jobs in the production and operational areas as well as in administrative areas. It is useful to divide the jobs in television production into three main areas:

- Production jobs
- Technical jobs
- Postproduction

There is crossover in some areas especially in operating portable equipment, such as camera and sound kit. For a production to work successfully both sets of personnel need to work harmoniously together. As multi-skilling becomes the norm on small productions there is often very little distinction between the two. To work in a technical area for a broadcast company, you need skills, training and television experience. If you are thinking of going into television it is a good idea to have knowledge of both areas, which can be obtained on a practical-orientated television degree course.

PRODUCTION JOBS

A team of hard-working enthusiasts who can pool their skills and experience come together with one aim – to transform an idea into a broadcastable television programme. This team is known as 'production'. Television is a producer-led medium and the **producer** is the head of a television production team. He or she starts the process of creating a show, and then goes about getting the money to make the show, and selecting the production personnel. It is the producer who selects the writer, and also picks the technical crew with the assistance of the director. The producer has overall responsibility for everything to do with the show. This includes the key matter of the budget, as well as health and safety considerations for location filming, and for actually getting the programme on the air. This is a creative job for a flexible, seasoned and experienced professional, and worth aspiring to. It is the producer who has the creative power and delivers the programmes. It is the producer who takes the blame, enjoys the fame, and accepts the BAFTA.

The television director

The director of any television programme is responsible for the look and staging of a show. The director takes a script and transforms it into the pictures and sound of a television programme whether it is factual, news, sport or drama. The director works closely with the producer and directs performers and technical crew. The exact role depends on the genre of the show, and the way it is made.

The main criteria for becoming a television director are the ability to understand and communicate the inner meaning of a script or programme idea, and visualise the action in a filmic way. This means seeing in the mind's eye how each line of the script will appear on the screen, and how the whole story will fit together. He or she will supervise the editing, select the music, work closely with the producer, and make sure the production is of the highest quality for the broadcast slot.

The **drama director** will understand and be able to develop characterisation, narrative and be cognisant of the language of directing. This director will visualise a way of compressing ten minutes, or ten years, of real time into a few screen moments, as well as showing the audience clues about character and back-story without being obvious. The director positions actors and choreographs scenes. The director decides on pace, timing and structure as well as unravelling what the script is all about. The director chooses where to put the camera on location and works with the camera operator to select framing, shot size and camera angle.

A **TV studio director**'s main job is to direct a multi-camera television studio set up. This will involve creating a camera script, rehearsing front of camera talent (the performers) and some involvement with the content and look of the show. A studio show may go out live, or be recorded as live, so the director's job is crucial on the day of recording. However, much of the preproduction will be set up by a large production team headed by the producer. Before the studio day the director will collect all the information about the show and put it all down in a camera script. This is a complex document that assigns each shot to a camera and sets out precisely how each shot will look, where music will come in and how videotape inserts will be integrated into the programme. Live sports shows rely on the director's ability to follow the action, and cut to the correct camera at the right time. This is a job that needs lightning quick reflexes, a calm and measured way of working and an understanding of what the viewer needs to see at any one time. It is not for the faint-hearted.

The **factual director** selects the locations, decides on camera angles and shot sizes, positions the presenter and sets up all the filming, and quite often writes lines for the presenter to say as well as asking the questions in an interview. The factual director thinks about how to shoot a scene in the most economical way. Only Hollywood has huge budgets.

More and more documentary and factual programmes are produced and directed by the same person. This is not just a cost-cutting development. Modern digital equipment and processes have cut down the production time needed to make a programme. One person doing both jobs can be in a better position to make fast decisions and take quick action, especially when working with a small team on location. More independent companies are making mainstream programmes. This allows specialist programme makers to create their own style of programming and offer the networks reasonably priced factual or reality programming – e.g. all those programmes about relocating to somewhere sunny abroad.

The independent director/producer researches, sets up and directs the filming of the programme, and then supervises the editing. In some cases where perhaps access is restricted, such as remote parts of the world, the producer/director will also film the programme using a lightweight professional camera. Anyone aspiring to work in factual television should develop skills in production and directing, as well as good camera techniques.

Are you a TV director?

Try doing this exercise. Show how you would shoot these scenes for maximum visual dramatic effect. Draw stick-men pictures inside a TV frame (a storyboard) to tell the story visually. There is no dialogue.

- *Drama.* A blonde woman in a mask holds up a bank while her boyfriend/accomplice waits on a motorcycle nearby. They make off with the money but leave a telltale object behind.

- *Drama.* A young man flies to Venice for an important business meeting. He agrees to start a mysterious job. He has to tell his girlfriend back in London that he cannot make the wedding of her best friend, set for two days' time. Work out how you can shoot this scene economically to bring out the main character's inner motivation.

- *Factual programme.* You are interviewing a well-known celebrity. You are in a major city. You can do the interview in a hotel room. Describe what other shots you need, so that you do not just have a talking head. What can you ask your celebrity to do to make the interview interesting? What locations can you use?

See Part 5 Television Drama for details of visual grammar and storyboarding. See Part 3 for Factual Television production.

Researcher

A researcher in television is often the first production job for a new recruit into the business. In fact this is a demanding and absorbing job that requires a number of skills. A researcher must be good with people, able to come up with stunning ideas for a programme and have excellent organisational skills. This is not the same as a simple academic research task, such as logging on to Google and finding out who won the Oscars last year. The main job for most factual programmes is to actually find people to take part in TV programmes. This takes patience, stamina and lateral thinking. Researchers have an extraordinary ability to persuade people to take part in a television programme that they may never have heard of.

Look at the schedules of the terrestrial broadcasters. Any day of the week includes programmes with so-called 'real' people. Diligent researchers have unearthed all these contributors. It appears to be less difficult to persuade someone to take part in a programme than it used to be, but finding suitable, interesting subjects can still take an enormous amount of telephoning and emailing. The researcher keeps a list of everyone who has been contacted with dates and times. The researcher has to be scrupulous in checking facts and checking all personal details to avoid bogus contributors.

Broadcasters and production companies require researchers with some experience to make short film items working from the initial idea right up to transmission. The modern TV researcher is able to not only think up, budget, research and find contributors for a programme, but also shoot and edit a simple story about a possible contributor. This is multi-skilling. Communication is most important as the producer has to be kept informed of what is happening and how each story is going at all stages. The researcher has to be able to write a treatment (see Part 3) and show how that item can be delivered for the allocated – probably very small – budget. When going for a researcher interview it is a good idea to have a file of possible stories and good ideas relevant to the programme genre of the company.

Production Assistant

The PA works closely with the producer and the director on the paperwork for all types of production. She, and it is nearly always a woman, is a formidable communicator and an essential part of every production. She will work on the shooting schedule, set up filming and will be involved in the day-to-day activities of the production team. She may well do much of the research. On a factual programme the PA organises payments for contributors, arranges flights, books hotels and hire-cars and deals with the budget, among many other responsibilities. She will ensure contributors sign release forms, as well as organising location permissions.

On a TV drama the PA's role is more specialised. She will be closely involved with the production of the script. She will work on scheduling the whole shoot with the production manager. Some shoots may require her to look after continuity on set. She will be responsible for drawing up a comprehensively marked-up editing script after each day's shoot. (For a profile of a TV studio PA see Chapter 20.)

Production Manager

The production manager is in charge of resources for a production and is answerable to the producer. He or she works closely with the director. This is an essential and important job in producing a drama. Before filming begins the production manager budgets and schedules complex activities and aims to save money wherever possible. Responsibilities include managing locations, scheduling the film crew, negotiating daily rates and terms of technical contracts, being responsible for health and safety and insurance, and arranging technical facilities. This means getting the crew, the actors and everyone else to turn up at the right time in the right place. Then if it rains, or a leading actor is ill, thinking on your feet and getting the whole show to another location.

The ideal PM is cool and calm under stress, and brilliant at organisation as well as being up to speed with the latest technical developments and costs in the industry. The PM will be involved with finding locations, drawing up the shooting schedule, the daily call sheets, and seeking permissions from land owners, the police and local authorities. For someone entering the television industry this is a job to only aspire to, as it requires a great deal of experience. One way towards becoming a production manager is to work first as a runner and then as an **assistant director** (AD).

Runner

A runner works to the production manager on the set, and 'runs' for anything that is needed at the time. Many professionals working on television dramas say that this job is the best way to learn the business. Certainly you see every aspect of the production by actually being on set nearly all the time. However, you do not usually see how a production is set up in preproduction, or the editing process in postproduction. It is worth asking for work experience in these areas.

Assistant Director (AD)

ADs are usually found on drama shoots. There are several ADs. The important post of first AD does much of the organisational work on a shoot. The first AD can line up shots, set up locations, supervise rehearsals and be responsible for the actors. The first AD is assisted by the second AD, the third AD and on large shoots the fourth AD. Each has a specific role. Often the third AD is in charge of the extras. This can mean marshalling large crowds or making sure a few extras are in exactly the right place for a shot. The fourth AD can be a suitable job for a trainee, often helping the third AD.

Assistant Producer

This is a post usually found on factual productions. As the title suggests the main function is to work closely with the producer. The assistant producer on a factual series is often the director and researcher and even the editor. He or she will research and set up a story, shoot it, edit it and then finalise the graphics and music in postproduction. On a studio-based programme the assistant producer is often the studio director. Large broadcasting companies, such as the BBC, employ assistant producers on many productions. The next step up for a researcher can be to assistant producer. The post is very good training to be a studio or location director, and/or a television producer.

An assistant producer needs skills and experience in television production, some of which may be gained with work experience, and on a good practical degree course in media production. This is unlikely to be a first job. If you really want to work in factual programming and for a large TV company then this is the job to aim for. It helps if you have expertise in another area. Large TV companies run factual programme strands such as science, the arts, gardening, motoring, travel, history and wildlife. Newer areas include the housing market, archaeology, leisure and tourism, collecting and antiques, and all the social areas of 'reality' TV. You may have a particular interest in British cinema, or energy and the environment, or vintage cars. This is worth highlighting on your CV. It is worth thinking up programme ideas based on any expertise you have in any area, however obscure, and writing them down as short one-page treatments (see Part 3: Chapter 10).

Production executives

Any large-scale television production will have an **executive producer**. This is the person who has originally commissioned the programme and has sanctioned the budget. You may never see the EP on the set, but the EP will have had an important role in setting up the show. In television, the EP will probably work within a genre, such as factual programming for young people, Reality TV, arts, current affairs or science. He or she will have a certain number of shows to deliver and is always looking to commission new ideas and talent.

Another important role especially on an expensive drama is the **associate producer**. The associate producer is heavily involved in devising a realistic budget in pre-production, and has a large say in the way the budget is spent. The associate producer can be responsible for increasing funding for a particular series though co-production with a broadcaster from another country. The associate producer on any production will be looking to arrange deals for technical resources, as well as ways of maximising sales of the finished product in order to bring cash into the production.

TECHNICAL JOBS

Lighting cameraperson

This role is also often known as the **director of photography** (DOP), and is the supervising cameraperson who works with the director to achieve a distinctive 'look' for a production. The DOP is in charge of the technical crew on a location set. On a large production, such as a drama, the DOP will work with the chief electrician and supervise the team of electricians (sparks) to set up the lighting for a scene. This may involve dozens of different lights; all need to be carefully placed not to cast shadows that may be 'in shot', and to light the area where the action takes place. The DOP will work with the **camera operator** to select the right lens, the most suitable camera mounting – dolly, tripod or steadicam – and any lens filters for a scene, as well as actually framing the shot. The camera operator will move the camera, operate the controls and is responsible for the technical quality of the pictures. On a small production, the DOP will operate the camera as well as supervise the electricians to position the lights, place reflectors, and light the scene according to the mood suggested by the director. On a small factual programme shoot for television, the camera operator will operate the digital camera, and carry a set of lights to light small areas, such as a room for an interview. In news, the camera operator will operate a camera with a light attached to it, or carry a battery-powered light for street interviews and will also be responsible for sound for an interview or piece to camera.

Camera assistant

This job is a good way of learning the skills of being a good camera operator. He or she handles the tripod, makes sure batteries are charged, loads and labels tapes or hard discs, and sets up the camera with the correct timecode at the beginning of each scene. The camera assistant might also be the focus puller on a shoot (setting the correct focus for a shot). He or she does a lot of carrying of equipment, like tripods, lenses and batteries.

Sound recordist

The sound recordist is in charge of recording all the location sound. For television he or she uses a small portable sound mixer that receives the output from the microphones either by cable or radio link. The mixer is cabled to the camera. The sound is recorded onto the digital tape or hard disc in the camera. For drama productions made on film or HD video the sound recordist may work with a portable sound recorder such as a Nagra and record a separate sound track. A clapper board is used to later put the recorded sound 'in sync' with the actors' lip movements. Two or more microphones can be set up and the sound monitored by the recordist on headphones. Television programmes are recorded in stereo. The sound recordist is not just responsible for sound quality. He or she ensures that there is no overlapping sound – voices talking over each other – in interviews or in drama, and that there is a good balance between background sound and speech. The aim is to deliver clean uncluttered sound to the editor that retains the ambience of the location and the full resonance of the speech.

Sound assistant

He or she works with the sound recordist setting up microphones, operating sound equipment in the TV studio sound gallery, and holding the mic boom on location. If you are interested in sound and have some knowledge of microphones, this can be a good first job.

Gaffer

This is a term (deriving from feature film-making) for the chief electrician on a shoot who is responsible for all the other electricians operating lights and lighting equipment. He or she works with the DOP to light a scene. Electricians working on lighting in television are fully qualified electricians; assistants can be in training to qualify.

Grip

The grip is a member of the camera crew, and works to the DOP or lighting camera operator. The main function of the grip is to set up the camera dolly and lay the track for the dolly. The grip will also move the camera along the track smoothly at the required speed, stopping at exactly the right point. He or she needs experience and knowledge of video/film cameras.

WORKING IN POSTPRODUCTION

Much of the work in creating a television programme happens after all the material has been shot. This is the process of postproduction. At the core of this process is the editing of the programme. This is the stage where the fragmented shots and sequences are brought together and reassembled into the illusion of three-dimensional space that we know as broadcast television. Editing brings together

PROFILE

Sports camera operator and technician: Daniel Barnard

Daniel's first job, after studying for a degree in Media Technology from Farnborough College of Technology in North Hampshire, was to work for Aerial Camera Systems based in Surrey and operating all over the country.

FIGURE 22.1
Sports camera operator/technician – Daniel Barnard

I went straight into this job from leaving university. I really enjoy the job because it is varied and I am working on live productions. At university I learned how to set up and make television programmes, so that when I meet other professionals I know what they do and I don't get in their way. All the theory was useful too. The practical part of my degree was really useful to my work. I learned how to plug up equipment. I worked on many live radio programmes on the College's radio station, which helped with the flexibility and quick reactions you need for a live TV sport transmission. The TV studio work helped too – I know what the director is talking about when he calls for shots – it gives you confidence.

A typical day is to drive with a colleague in a company van to the McAlpine stadium in Huddersfield for a rugby match, to set up pan and tilt remote control cameras behind the goals. We also fit a camera in each dressing room and test them for the evening transmission. We check the cameras all morning, and rehearse with the live match director until transmission in the afternoon. You have to be able to sort something out if it goes wrong.

I got into television because of that feeling of liveness. An inner feeling of enjoyment working to a live audience. If there is a downside it is the long hours away from home. The great thing is you concentrate hard when you are working, but afterwards you get a whole day off with no paperwork. We also do foreign trips.

PROFILE

Daniel remembers that the interview for the job was quite easy.

They asked me if I could operate a camera, what my interests are, and did I mind being away from home. The company get at least half a dozen CVs a week, but few people actually follow up their CV. This job was advertised on the college notice board. My holiday work experience at Southampton FC television service helped a lot. I would really like to stay with the company as there are many opportunities to learn different skills. We have specially shock proofed cameras for putting on helicopters for movies, or the Olympics blimp. Lots to learn. It's great to have such a varied and interesting job.

different perspectives on the same scene and balances the pictures and the sound to create a cohesive whole. It is essential in creating the narrative thrust of a programme, since editing decisions guide the audience through the movement of sound and images that make up the programme.

Video editor

There are many employment opportunities within the postproduction area. The main job is video editor. A video editor will typically have several years experience as an **assistant video editor**, or in some other area of video postproduction. The job requires a very good sense of narrative and picture composition, a profound understanding of the medium and some technical ability. Modern editing for television is a non-linear, digital, computerised process that allows the editor an extraordinary amount of freedom in creating the finished programme from the filmed material. There are a number of industry standard software systems for video editing. Apple's Final Cut Pro is popular with many editors and one of the best known, and has systems for editing drama, news and factual programmes. Adobe Premiere is an effective system for low-budget productions, or for home editing. Whether on digital video tape or disc the editor sees pictures on a monitor, and manipulates them with a mouse and a keyboard.

Many experienced video editors set up on their own and work from a small office with just a high-end Apple computer, an HD screen and Final Cut Pro. For larger productions an independent editor may be pleased to have some help and this is a good way to get experience. A finished broadcast programme can be produced on Final Cut Pro although some extra sound dubbing and picture colour balancing may be necessary.

Facilities house

Many people working in the television business found their first job in the post-production area. These are often at facilities houses. A facilities house is a commercial company offering a range of TV production facilities for hire on a daily or hourly rate. Some companies offer solely video-editing suites and equipment, while others offer all the equipment you need for the full postproduction process, including sound dubbing. An assistant may be helping with the collection of tapes, or setting up and loading videotape machines or transferring rushes for clients. Some of the work may be copying tapes, looking after clients, opening the mail and helping around the office. It is all good experience. Postproduction also includes sound dubbing where the final sound mix is created in a specialist dubbing suite from the original rushes. There is possible work here as a sound assistant, where knowledge of sound/music mixing is essential. There are now college courses in audio technology which provide training in this area.

Television production companies

Until the advent of Channel 4, most television programmes were made in-house by the broadcasting companies. Channel 4 is not a producer of programmes. It is effectively a publisher as all its output is contracted from outside production companies. Over 25 per cent of the BBC's television production is now made out-side the organisation, and this has led to the growth of small and large production companies often specialising in one genre of programme. Lion TV in west London, for example, make a wide variety of factual programmes for terrestrial and satellite broadcasting companies. Other companies, such as Hat Trick, are known for their comedy output.

There are many smaller companies working on just one or two commissions at any one time. Many companies are looking to recruit enthusiastic and flexible people to work on a variety of roles on their productions. There are other more technical companies who provide camera crews for a whole range of specialist and standard types of production. These range from high-quality outside broadcast units to smaller cameras hiring out low-budget DV cameras or providing camera crews and other personnel.

It is worth sending your CV to any company in your area that you think is involved in television production. Telephone them to see whether work is available, and/or send a CV that is aimed at whatever job you think they may have. Always follow up a posted CV with an email or phone call. Job vacancies can arise very quickly. Be prepared to do some work experience for a few weeks for very little money.

Your CV should be only one/two pages long. Notice that any television experience and skills you have acquired at university or on work experience are at the top of the page, before your qualifications.

SAMPLE CV

Your address
Your name
The date

What is the job you have most experience at doing?

Describe in one or two sentences what you do best in television.

TELEVISION RESEARCHER

An experienced television researcher with a particularly strong track record in researching distinctive factual programmes, finding and selecting contributors and making short films for independent television companies.

TELEVISION EXPERIENCE

I have been working with independent production companies on broadcast television programmes for two years, including location programmes for Channel 4, and make-over programmes for the BBC. I find and select contributors, check that all their details are correct, make a short video about them, and recommend suitable ones to the producer. I direct short inserts for the programme. I have written, produced and directed a ten minute short which was shown at the London Film Festival. I would like to work in television production management.

SKILLS

I have an approachable and direct telephone manner with strong interpersonal skills. This is an asset in recruiting exciting programme contributors. I am able to direct actors and presenters in single-camera or multi-camera formats, and film sensitively with members of the public. I have a good knowledge and understanding of digital-video equipment and editing. I have experience and expertise in developing scripts, and shooting short dramas and factual programmes. I have a range of experience in postproduction techniques, including working with AVID and Premiere.

TRAINING

SKILLSET researcher's course [4 wks]
Writing for the media LFS

Equal Opportunities in Broadcasting BBC

EDUCATIONAL QUALIFICATIONS

BA (Hons) Film with television studies (2:1), Warwick University.

Three A levels: Media Studies (A), Business Studies (B) and French (B)

RESEARCH

'The Daring Task of Literacy in India'

Research study of literacy in southern India, undertaken in gap year.

INTERESTS

I enjoy the Arts: theatre, music and film

I also participate in active leisure. I play tennis regularly.

I take colour and B & W photographs for publication in books and periodicals. I have an informed interest and concern for green issues.

Finally, repeat your name, address and mobile phone number at the bottom of the page.

Many people contribute to the making of a television programme. Depending on the type of show there will be people from make up, graphic design, costume, as well as a property buyer – for on-set moveable props – and an art designer for making and maintaining the set. Nearly all these personnel have assistants.

If you are interested in any of these areas it is sometimes possible to gain work experience as an assistant to see whether that area of television production is for you. If you are interested then apply for a job as a full-time assistant. You will need a media friendly CV. All jobs in television attract a large number of applications especially if they are advertised in the *Guardian*, one of the main sources of media jobs. Job applications should not just indicate your interest in a job. You will need to highlight the extent of your work experience in that particular area. It is no good going for a job as a sound assistant if you know nothing about how sound is recorded, or lack basic knowledge about microphones. The company will expect you to have some experience of working with a sound recordist on location or in a TV studio. You will want to personalise your CV according to your skills, experience and qualifications. If you would like to work in the television business there are various ways you can gain work experience to see whether this is the industry that appeals to you. A good place to start is at the industry's training forum SKILLSET, whose website is www.skillset.org. They publish *A Career Handbook for TV, Radio, Film, Video and Interactive Media*, by Shiona Llewellyn and Sue Walker. Part of the same organisation is www.skillsformedia.com, which has information about entering or progressing in the media industry and has links to media jobs.

PROFILE

Assistant video/film editor: Matthew Loxterkamp

Matthew studied practical television and film at university. He was particularly interested in film studies. Looking around for a part-time job in the media industry, he took on part-time work at BAFTA in London. They wanted help with organising all their archive material collected since the BAFTA awards began in 1947. When Matthew's degree course finished, BAFTA took him on full time to continue putting all the photos, videos and press cuttings into an accessible archive. He found the work gave him a chance to improve his knowledge of British film and television

FIGURE 22.2
Mathew Loxterkamp

and work in a professional environment. He designed a database for the archive, and then in Spring 2004 found himself out of a job. The BAFTA building was being completely renovated and the archive was stored elsewhere.

Wanting to keep on working with film and TV, he sent out eighty-seven emails and mailed forty-one CVs to directors, TV production managers and a few film producers. He received twenty emails in reply, but none offering him any work. They said they would keep his CV on file. Eventually he saw an advertisement for a trainee assistant video editor with Vertigo films in Kentish Town, London. This company had a good track record of editing films including *Human Traffic* and *Football Factory*. The job offered turned out to be four weeks' work experience, with only expenses paid. Learning editing techniques on Final Cut Pro and AVID, he was able to bring his experience of graphics work with Photoshop to help create press material for the company's films. This and his impressive interpersonal skills led the company to offer him a more permanent job as an assistant video editor. Matthew says: 'it helped that I know Photoshop and that I was able to show that I was competent with editing software. Even though I didn't know the particular one they were using.'

Matthew is very aware of how hard it is to get that first job:

> It's all about personality. You need to be adaptable and get on with everybody from day one. I wrote everything the editor told me down, so that I wouldn't forget anything. The editor liked the fact that I knew about film analysis and character and plot – so the media degree course was worth it just for that. He asks my opinion. He seems to like my input on the film he is editing, but I am careful what I say!

Matthew is using this job as experience in order to move into drama production: 'My ambition is to try and work on major movies or TV dramas. I only earn £200 a week, and the hours are very long. But I am getting priceless experience, and working with really nice people.'

PROFILE

REFERENCES AND FURTHER READING

Hart, C. *Television Program Making*, Oxford: Focal Press, 1999.

Millerson, G. and Owens, J. *Television Production*, 14th edn, Oxford: Focal Press, 2009.

Orlebar, J. *Digital Television Production*, London: Arnold, 2002.

Orlebar, J. *The Practical Media Dictionary*, London, Arnold, 2003.

Tunstall, J. *Television Producers*, London: Routledge, 1993.

Tunstall, J. (ed.). *Media Occupations and Professions: A Reader*, Oxford: Oxford University Press, 2001.

CHAPTER 23

Television and the law

PRIVACY

Programme makers need to respect the privacy of individuals at all times. The only justification for bringing someone's private life into the public domain is that there is a wider public interest. Traditionally in English law, there has been no right to privacy. However, there has been a clutch of recent court cases where famous people have won over privacy issues. Catherine Zeta-Jones and Michael Douglas sued and won against *Hello!* magazine for publishing unauthorised photos taken at their wedding. Supermodel Naomi Campbell won a privacy case against the *Mirror* newspaper, which had made public her battle against drug addiction. These cases were argued under the European Convention of Human Rights which came into force in British law in October 2000. Article 8, section 1, of the convention states: 'Everyone has the right for his private and family life, his home and his correspondence.' This can cause legal difficulties as it appears to sit awkwardly with Article 10 which enshrines the right to freedom of expression.

In the UK programme makers may film anyone in a 'public situation', such as walking in the street, or in a public shopping area. Even a quiet beach can be considered a public place, and this is where the paparazzi take shots of famous people sunbathing. Some well-known people are questioning this intrusion on their privacy. Newsreader Anna Ford was dismayed when first the Press Complaints Commission then the High Court refused to agree that paparazzo pictures taken of her on holiday breached her privacy. It was ruled that a publicly accessible beach in Majorca in August was not a place where she could reasonably have expected privacy.

In Naomi Campbell's case, the newspaper broke the law by publishing the times and nature of her medical treatment. Keeping medical data private is the right of any individual. So although there is no law of privacy in the UK, individuals may be able to use the law of confidentiality to protect their privacy. In terms of making television programmes this could raise some difficult issues in some circumstances. In all cases of using photographs, correspondence or diaries, permission from the owner must be sought. In cases where this would put the programme in jeopardy, legal advice should be obtained to see if there is a justification that the material is in the public interest.

COPYRIGHT

In the multi-platform digital television environment intellectual property, or copyright, has become a major issue. All created content is owned by someone and if it is published then it is subject to copyright laws. Television programme making is about bringing together ideas and creative people and their work. Much of this work, such as music and scripts, and the actual television programme itself, is protected from unlawful copying by copyright.

Copyright goes back a long way. Writer Jonathan Swift instigated the first copyright Act which was passed in 1709, with published books protected for twenty-one years. Copyright is an intellectual property right. It is a way of protecting the tangible result of creative work – such as music or writing – from being used by someone else for their gain. Throughout the world copyright exists. National laws cover different countries. The principles remain broadly the same. Always check before using copyright material. The 1988 Copyright, Designs and Patents Act in the UK covers copyright of all types, including intellectual property. The Copyright and Related Rights Regulations amended this for the digital age in 2003.

Ideas cannot be copyrighted, but the expression of an idea in a tangible form can be. This includes online creative work. Copyright protects the originator from the piracy and copying of original work. It could be a script, a film, a play or a TV programme format, or an original musical work such as a pop song. The most obvious use of copyrighted material on television is the use of commercial music.

THE 1988 COPYRIGHT, DESIGNS AND PATENTS ACT

The 1988 Copyright, Designs and Patents Act protects the tangible result of creative work from unfair exploitation. The act covers:

Original literary, dramatic and musical works

Not just books, plays, film scripts and magazines, but programme schedules, opinion polls and airline timetables. TV signature tunes and thirty-second radio ads are covered by the Act. Today literary, artistic, musical and dramatic works are protected for seventy years from 31 December of the year in which the author died. Using extracts from books and publications in television programmes for review purposes is usually acceptable, if the publication is fully referenced. Readings on television from novels or adaptations of any published work must be cleared for copyright. Even an extract from Shakespeare or Keats is likely to come from a copyrighted published edition.

Original artistic works

All works of art such as paintings, drawings, art videos, maps, photographs and plans are covered by the Act, and protected for seventy years. It is not safe to assume that because the artist has been dead a long time a reproduction of Van Gogh's sunflowers can be used in a gardening programme. The colour photograph of the painting is almost certainly covered by copyright. Museums and galleries jealously guard their copyrighted reproductions, but may be open to negotiation.

Sound recordings

All sound recordings are copyrighted for fifty years from the end of the calendar year in which the recording is made. This mainly refers to music copyright. Music copyright is complicated because any or all of the people involved in producing a commercial CD, or downloadable song, may have rights – composer, lyricist, instrumentalists, singers, the record company, the arranger and the publisher of the music. Working in television involves obtaining music clearance to broadcast music on a programme. Commercial sound recordings have three basic sets of rights in: the rights in the musical work, the rights in the recording of that work onto CD, and the rights to broadcast it. The first rights are the musical work itself, known as 'the song'. The rights to the mechanical copying of the musical work are obtained from MCPS, or the copyright-owner. The second rights are to the sound recording made by the record company. To copy that sound recording the rights are obtained from the record company, or through one of the copyright societies – PPL, VPL or BPI. The right to broadcast any commercial recording – or play a CD in a club, restaurant or pub is cleared through the Performing Rights Society (PRS).

Composed music

A programme maker may ask a composer to write music for a forthcoming broadcast production. This music will be composed, performed and recorded exclusively for the production. This can be music recorded 'live', or created electronically on computer, or a mix of both. This is known as specially commissioned music and the production usually buy out the global all platform rights to the music. This can be expensive but allows the programme to be exploited in all markets including the internet, satellite and cable.

The spoken word

This covers all broadcasts, such as Sky News, and a non-broadcast interview. In an interview recorded by a reporter with a politician, the politician owns the copyright in the words. The broadcasting organisation owns the copyright in the recording that the reporter makes while working for that broadcaster. The broadcasting company can use the recording in the way agreed, but the speaker has some defence against the words being used in a different context, or being deliberately distorted. Once an interview is freely given, the interviewee cannot change their mind and say it cannot be transmitted. A refusal to be interviewed can be broadcast, as the Act cannot be used as a form of censorship of free speech.

Copyright on the internet

Contrary to what many people think, much of the original work on the internet is copyright. Look for the copyright logo on a web site. It is hard to enforce copyright on so much internet material although music and film publishers are policing YouTube and requiring some cases of copyright infringement to be taken down from the site. It is best to assume creative material cannot be copied and broadcast, especially visual material such as pictures without permission from the owners.

Feature films

There is copyright on all commercial films. Copyright is seventy years from the death of the last survivor out of the principal director, the screenplay author, author of the dialogue or the composer of the specially written music. Extracts released by the film distributor can usually only be broadcast in the week of release, but always check with the distributor. Using extracts from movies is possible but must always be negotiated. The exact use of the extract and the context will be closely examined. A documentary on disco could negotiate for a clip from *Saturday Night Fever* by arguing that the film had an inspiring effect on the disco movement. It is likely to be expensive to get copyright clearance to use extracts from Hollywood films. All broadcasters have an agreement with, and pay fees to the MCPS-PRS Alliance to broadcast commercial music. The royalty collection societies MCPS and PRS have joined together to collect royalties for music writers, composers and publishers. See www.prsformusic.com.

COPYRIGHT FREE MATERIAL

For students there is a special exemption on the copying of commercial discs. For projects where copyright discs are copied on a student video as part of an educational course, and used only within an educational establishment, such as a college or university, no copyright payment or clearance is required. The video must not be used outside the educational establishment. This concession does require the logging of all music details.

DEFAMATION AND THE LAW OF LIBEL

The one area of law that most affects broadcasting organisations and programme makers is defamation, and particularly the law of libel. The simplest definition of libel is telling lies about someone. The libel laws in the UK protect the individual through the Defamation Act of 1996. Lord Justice Beldam defined this as: 'The (right to) protection against attacks on reputation and honour is as important in a democratic society as the right to freedom of the press . . .' (*Kiam vs Neil*, 1996).

Working in television it is essential to know just what committing libel means. It is possible to libel individuals, groups or organisations. To commit libel a broadcaster would have to broadcast something that is defamatory. The courts normally apply these criteria to test whether a statement is defamatory.

- Does it expose a person to hatred, ridicule or contempt?
- Does it injure the person in his or her profession or trade?
- Does it cause a person to be shunned or avoided?
- Does it reduce a person in the eyes of right-thinking people?

Only one of these criteria has to be violated for there to be grounds for a case. The broadcasting company as the publisher of the television programme or online content is responsible for making sure that a libel does not occur. The broadcaster is responsible if a libel is committed by a guest on a TV programme or by a contributor to an online forum. An individual who sues a broadcasting organisation for libel has to prove three things in court: that the alleged libel is defamatory, that it relates to that person, and has been broadcast to a third party. Secondary libel can occur when a broadcaster repeats a libel that has been made elsewhere, in a newspaper for example.

There are three principal defences against libel that the lawyer for a broadcaster could use.

- *Justification*. This is the ability to prove that the facts as given in the programme are true, and that the broadcast material is telling the truth.

- *Fair comment.* This is where the broadcast material was made as a fair comment on a matter of public interest. The criteria are that the comment is fair, accurate and based on fact, without malice and of public concern.

- *Privilege.* Privilege refers to statements in broadcasts of court proceedings, or of parliamentary proceedings or other public meetings. The reports of these proceedings must be fair and accurate, and contemporaneous. In qualified privilege the reports must not be motivated by malice. The defence of privilege acknowledges that occasionally it is necessary for a person to freely speak their mind, even if when doing so he or she falsely damages another person's reputation.

CONTEMPT OF COURT

Television production staff need to know about the law of contempt (Contempt of Court Act 1981). The law of contempt aims to uphold the integrity of the legal process. A broadcaster risks contempt of court by broadcasting an interview, or any material that may influence the jury, and prejudice a fair trial, or make a statement that risks impeding or prejudicing the course of justice.

When a suspect is arrested and charged with committing a crime, or when a summons is issued in a civil case, the case becomes 'active'. This means there are restrictions on what a broadcaster can do. The 'active' period ends once sentence has been passed in criminal cases, and on judgment in civil cases. A reporter hoping to interview people involved in a court case, or report on court proceedings, should be aware of the following:

- Do not broadcast pictures, or comment, that could influence people involved in the case – witnesses, jurors, lawyers. Details of evidence could fall into this category.
- Do not broadcast anything that could prejudice the case.
- Do not broadcast interviews with witnesses or have dealings with them that could prejudice the case, before the case is over.
- Never speak to a juror about the case at any time, even after the case is over.
- Do not speculate or comment about the outcome of a case.
- Do not go against the court's wishes, or report what a judge has said must not be reported.

Contempt of court is a very serious offence. Dangers arise when the case comes to court and material is discussed on air that might be considered background material. Newspapers are most likely to be involved in this type of background piece, but a broadcasting organisation must not repeat material likely to prejudice the case. One of the most high-profile cases was the collapse of the trial of two Leeds United footballers in 2002. The *Sunday Mirror* was fined £75,000 for contempt of court by publishing an interview with the victim's father who said his son was the victim of a racial attack. The trial judge had said in court that there was no evidence of a racial motive. The interview was published while the jury was still considering its verdict. Because of the contempt of court the trial was abandoned, and a retrial ordered, at a total cost of over two million pounds. Inaccurate court reporting can lead to contempt proceedings.

A broadcaster or journalist has the right to report a 'fair-and-accurate' account of court proceedings, where there are not reporting restrictions. Reporting restrictions are lifted when a case reaches a conclusion. This is when the defendant is: acquitted or sentenced; freed without charge; is unfit to plead; an arrest warrant has expired; the case is discontinued. If there is to be a retrial, as in the case of the two Leeds United footballers, care must be taken that the retrial will not be prejudiced. There are real dangers in live talk shows, or discussion programmes, where issues of the day are aired. This is where careful briefing and some knowledge of contempt law is essential.

REFERENCES AND FURTHER READING

Banks, David and Hanna, Mark. *McNae's Essential Law for Journalists*, 20th edn, Oxford: Oxford University Press, 2009.
Kiam vs *Neil*, 1996. Carter – Ruck: http://www.carter-ruck.com/Media%20Law/publicationDetails.asp?ID=16.

Glossary

active audience: television audiences regarded not as passive consumers of meanings, but as negotiating meanings for themselves that are often resistant to those meanings that are intended or that are discovered by close analysis.

actuality footage: television pictures representing an event that was filmed live. The term usually refers to pictures of news events.

AFM (assistant floor manager): In a television studio the AFM works to the floor manager and looks after the actors and helps co-ordinate studio production.

ambient noise: The background sound present at any location recording such as the rumble of traffic or air conditioning.

analogue: representation in electrical terms of a physical quantity. Analogue broadcasting signals are in waves of varying frequency.

animation: a style of filming that creates movement from still images. Drawings, computerised images, or models are filmed or videoed frame by frame. Modern animation is computer generated animation (CGA).

aperture: controls the amount of light that enters a camera. This alters the exposure and also controls the depth of field. A lens may be 'opened up' or 'stopped down'.

archive: film, video or sound recording that is stored in a film archive or library.

aspect ratio: the ratio of height to width of a television picture. Standard TV picture aspect ratio used to be 4:3. Modern broadcast television aspect ratio is 16:9.

Aston: industry standard brand text and graphics generator usually found in a TV studio or in a postproduction facility.

audience share: the percentage of viewers estimated to have watched one channel as opposed to another channel broadcasting at the same time.

Autocue: brand name and colloquial term for prompting equipment that shows the words for a presenter to read in front of the lens of a TV camera. This allows the presenter to read the script while looking straight at the camera.

Avid: brand name for broadcasting standard computer video-editing system.

back lighting: lighting the subject of a shot from behind to provide depth by separating the subject from the background.

balance: the requirement in television news and current affairs to present both sides of an argument or issue.

BARB (Broadcasters Audience Research Bureau): the independent body that gathers and reports viewing statistics on behalf of UK television institutions.

barn doors: moveable side flaps fitted to a portable or studio TV lamp, used to restrict the amount of light that spills into unwanted areas.

BCU (big close up): Typically shows just the face of a person. See **shot size**.

binary opposition: two contrasting terms, ideas or concepts, such as inside/outside, masculine/feminine, or culture/nature.

blimp: a soundproof cover for a camera.

blonde: 2,000watt, variable-beam, portable, television and film lamp, so called because of the yellow colour of the lamp's head or metal casing.

bluescreen: blue sheet or screen that allows an image or series of images to be overlaid on part of another image. Also known as **chromakey**.

boom: long adjustable telescopic pole, or arm, that holds a microphone or camera. Can be a portable fishpole boom for a microphone, or a large boom with adjustable extensions mounted on a moveable base and usually found in a TV studio.

broadband: refers to a fast internet connection with permanent access, suitable for video streaming, good-quality video downloads on demand, and other multimedia functions.

Broadcast **magazine:** the leading weekly trade magazine for the UK broadcasting industry, www.broadcastnow.co.uk.

camcorder: video camera that records video and sound digitally onto disc, tape or hard disc, or memory card.

CCD (charge coupled device): a rectangular grid of detectors which are able to sense light, and are the picture sensing elements in a digital camera. The light arrives through the lens on to the CCDs. The millions of tiny pixels that make up the CCD convert this light into electrons which are then measured and converted to a digital value.

censorship: the omission of sensitive, prohibited or disturbing material at any stage in the production process from the initial idea to its transmission.

churn rate: a ratio setting the numbers of new subscribers to a paid-for television service against the number of subscribers cancelling their subscription.

close-up: a camera shot where the frame is filled by the face and neck of a person showing just the top of the shoulder. Close-ups may show details of an object or place.

CNN (Cable News Network): the first international satellite news channel, operating from the United States.

code: in semiotics, a system or set of rules that shapes how signs can be used, and therefore how meanings can be made and understood.

commissioning: the process by which an idea for a programme is selected to go into production.

computer generated imaging (CGI): the creation of images by programming computers with mathematical equations that can generate realistic two-dimensional pictures.

connotations: the term used in semiotic analysis for the meanings that are associated with a particular sign or combination of signs.

conventions: the frameworks and procedures used to make or interpret texts.

convergence: the process whereby previously separate digital media technologies merge together via the internet.

copyright: the legal right of ownership over written, visual or aural material, including the prohibition on copying this material without permission from its owner.

couch potatoes: a derogatory term for television viewers supposedly sitting motionless at home watching television passively and indiscriminately.

crane: counterweighted long metal arm with a flexible camera mounting that can raise or lower a camera to show high shots of the action.

crew: skilled technical personnel who operate equipment on a television set. Colloquially refers to the camera crew on location.

cue: signal to an actor or presenter to start talking, or to begin an action.

cut: the moment at which one camera shot ceases and another begins, where no transitional visual effect (such as a fade or a dissolve) is used.

cutaway: in fictional dialogue or interviews, shots that do not include people speaking. Cutaways often consist of details of the setting or of interviewees (such as hands).

cyclorama: large backing cloth or curtain that covers the entire back wall in a TV studio and can be pulled on rails to surround and give a background to the set.

demography: the study of population, and the groupings of people (demographic groups) within the whole population.

denotation: in semiotics, the function of signs to portray or refer to something in the real world.

diegesis: the distinction between showing (mimesis) and telling (diegesis) suggests the way a story may be told in images. Diegetic sound is sound material that directly relates to the scene, and is recorded, or appears to be recorded at the same time as the pictures.

digital television: television pictures and sound encoded into the ones and zeros of electronic data streams.

digitise: to convert an analogue electronic signal into a digital form as a series of electronic impulses that can be saved on a computer. Term used in digital video editing.

director: the person responsible for the creative process of turning a script or idea into a finished programme, by working with a technical crew, performers and an editor.

discourse: a particular use of language for a certain purpose in a certain context (like academic discourse, or poetic discourse), and similarly in television, a particular usage of television's audio-visual 'language' (news programme discourse, or nature documentary discourse, for instance).

dissolve: the gradual merging and replacing of one shot with another. Also called a mix.

documentary: a form aiming to record actual events, often with an explanatory purpose or to analyse and debate an issue.

docusoap: a television form combining documentary's depiction of non-actors in ordinary situations with soap opera's continuing narratives about selected characters.

dolly: a wheeled camera platform. A 'dolly shot' is a camera shot where the camera is moved forward or back using this platform.

drama-documentary: a television form combining dramatised storytelling with the 'objective' informational techniques of documentary. Abbreviated as 'drama-doc' or 'docudrama'.

dubbing: replacing the original speech in a programme, advertisement etc. with speech added later, sometimes to translate speech in a foreign language.

dumbing-down: the notion that television has reduced in quality as compared to an earlier period, showing programmes that are more 'dumb' or stupid and addressing its audience as if they were stupid.

duration: the exact length in minutes and seconds of a television programme.

DV (digital video): Video recording format widely used in television field production and in domestic camcorders.

DVCAM: digital video tape of the same size as DV tape but recording at a faster speed and with higher quality.

DVD (digital versatile disc): a 12cm disc that stores high-quality digital video and audio for playback and recording.

DVE (digital video effects): electronic equipment typically located in a TV studio gallery for creating video effects such as wipes and chromakey.

editing: the process of selecting and placing together different images and sounds to tell a factual or fictional story for television. Video editing for television is non-linear and is done on a computer using a proprietary video-editing system such as Final Cut Pro.

effects: measurable outcomes produced by watching television, such as becoming more violent or adopting a certain opinion.

electronic news gathering (ENG): the use of lightweight cameras and digital technology to record and transmit news pictures and sound.

embargo: a date before which a certain news item, or defined commercial information, cannot be broadcast, or published in the press.

exposure: the amount of light that enters the lens of a camera through the aperture.

exterior: denotes that the location of a scene in a television programme is outside, and not inside a building or studio.

eyeline: the direction in which the eyes of an actor or contributor are looking as seen by the camera.

fade: a fade-out is the gradual darkening of the shot until the image disappears leaving a blank screen. A fade-in is where the shot emerges from a black screen.

fan culture: the activities of groups of fans, as distinct from 'ordinary' viewers.

final cut or fine cut: the final edited version of a programme that is delivered to the television institution for broadcast.

flashback: a television sequence marked as representing events that happened in a time previous to the programme's present.

flow: the ways that programmes, advertisements etc. follow one another in an unbroken sequence across the day or part of the day, and the experience of watching the sequence of programmes, advertisements, trailers, etc.

fly-on-the-wall: a documentary form where the subject is observed without the programme maker's intervention.

focal length: the distance, in millimetres, a camera lens takes to focus the parallel rays of light from a subject.

focus groups: small groups of selected people representing larger social groupings, such as people of a certain age-group, gender or economic status, who take part in discussions about a topic chosen for investigation.

foldback: sound played through a speaker or headphones on the TV studio floor that can be heard by performers, but does not feed back into the final sound mix.

format: the blueprint for a programme, including its setting, main characters, genre, form and main themes.

frame: a rectangular image that is the basic unit that makes up a video or film. The PAL video system used in the UK runs at twenty-five frames a second.

Frankfurt School: a group of theorists, notably Theodor Adorno and Max Horkheimer, centred in Germany in the mid-twentieth century who worked on theories of contemporary culture from a Marxist perspective.

freelance: self-employed worker of any category in the media industry.

free-to-air: television programming for which viewers make no direct payment.

f-stop: the measurement of the size of a camera lens aperture. The smaller the stop number the larger the aperture, e.g. f-2 lets in more light than f-11.

gallery: the control room in a television studio where the studio director, vision mixer, and the sound and video supervisors observe the production of a programme.

gatekeepers: the critical term used for the people and institutions (such as television commissioning producers, or regulatory bodies) who control access to television.

gender: the social and cultural division of people into masculine or feminine individuals. This is different from sex, which refers to the biological difference between male and female bodies.

genre: a kind or type of programme.

globalisation: the process whereby ownership of television institutions in different nations and regions is concentrated in the hands of international corporations.

graphics: images and words created by drawing, lettering, or by computer, and used in a television programme.

grip: member of the camera crew who sets up the camera dolly, controls it, and lays track for it to run on.

gun mic: long thin unidirectional microphone often seen encased in a hairy wind shield and used by a news film crew.

HDTV (High Definition Television): widescreen television with a very high resolution of at least 720 progressive vertical lines and 1280 horizontal lines.

hegemony: a term deriving from Marxist theories of society, meaning a situation where different social classes or groups are persuaded to consent to a political order that may be contrary to their benefit.

Hertz (Hz): electrical measurement of frequency of radio or sound waves.

high-angle shot: shot where the camera is placed high above the eyeline of the action.

iconic sign: in semiotics, a sign which resembles its referent. Photographs, for example, contain iconic signs resembling the objects they represent.

identification: a term deriving from psychoanalytic theories of cinema, which describes the viewer's conscious or unconscious wish to take the place of someone or something in a television text.

idents: the symbols representing production companies, television channels etc., often comprising graphics or animations.

ideology: the set of beliefs, attitudes and assumptions arising from the economic and class divisions in a culture, underlying the ways of life accepted as normal in that culture.

indexical sign: in semiotics, a sign which is the result of what it signifies, in the way that smoke is the result of fire.

information society: a contemporary highly developed culture (especially Western culture) where the production and exchange of information is more significant than conventional industrial production.

insert tape: video tape/disc with all the recorded items for a television programme.

interactive: offering the opportunity for viewers to respond to what is broadcast, by sending signals back to the broadcaster (along a cable or phone line, for example).

interior: indication of the location of a scene that is set inside a building.

intertextuality: how one text draws on the meanings of another by referring to it, by allusion, quotation, or parody, for example.

iris: the iris in a camera, made of overlapping metal flaps controls the aperture or opening through which the light reaches the CCD or unexposed film.

jump cut: a cut in continuous action from one shot to the same shot size, disturbing the visual continuity of the scene.

key light: the main light source in any television lighting set up that provides the 'key' to the scene's appearance.

libel: legal term for broadcasting a statement that is an unfair, untrue or unreasonable defamation of a person's character.

licence fee: an annual payment by all owners of television sets, which is the main source of income for the BBC.

lighting cameraman: the leading male or female cameraperson in a television location production, who is responsible for the framing and lighting for each scene.

lip sync: the synchronisation of an actor's lip movements with the dialogue he or she is speaking.

location: any place in which television images are shot, except inside a television studio.

long shot (LS): shot showing the full length of a person including the setting and background with a wide field of vision.

low-angle shot: shot where the camera is placed below the eyeline looking up at the subject, often giving the impression of power.

magazine programme: television programme made up of a number of different items and stories often in genres such as travel, business or sport.

master shot: a wide shot in a drama production that includes all the main action in a scene.

media literacy: the skills and competence that viewers learn in order to easily understand the audio-visual 'languages' of media texts.

medium close-up (MCU): a camera shot much used in television studio interviews and chat shows. Wider than a close-up, it includes the head and shoulders of the subject with the bottom of the frame along the line of the top pocket on a man's jacket.

medium shot (MS): shot of the top half of a person with the bottom of the frame running along the waist. Also called a mid shot.

melodrama: a form of drama characterised by exaggerated performance, a focus on reversals of fortune and extreme emotional reactions to events.

merchandising: the sale of products associated with a television programme, such as toys, books or clothing.

metaphor: the carrying-over from something of some of its meanings onto another thing of an apparently different kind. For example, a television narrative about life aboard ship could be a metaphor for British social life (the ship as a metaphor for society).

metonymy: the substitution of one thing for another, either because one is part of the other or one is connected with the other. For example, 'the Crown' can be a metonym for the British state.

mise-en-scène: literally means 'putting on stage' all the elements of a shot or sequence that contribute to its meanings, such as set design, costume, lighting and camera position.

mix: gradual transition from one shot to another, where the first shot gradually dissolves into the incoming shot.

mixer: usually refers to audio equipment that combines different sound sources. Can be portable or in a sound suite.

modality: the fit between a fictional representation and the conventional understanding of reality. High modality describes a close fit, and weak modality a distant one.

monitor: high-quality television set used to view or monitor television pictures.

multi-accentuality: the situation where meanings are able to be read in different ways by different groups of viewers because a text offers multiple meanings at the same time.

multiplex: agencies that carry many disparate digital television and radio channels, using less bandwidth than conventional terrestrial television transmissions.

mute: means silent; refers to a video or film recording made with no diegetic sound.

name super: the superimposition of a contributor's name over the person's image in the lower third of the screen. Also known as a caption.

narration: the process of telling a story through image and sound. Narration can also refer to the spoken text accompanying television images.

narrative: an ordered sequence of images and sound that tells a fictional or factual story.

natural break: a vague term meaning a point at which a programme can be interrupted without causing undue disruption to the ongoing flow of the programme.

naturalism: originally having a very specific meaning in literature and drama, this term is used to denote television fiction that adopts realistic conventions of character portrayal, linear cause and effect narrative, and a consistent and recognisable fictional world.

negotiated reading: a viewer interpretation of a television text where the viewer understands meaning in relation to his or her own knowledge and experience, rather than simply accepting the meaning proposed by the text.

news agency: a media institution that gathers news reports and distributes them to its customers (who include television news broadcasters).

news value: the degree of significance attributed to a news story, where items with high news value are deemed most significant to the audience.

niche audiences: particular groups of viewers defined by age-group, gender or economic status, for example, who may be the target audience for a programme.

noddy shot: in television interviews, shots of the interviewer reacting silently (often by nodding) to the interviewee's responses to questions.

non-linear editing: video or film editing where the shots are assembled and reassembled in any order. Video editing on a computer is non-linear.

non-sync: a recording made on film or video with no synchronised sound. This is different from 'out of sync', where the sound is not correctly synchronised with the dialogue.

NTSC (National Television Standards Committee): The standard colour television system used in the USA, Japan and some South American countries.

OB: see **outside broadcast**.

observational documentary: a documentary form in which the programme maker aims to observe neutrally what would have happened even if he or she had not been present.

Ofcom: Ofcom is the independent regulator and competition authority for the UK communications industries: www.ofcom.org.uk.

off-line editing: the first stage of editing a completed programme, where the sequence of shots, sounds and music are established, using inexpensive copies of the original high-quality pictures and sound. Largely replaced by non-linear computer editing.

off mic: when a recorded sound is audible but muffled or obscure and not crystal clear it is said to be off mic.

180 degree rule: the convention that cameras are positioned only on one side of an imaginary line drawn between two performers in a scene. This produces a coherent sense of space for the viewer. Also known as not crossing the line.

online editing: the final stage of editing a completed programme, where effects are added and a high-quality version of the programme is produced.

outside broadcast (OB): the television transmission of outdoor events such as sport or ceremonial occasions, using equipment set up in advance for the purpose.

outtake: a shot or sequence which was omitted from a finished programme, because of a mistake during production or an artistic decision.

overlay: the combining of two picture sources to make one composite image, usually through a TV gallery DVE console.

PAL: Phase Alternate Line transmission of television pictures; a German technical standard introduced in the 1960s still used in the UK today for all TV transmissions.

pan: a shot where the camera, mounted on a tripod or dolly, is moved in a horizontal arc from left to right, or right to left. The term derives from the word 'panorama', suggesting the wide visual field that a pan can reveal.

pantograph: a moveable arm with a lamp attached, which is part of a TV studio lighting rig enabling the lamp to be hoisted up or down.

pastiche: the imitation of forms or conventions in another text. The term can convey a negative view that the imitation is less effective or valuable than the original.

pedestal: steady, camera mounting on wheels for a heavy, studio television camera operated by a cameraman.

personalities: people appearing on television who are recognised by audiences as celebrities with a media image and public status.

picture editor: another name for a video editor, often working in news.

pitch: a short written or spoken outline for a programme used to try and persuade a commissioning producer to commission the programme.

pixel: pixels are the light sensing elements of a CCD in a digital camera that create the picture on a TV screen or computer monitor.

point of view (POV) shot: a camera shot where the camera is placed in, or close to, the position from where a previously seen character might look.

polysemia: the quality of having multiple meanings at the same time. Texts like this are called 'polysemic'.

postmodernism: the most recent phase of capitalist culture, the aesthetic forms and styles associated with it, and the theoretical approaches developed to understand it.

postproduction: the work done on a programme after the video recording or filming has taken place leading to the completion of the production.

preferred reading: an interpretation of a text that seems to be the one most encouraged by the text, the 'correct' interpretation.

preproduction: the work done, including planning and research, on a television programme before any video recording or filming takes place.

prime-time: the part of a day's television schedule when the greatest number of viewers may be watching, normally the mid-evening period.

private sphere: the domestic world of the home, family and personal life.

producer: the person working for a television institution, or independent production company, who is responsible for making a television programme or series.

production values: the level of investment in a television production as seen on the screen, such as the amount spent on costumes, props, effects and sets.

PSC (portable single camera): describes a cameraman working in the field with a video camera usually for acquisition of news material.

PTC (piece to camera): on location, a television presenter looking straight into the camera reading an autocue, or delivering a memorised script, is doing a piece to camera.

public service broadcasting (PSB): in television, the provision of a mix of programmes that inform, educate and entertain in ways that encourage the betterment of audiences and society in general.

public sphere: the world of politics, economic affairs and national and international events, as opposed to the 'private sphere' of domestic life.

quality: in television, kinds of programme that are perceived as more expensively produced and, especially, more culturally worthwhile than other programmes.

ratings: the number of viewers estimated to have watched certain programmes, as compared to the numbers watching other programmes.

realism: the aim for representations to reproduce reality faithfully, and the ways this is done.

Reality TV: programmes where the unscripted behaviour of 'ordinary people' is the focus of interest.

recce: to recce a location is to check it out both for suitability for the programme, and for practical considerations such as the availability of an electrical power source.

redhead: a lightweight, variable beam, 800 watt television light.

reflexivity: a text's reflection on its own status as a text, for example, drawing attention to generic conventions, or revealing the technologies used to make a programme.

register: a term in the study of language for the kinds of speech or writing used to represent a particular kind of idea or to address a certain audience.

regulation: the control of television institutions by laws, codes of practice or guidelines.

release form: a form signed by a contributor to a television programme giving permission for his or her contribution to be broadcast.

representation: the way different people of different gender, race, ethnicity and from different backgrounds are portrayed on television.

rostrum camera: video camera set up on an overhead rig to record drawings, still photos or any object that can be placed on a flat platform.

rough cut: the first edited version of a television programme, which is generally too long and needs a good deal of further editing.

runner: the most junior member of a television or film production team.

running order: a list of the duration, source and description of the items in a television programme in the order in which they will appear in the programme.

rushes: all the audio and visual material that has been shot during the production period, including bad takes and other unwanted material.

satellite television: television signals beamed from a ground transmitter to a stationary satellite that broadcasts the signal to a specific area (called the 'footprint') below it.

satire: a mode of critical commentary about society or an aspect of it, using humour to attack people or ideas.

scanner: the large vehicle housing the mobile control room for an outside broadcast.

schedule: the arrangement of programmes, advertisements and other material into a sequential order within a certain period of time, such as an evening, day or week.

screenplay: a script that is written specifically to be made into a television drama or film.

semiotics: the study of signs and their meanings, initially developed for the study of spoken language, and now used also to study the visual and aural 'languages' of other media such as television.

serial: a television form where a developing narrative unfolds across a sequence of separate episodes.

series: a television form where each programme in the series has a different story or topic, though settings, main characters or performers remain the same.

set: the arrangement of scenery in a studio, or on location, where scenes for a television programme will be shot.

shooting ratio: the number of minutes of film used to film a scene or complete programme as compared to the screen-time of the finished scene or programme.

shot: a single shot runs from the point at which the camera is turned on to where it is paused, or turned off. A shot is identified by the video time code or by a clapperboard.

shot size: the size of the subject within the frame of a shot, usually referred to by abbreviations such as CU for close-up.

Skillset: the national training and careers advice organisation for the film, broadcasting, video and multi-media industries: www.skillset.org.

sign: in semiotics, something which communicates meaning, such as a word, an image, or a sound.

simulation: a representation that mirrors an aspect of reality so perfectly that it takes the place of the reality it aims to reproduce.

slot: the position in a television schedule where a programme is shown.

soap opera: a continuing drama serial involving a large number of characters in a specific location, focusing on relationships, emotions and reversals of fortune.

sound effects (fx): the extra sounds that are added in the editing process to the natural sounds in a scene.

spin-off: a product, television programme, book, etc. that is created to exploit the reputation, meaning or commercial success of a previous one, often in a different medium from the original.

sponsorship: the funding of programmes or channels by businesses, whose name is usually prominently displayed in the programme or channel as a means of advertising.

sparks: colloquial name for the electricians who are responsible for the lights on a production. They take their instructions from the lighting cameraperson.

steadicam: a camera mounting that straps the camera to the body of the operator and incorporates a device that keeps the image steady.

stick mic: quite long, stick-like, hand-held microphone typically used by a presenter.

stills: non-moving images used in a television production such as photographs.

sting: a brief musical or visual insert used as punctuation in a programme.

stock footage: video and film that is kept in an archive or library and can be used as illustrative material in a programme.

storyboard: a sequence of drawn images showing the shots to be used in a programme.

strand: a linked series of programmes, sharing a common title.

stripping: in television scheduling, placing a programme or genre of programme at the same time on several days of each week.

subtitle: written text appearing on the television screen, normally to translate speech in a foreign language.

sungun: a hand-held television light that runs from belt batteries and can give an intense beam.

superimpose: to introduce a new image or graphics and superimpose it over an existing picture. Typically created by the vision mixer in a TV studio gallery.

symbol: a representation which condenses many meanings together and can stand for those many meanings in a certain context. For example, a brand-new car could be a symbol of wealth, social status and masculine prowess.

symbolic sign: in semiotics, a sign which is connected arbitrarily to its referent rather than because the sign resembles its referent. For example, a photograph of a cat resembles it, whereas the word 'cat' does not: the word is a symbolic sign.

sync sound: abbreviation for synchronised sound, meaning sound that is shot simultaneously with the pictures, and matches the lip movements of the actors or contributors.

syntagm: in semiotics, a linked sequence of signs existing at a certain point in time. Written or spoken sentences, or television sequences, are examples of syntagms.

take: a repetition of the action when recording a scene. Each recording of the same scene will have a take number.

talking heads: the term used for interviews or other head and shoulder shots of contributors to a programme.

teaser: a very short television sequence advertising a forthcoming programme, often puzzling or teasing to viewers because it contains little information and encourages curiosity and interest.

terrestrial: broadcasting from a ground-based transmission system, as opposed to broadcasting via satellite.

text: an object such as a television programme, film or poem, considered as a network of meaningful signs that can be analysed and interpreted.

textual analysis: a critical approach which seeks to understand a television text's meanings by undertaking detailed analysis of its image and sound components, and the relationships between those components.

three-point lighting: standard way to light an interview or small scene for television. So called because it uses three lights in different positions.

three shot: shot with three people in the frame.

time code: the electronic process that gives each frame of video its own numerical identification, displayed on the screen as a series of numbers that show the tape number, hours, minutes, seconds and frames.

timeline: visual reference for computer video editing, showing video tracks, edit points and audio tracks along a time reference scale.

title sequence: the sequence at the opening of a television programme in which the programme title and performers' names may appear along with other information. Colloquially known as 'titles'.

tracking shot: a camera shot where the camera is mounted on a dolly and records moving along a track similar to a miniature railway track.

trailer: a short television sequence advertising a forthcoming programme.

transition: change from one shot to the next different shot, typically using a dissolve or wipe.

transmission: the process of broadcasting a television programme to an audience.

treatment: a short written outline for a programme, usually written for a commissioning producer to read, specifying how the programme will tell its story or address its subject.

tripod: three-legged camera mounting used to obtain professional-looking shots.

tungsten lamp: television lighting lamp with a tungsten filament that has to be colour balanced for daylight with a blue gel.

turn over: instruction given by the director to start the camera and sound recording.

variety programmes: entertainment programmes containing a mix of material such as songs and comedy sketches.

vérité: a French word that describes observational filming that follows events rather than reconstructs them, or uses other cinematic devices.

vertical integration: the control by media institutions of all levels of a business, from the production of products to their distribution and means of reception.

vision mixer: operates the vision mixing desk in the gallery of a multi-camera TV studio.

voice-over: speech accompanying visual images but not presumed to derive from the same place or time as the images.

vox pop: literally meaning 'the voice of the people', short television interviews, answering just one question, conducted with members of the public, usually in the street.

voyeurism: gaining sexual pleasure from looking at someone or something that cannot look back.

VU meter: volume unit meter found on audio equipment that displays the intensity of a sound source measured in decibels.

watershed: the time in the day (conventionally 9.00 pm) after which programmes with content that may disturb children can be shown.

whip-pan: a very rapid panning shot from one point to another.

white balance: a way of making the colour of the pictures from a video camera accurately represent the true colours of the scene, by pointing the camera at a white surface that reflects the light temperature of the scene.

widescreen: standard broadcasting format for television programmes with an aspect ratio of 16:9.

wildtrack: sound recording taken at the time of shooting on location but without pictures. The wildtrack sound is used in editing, sometimes as background sound.

zapping: hopping rapidly from channel to channel while watching television, using a remote control (a 'zapper').

zoom lens: a lens with a variable focal length.

Index